Vest Pocket
RUSSIAN

TITLES IN THIS SERIES

VEST POCKET SPANISH

VEST POCKET FRENCH

VEST POCKET GERMAN

VEST POCKET ITALIAN

VEST POCKET RUSSIAN

VEST POCKET MODERN GREEK

VEST POCKET JAPANESE

VEST POCKET ARABIC

VEST POCKET ENGLISH
(Inglés En El Bolsillo)

VIETNAMESE IN A NUTSHELL

Vest Pocket
RUSSIAN

Formerly published as: RUSSIAN IN A NUTSHELL

By
MARSHALL D. BERGER, Ph.D.
City College of New York

PUBLISHED BY
INSTITUTE FOR LANGUAGE STUDY
Montclair, New Jersey 07042

DISTRIBUTED TO THE BOOK TRADE BY
BARNES & NOBLE BOOKS
A DIVISION OF HARPER & ROW, *PUBLISHERS*

Library of Congress Catalog Card Number: 60-9758

GETTING THE MOST OUT OF YOUR COURSE

T HE WORLD is growing smaller every day. Far-sighted people who recognize the value of speaking a second language will reap the benefits of greater business success, more traveling enjoyment, easier study and finer social relationships.

VEST POCKET RUSSIAN will unlock for you the treasure house of learning a language the easy way, with a fresh, new approach—without monotonous drills. Before you know it, you'll be speaking your new language easily and without embarrassment. You will be able to converse with fascinating people from other lands and read books and magazines from their country in the original language.

Much research and painstaking study has gone into the "Vest Pocket" method of learning a language as easily as possible. This Course is the result of that research, and for the reader's convenience it is divided into several basic, closely related sections:

The KEY TO PRONUNCIATION explains the sounds of the language. Each sentence is accompanied by the phonetic spelling to help you learn the pronunciation. This method has been tested extensively and is found to be the best to enable the student to associate sounds with written forms.

The BASIC SENTENCE PATTERNS are the unique new approach to sentence construction. Here you will find sentence patterns needed in general conversation. On these basic patterns you can build sentences to suit your own particular needs.

The EVERYDAY CONVERSATIONS form the main section of this book. Here you will find a large number of situations useful for general language learning and traveling purposes. You will learn hundreds upon hundreds of conversational sentences you may need to make yourself understood. Even more important, the material is organized to provide you with a wide basis for varying the vocabulary and sentences as much as your interest and ingenuity might desire.

The OUTLINE OF GRAMMAR provides a rapid understanding of the grammatical structure of your new language. The "Basic Sentence Patterns" are closely correlated with this section to give you a quick knowledge of the language.

The two-way DICTIONARY of over 6500 entries includes all the words used in the Everyday Conversations and contains another 3000 frequently used words and expressions. It thus forms a compact and invaluable tool for the student.

Here are the tools. Use them systematically, and before you know it you will have a "feeling" for the new language. The transcriptions furnish authentic reproduction of the language to train your ear and tongue to the foreign sounds; thus you can SEE the phrase, SAY the phrase, HEAR the phrase, and LEARN the phrase.

Remember that repetition and practice are the foundation stones of language learning. Repeat and practice what you have learned as often as you can. You will be amazed (and your friends will, too) how quickly you have acquired a really practical knowledge of Russian.

THE EDITORS

ACKNOWLEDGEMENT

I wish to express my thanks to Dr. Zoya Yurieff and Mr. Hans ter Laan for their valuable assistance in the preparation of the dictionary; to my wife Gale Dashuck Berger and to Anton and Ludmila Kolomatsky for their invaluable help in assuring the idiomatic accuracy of the Russian text; and most of all to the editors of the Institute for Language Study, my good friend and colleague Dr. George C. Pappageotes and Mr. Benedict Kolthoff, for their careful and conscientious editorial work.

M. D. B.

———

Many of the Russian sentences in the Everyday Conversations have been based on materials found in the *Language Guide* by S. Abrahm and Ph. Silpert (Moscow: Mezhkniga, 1934). The phonetic transcription is entirely the author's.

TABLE OF CONTENTS

7

KEY TO RUSSIAN PRONUNCIATION

RUSSIAN PRONUNCIATION AND SPELLING

Russian spelling is not consistently phonetic. One cannot simply read off the approximate English equivalents of each Russian letter to arrive at a good, or even understandable, pronunciation of Russian.

For this reason, one must resort to the use of a system of phonetic writing. Such a system represents the basic sounds and sound combinations of the language as simply and consistently as possible. In such a system, each symbol stands for one sound, and one sound only. There are no exceptions.

RUSSIAN CONSONANT SOUNDS

Russian consonant sounds, with a very few exceptions, come in pairs. Of each pair, one member is *plain* and the other *palatalized.* *

1. Plain Consonants

A listing of plain consonant phonetic symbols and Russian letters follows:

PHONETIC SYMBOL	DESCRIPTION	RUSSIAN LETTER	EXAMPLE	
b	For all practical purposes,	б	бас	(bass [voice])
m	identical with the equiva-	м	мáма	(mama)
g	lent English sounds.	г	газ	(gas)
f		ф	факт	(fact)
v		в	вáза	(vase)
s		с	сорт	(sort)
z		з	зóна	(zone)
p	Same as the English sounds	п	пáпа	(papa)
t	except that they are pro-	т	такт	(tact)
k	duced with less force of breath.	к	кáрта	(card)

* The traditional Russian term for *palatalized* is "soft." For *plain* the traditional term is "hard."

PHONETIC SYMBOL	DESCRIPTION	RUSSIAN LETTER	EXAMPLE
t	Same as the English sounds	т	такт (tact)
d	but with the tongue tip	д	да (yes)
n	placed lower, i.e. on the	н	нос (nose)
l	backs of the upper teeth.	л	лáмпа (lamp)
r	Trilled by vibrating the tongue tip against the upper gum ridge.	р	ráса (race [of people])
ḥ	Similar to the English h sound but breathier. Somewhat like the sound produced when "clearing the throat."	х	халвá (halva [candy])
sh	Similar to the English sound but in Russian the tongue tip is curled up toward the roof of the mouth, producing a "thicker," "deeper," "harder" sound.	ш	шок (shock)
zh	This symbol stands for the sound of z in seizure with the same tongue curling described for sh and with the same "thick" effect.	ж	жандáрм (gendarme)
ts	Same as in English but it comes at the beginning of Russian words as well as medially and finally.	ц	царь (tsar)

A preliminary note about Russian vowels

In the Russian words given above, the reader will note that the familiar vowel letters **a** and **o** are used. As in many languages other than English, these letters have their so-called continental values, i.e., the *ah* sound of *father,* but shorter and more clipped, and the *aw* sound of *law* or *sort,* but shorter and more strongly lip-rounded.

Another basic Russian vowel, not shown in any of the earlier examples, is like the *oo* of *food*, but is shorter and has a "deeper" quality. This sound is represented in Russian spelling by the letter **y**:

суп (soup)   **футбóл** (football)

2. Palatalized Consonants

Palatalized consonants are formed in the same manner as plain consonants, i.e. with the same organs and in the same places in the mouth, but with a simultaneous raising of the front of the tongue toward the roof of the mouth or hard palate.

This produces the effect of a *y*-sound (as in *yes*) being attached to the basic consonant sound. At first blush, this may not seem like much, since the initial sounds of such English words as *beauty, music* and *few* are made in a similar manner.

In English, however, there are three fairly distinct movements from the first consonant to the *y*-sound to the vowel sound of long *u*, whereas in Russian the basic consonant and the *y*-sound are made in one simultaneous movement with the vowel sound coming tumbling after.

A possible representation of this pronunciation might well be *p^y, t^y, l^y, d^y, s^y* and the like, but since so many *y*'s would be rather difficult to read and even harder to print we have used an apostrophe instead: *p', t', l', d', s',* etc. The apostrophe, then, is the equivalent of such a small *y*.

There are a few Russian consonants which do not have either plain or palatalized counterparts:

1) The sounds represented by the letters **ш, ж** and **ц** are always plain (see earlier discussion).

2) Russian *ch* (spelled **ч**) and *shch* (spelled **щ**) are always palatalized, even though in our transcription the palatalizing apostrophe is omitted.

3) Palatalized *zh'zh'* occurs in the word уезжáть (to go away) and a few others.

4) The sound of *y* (as in *yes*) itself is a full-fledged Russian sound, and—although it is palatal, not really palatal*ized*— it clearly belongs with the palatalized group in any sensible system of classification.

Spelling of the y-sound and other palatalized consonants

The sound of *y* coming at the beginning of a word or syllable is not represented by a separate letter in Russian. For the common sequences *ya, ye, yo,* and *yu* (continental values of the vowel letters), Russian uses the single letters **я**, **е**, **ё**, and **ю**:

я (I)	**ёлка** (fir tree)
ел (ate)	**юг** (south; cf. *Y*ugoslavia)

The same single letters are used to indicate that a preceding consonant letter represents a palatalized rather than a plain sound. Note the following three-way contrast:

ёлка [YOL-kə], fir tree	**толк** [tolk], sense
тёлка [T'OL-kə], heifer	

Two-way contrasts:

он знал [on znal], he knew	**он снял** [on sn'al], he took off
нос [nos], nose	**нёс** [n'os], was carrying
лук [luk], onion	**люк** [l'uk], trapdoor

At the end of words or syllables, palatalization is indicated by a special symbol called a "soft sign" and spelled **ь**:

сталь [stal'], steel	**пальма** [PAL'-mə], palm tree
брать [brat'], to take	

In some cases a *plain* consonant or a *palatalized* one may make all the difference between one possible meaning and another. At the very least, proper placement of these consonants is essential to correct pronunciation:

стал [stal], became   **брат** [brat], brother   **палка** [PAL-kə], stick

FURTHER DISCUSSION OF VOWELS: SOUNDS AND LETTERS

Like я, ё, and ю, the Russian letter **е** also appears after consonant letters to indicate the palatalized character of the preceding consonant sound:

тень [t'en'], shade, shadow	
нет [n'et], no	
где [gd'e], where	

Strange to say, the sound of [e] after *plain* consonants is represented by the same letter:

шесть [shest'], six	теннис [TE-n'is], tennis *
жест [zhest], gesture	купе [ku-PE], train compart-
центр [tsentr], center	ment *

The letter **э**, which also stands for [e], is never used after consonant letters, but is restricted to the initial position of words or syllables:

| это [E-tə], this, that | дуэт [du-ET], duet |
| эхо [E-hə], echo | поэт [pa-ET], poet |

The vowel [i] as in *machine*, but somewhat shorter, is found only after *palatalized* or "soft" consonants, or at the very beginning of words. The letter **и** is used to represent the vowel sound and, if necessary, to indicate the palatalized character of the preceding consonant sound:

| бить [b'it'], to beat | эти [E-t'i], these, those |
| и [i], and | лифт [l'ift], elevator |

After *plain* or "hard" consonants an *i*-type of sound does occur, but it undergoes an important change. Since the front of the tongue cannot rise toward the palate after a plain consonant (such a movement would convert it into a palatalized consonant), the middle or even the back of tongue rises instead. The result is a special form of *i*, which may sound or feel strange to the non-Russian, but is not difficult to make if the *plain* or "hard" consonant is produced properly in all basic respects (review earlier discussion of plain consonants). The consonant conditions the quality of the vowel.

Considering that this vowel is a centralized *i*, the phonetic symbol [ɨ] is used to represent it. The Russian spelling is **ы**, except after **ш** and **ж**, where **и** is used in spite of the pronunciation. After **ц**, both **и** and **ы** are found:

дым [dɨm], smoke	жить [zhɨt'], to live
быть [bɨt'], to be	цирк [tsɨrk], circus
сын [sɨn], son	отцы [at-TSɨ], father

DIPHTHONGS

The sound of *y* (as in *yes*) can combine with any Russian vowel to form a diphthong. The *y*-sound in this position usually is represented by the letter **й**:

---

* Recent borrowings from English and French.

[ay]	as in	**дай**, give!	(like *die*, but shorter)
[ey]	„ „	**ей**, to her	(like *yay*, but tenser)
[iy]	„ „	**кий**, billiard cue	(like *key*, but tenser and longer)
[iy]	„ „	**милый**, dear	(like *mealy*, but with a "harder" l)
[oy]	„ „	**бой**, battle	(like *boy*, but shorter)
[uy]	„ „	**фуй**,* faugh!	(like *phooey*, but much shorter)

VOWELS IN UNSTRESSED SYLLABLES

Russian words, no matter how long, have only one stress. There are almost no secondary stresses. Consequently, vowel sounds in unstressed syllables tend to be obscured or merged with one another. There are similar tendencies in English.

For this reason, the spelling and pronunciation rules for vowels taken up in the preceding sections are valid only for the stressed syllables of plurisyllabic words.

In the unstressed syllables of words of more than one syllable. two basic mergers take place:

1) After *plain* consonants, [a] and [o] fall together into [a].

сама [sa-MA], herself   **дома** [da-MA], houses

2) After *palatalized* consonants, [a], [e], and [i] fall together into [i].

восемь [VO-s'im'], eight   **девять** [D'E-v'it'], nine

3) [u] remains unchanged.

культуру [kul-TU-ru], culture (accus. case)

In unstressed syllables other than the one directly before the stressed syllable of the word, [a] is further weakened to [ə] (a neutral, murmured vowel identical with the first vowel sound of *along* and the last one of *sofa*):

хорошо [hə-ra-SHO], good, well   **понимаю** [pə-n'i-MA-yu],
                                                                  I understand
можно [MOZH-nə], possible   **спасибо** [spa-S'I-bə], thank you

These rules apply to all Russian words and names. Be especially careful about the pronunciation of familiar words such as the Russian counterparts of telephone, American, and officer:

телефон	[t'i-l'i-FON]	(*not*: te-lə-FON)
американец	[a-m'i-r'i-KA-n'its]	(*not*: a-me-rə-KA-nəts)
офицер	[a-f'itSER]	(*not*: o-fə-SER)

---

* Фу, however, is much more commonly used.

MUTUAL CONSONANT INFLUENCES

Russian spelling does not mirror faithfully and consistently the influences that neighboring consonant sounds in a word or phrase exert upon one another:

1) Russian permits only voiced or voiceless consonant sequences. The determining consonant is the last one in the sequence, i.e. only [g] can precede [z], never [k]; only [k] can precede [s], etc.:

вокзал [vag-ZAL], railroad station **футбол** [fud-BOL], football (soccer)

в кино [f k'i-NO], in the movies **завтра** [ZAF-trə], tomorrow

в городе [v GOR-ə-d'i], in the city

2) Final consonants before a pause (the very end of the word with only silence following) are voiceless. The pause may be said to have the force of a voiceless consonant:

багаж [ba-GASH], baggage **город** [GOR-ət], city **зуб** [zup], tooth

3) Palatalized consonants sometimes occur in groups, too, notably those which contain *t'*, *d'*, *n'*, *s'* and *z'* before another palatalized consonant. Russian spelling usually shows the palatalization only of this last consonant:

здесь [z'd'es'], here **шесть** [shes't'], six **кончил** [KON'-chil], finished

In the text of this book the palatalizing apostrophe is generally placed after the last member of a consonant group, as in Russian spelling. There are a few instances, however, where extra apostrophes have been inserted to help the learner along.

MISCELLANEOUS SOUND AND LETTER PROBLEMS

The letter **ч** stands for [sh] instead of the normal [ch] in a few words:

что [shto], what **конечно** [ka-N'ESH-nə], of course

The letter **г** stands for [v] instead of the normal [g] in genitive endings:

его [yi-VO], him, his
ничего [n'i-chi-VO], nothing (*lit.*: of nothing)
сегодня [s'i-VOD'-n'ə], today (*lit.*: of this day)

The endings **-ся** and **-тся** are pronounced [sə] and [tsə], respectively, instead of [s'ə], [t's'ə] or [ts'ə]:

> **называться** [nə-zɨ-VAT-sə], to   **заблудился** [zə-blu-D'IL-sə],
> be called   got lost, lost one's way
> **называется** [nə-zɨ-VA-yit-sə],
> is called

In certain common conversational words, sounds are omitted:

> **пожалуйста** [pə-ZHA-lə-stə],   **здравствуйте** [ZDRAST-vuy-
> please   t'i], hello!

STRESS

Stress in Russian cannot be reduced to simple rules. In this book, placement of stress is indicated by the capitalizing of the stressed syllable, e.g. **сказать** [ska-ZAT'], to say. * Monosyllables are often capitalized, too, to indicate the stresses necessary for the rhythm of the particular sentence. Moreover, rhythms may vary from context to context:

> **Я американец.**
> *YA a-m'i-r'i-KA-n'its* or *ya a-m'i-r'i-KA-n'its.*
> I am an American.

SYLLABICATION

Each word of more than one syllable is broken up into syllables by means of hyphenation. The syllabication is not necessarily Russian, however. In many cases, the hyphen was placed where it would be helpful to the native speaker of English, even though the rules of Russian syllabication might be violated.

---

* In the Grammar and Dictionary sections at the end of this book, an acute accent is used to indicate the stressed syllable of a word, for instance as in **сказа́ть**. The letter **ё** always represents a stressed sound, as in **ёлка** [YOL-kə], fir tree.

THE RUSSIAN ALPHABET

PRINTED	WRITTEN	NAME OR VALUE
А а	*А а*	[a]
Б б	*Б б*	[be]
В в	*В в*	[ve]
Г г	*Г г*	[ge]
Д д	*Д д, д*	[de]
Е е	*Е е*	[ye]
Ё ё	*Ё ё*	[yo]
Ж ж	*Ж ж*	[zhe]
З з	*З з, з*	[ze]
И и	*И и*	[i]
Й й	*Й й*	short [i]
К к	*К к*	[ka]
Л л	*Л л*	[el]
М м	*М м*	[em]
Н н	*Н н*	[en]
О о	*О о*	[o]
П п	*П, П п*	[p]
Р р	*Р р*	[er]
С с	*С с*	[es]
Т т	*Т т, т, т*	[te]
У у	*У у*	[u]
Ф ф	*Ф ф*	[ef]
Х х	*Х х*	[ḥa]

19

PRINTED	WRITTEN	NAME OR VALUE
Ц ц	*Ц ц*	[tse]
Ч ч	*Ч ч*	[che]
Ш ш	*Ш ш, щ*	[sha]
Щ щ	*Щ щ*	[sh'cha]
Ъ ъ	*ъ*	separative sign
Ы ы	*ы*	[ɨ]
Ь ь	*ь, ь*	soft sign
Э э	*Э э*	reversed [e]
Ю ю	*Ю ю*	[yu]
Я я	*Я я*	[ya]

SAMPLE OF RUSSIAN HANDWRITING

Я тоже не беспокоилась бы много, если бы знала, что мой сын жив и здоров.

Ну, я отдохнул и чувствую себе лучше. Теперь, не спеша, пойду домой. До свидание, Анна Петровна. Желаю вам скорее получить хорошие новости от вашего сына.

Я тоже не беспокоилась бы   много, если бы   знала, что мой сын жив   и здоров.

Ну, я отдохнул и чувствую себя лучше. Теперь, не спеша,   пойду домой. До свидания, Анна Петровна. Желаю вам скорее   получить хорошие новости от вашего сына.

I, too, would not worry much if I knew that my son is alive and in good health.

Well now, I have rested and am feeling better. Now I shall go home without hurrying. Good-by, Anna Petrovna. I hope that you will get good news from your son as soon as possible.

BASIC SENTENCE PATTERNS
AND
EVERYDAY CONVERSATIONS

BASIC SENTENCE PATTERNS

In each language there are a few types of sentences which are used more often than others in everyday speech.

On the basis of such sentences, one can form many others simply by replacing one or two of the words of each of these basic sentences. The sentences selected to illustrate the basic patterns are short, useful and easy to memorize. Learning them before you enter the main section of Everyday Conversations will automatically give you an idea of the structure of the language. Through them, you will also learn indirectly some of the most important grammatical categories and their function in the construction of sentences. This is in fact the natural way of learning a language — the way a child absorbs its native language by hearing, repeating and using the words and constructions in actual practice.

Cross references have been supplied to establish a correlation between the Basic Sentence Patterns and the Outline of Russian Grammar in this book. The grammatical knowledge you will acquire from the basic sentences can thus be related to the systematic presentation of Russian grammar.

SIMPLE DECLARATIVE SENTENCES
(See Grammar 6.1-4; 1.0-1; 2.0-2)

Russian has no separate words for the verb forms *am*, *is* and *are*. Also, there are no equivalents for the articles *a* or *an* and *the*. The meanings of these words are derived from the context. Similarly, the context tells whether это means *this* or *that*.

Affirmative

Я понимаю по-русски.
ya pə-n'i-MA-yu pa-RU-sk'i.
I understand Russian.

Он говорит по-русски.
on gə-va-R'IT pa-RU-sk'i.
He speaks Russian.

23

Мы возьмём это.
mɨ vaz'-M'OM E-tə.
We'll take this (*or* that).

Вы заказали комнату.
vɨ zə-ka-ZA-l'i KOM-nə-tu.
You ordered a room (*or* the room).

Я американец.
ya a-m'i-r'i-KA-n'its.
I am an American.

Суп пересолен.
SUP p'i-r'i-SO-l'in.
The soup is oversalted.

Это нужно.
E-tə NUZH-nə.
This is necessary.

Моя фамилия Петров.
ma-YA fa-M'IL'-yə p'i-TROF.
My surname is Petrov.

Я хочу сесть.
YA ha-CHU S'EST'.
I want to sit down.

Иван будет завтракать.
i-VAN BU-d'it ZAF-trə-kət'.
John is going to have breakfast.

Он англичанин.
on an-gl'i-CHA-n'in.
He is an Englishman.

Это можно.
E-tə MOZH-nə.
That is possible (permissible).

Это правильно.
E-tə PRA-v'il'-nə.
That is correct.

Negative

Я не понимаю по-русски.
ya n'i pə-n'i-MA-yu pa-RU-sk'i.
I don't understand Russian.

Мы не возьмём это.
mɨ n'i vaz'-M'OM E-tə.
We won't take this.

Вы не заказали комнату.
vɨ n'i zə-ka-ZA-l'i KOM-nə-tu.
You didn't order a room.

Я не американец.
ya n'i a-m'i-r'i-KA-n'its.
I am not an American.

Суп не пересолен.
SUP n'i p'i-r'i-SO-l'in.
The soup is not oversalted.

Это не нужно.
E-tə n'i NUZH-nə.
This is not necessary.

Моя фамилия не Петров.
ma-YA fa-M'IL'-yə n'i p'i-TROF.
My surname is not Petrov.

Он не говорит по-русски.
on n'i gə-va-R'IT pa-RU-sk'i.
He doesn't speak Russian.

Я не хочу сесть.
ya n'i ha-CHU S'EST'
I don't want to sit down.

Иван не будет завтракать.
i-VAN n'i BU-d'it ZAF-trə-kət'.
John is not going to have breakfast.

Он не англичанин.
on n'i an-gl'i-CHA-n'in.
He is not an Englishman.

Это нельзя.
E-tə n'il'-Z'A.
That is not possible (permissible).

Это не правильно.
E-tə n'i PRA-v'il'-nə.
That is not correct.

SIMPLE QUESTIONS

With interrogative words

(See Grammar 4.5-6)

Что он понимает?
shto on pə-n'i-MA-yit?
What does he understand?

Кто говорит по-русски?
kto gə-va-R'IT pa-RU-sk'i?
Who speaks Russian?

Где Иван будет завтракать?
GD'E i-VAN BU-d'it ZAF-trə-kət'?
Where is John going to have breakfast?

Что это такое?
shto E-tə ta-KOY-ə?
What is that? (*lit.,* what that such?)

Что нужно?
SHTO NUZH-nə?
What is necessary?

Как ваша фамилия?
KAK VA-shə fa-M'IL'-yə?
What is your surname? (*lit.,* how ...?)

Что вы возьмёте?
shto vi vaz'-M'O-t'i?
What will you take?

Куда вы хотите сесть?
ku-DA vi ha-T'I-t'i S'EST'?
Where do you want to sit?

Кто он такой?
kto on ta-KOY?
Who is he? (*lit.,* who he such?)

Как это можно?
KAK E-tə MOZH-nə?
How is that possible?

Где комната?
GD'E KOM-nə-tə?
Where is the room?

Yes-or-no questions

(See Grammar 4.1, 4.4; 7.1)

The simplest and most common way of forming such questions in Russian is by the addition of an interrogative intonation to the declarative sentence. This intonation is often quite different from that heard in English, in that it consists of simply raising very high the most prominent syllable in the phrase or sentence. To English ears this sounds like a very emphatic statement, but it is nevertheless the commonest Russian way of asking a yes-or-no question. The English type of final-rising inflection is heard also.

Он понимает по-русски?
on pə-n'i-MA-yit pa-RU-sk'i?
Does he understand Russian?

Он не говорит по-русски?
on n'i gə-va-R'IT pa-RU-sk'i?
Doesn't he speak Russian?

Мы возьмём это?
mi vaz'-M'OM E-tə?
Will we take this?

Иван не будет завтракать?
i-VAN n'i BU-d'it ZAF-trə-kət'?
Isn't John going to have breakfast?

Суп пересолен?
SUP p'i-r'i-SO-l'in?
Is the soup oversalted?

Это можно?
E-tə MOZH-nə?
Is this possible (permissible)?

Ваша фамилия Петров?
VA-shə fa-M'IL'-yə p'i-TROF?
Is your name Petrov?

Вы заказали комнату?
vi zə-ka-ZA-l'i KOM-nə-tu?
Did you order a room?

Он англичанин?
on an-gl'i-CHA-n'in?
Is he an Englishman?

Это нужно?
E-tə NUZH-nə?
Is that necessary?

Это правильно?
E-tə PRA-v'il'-nə?
Is this correct?

An alternative, though less common, way of forming yes-or-no questions is by reversing verb and subject:

Понимает он по-русски?
pə-n'i-MA-yit on pa-RU-sk'i?
Does he understand Russian?

Нужно это?
NUZH-nə E-tə?
Is this necessary?

More commonly, the particle ли is added:

Понимает ли он по-русски?
pə-n'i-MA-yit l'i on pa-RU-sk'i?
Does he understand Russian?

Нужно ли это?
NUZH-nə l'i E-tə?
Is this necessary?

Англичанин ли он?
an-gl'i-CHA-n'in l'i on?
Is he an Englishman?

MORE COMPLEX DECLARATIVE SENTENCES

Indirect quotations

(See Grammar 6.5; 5.1-2)

Note use of ли as in yes-or-no questions type 3:

Я не знаю, понимает ли он по-русски.
YA n'i ZNA-yu pə-n'i-MA-yit l'i on pa-RU-sk'i.
I don't know if (= whether) he understands Russian.

Я не знаю, хочу ли я сесть.
YA n'i ZNA-yu ha-CHU l'i ya S'EST'.
I don't know if I want to sit down.

Я не знаю, англичанин ли он.
YA n'i ZNA-yu an-gl'i-CHA-n'in l'i on.
I don't know if he is an Englishman.

Я не знаю, нужно ли это.
YA n'i ZNA-yu NUZH-nə l'i E-tə.
I don't know if that is necessary.

Other types:

Я не знаю, что он понимает.
ya n'i ZNA-yu shto on pə-n'i-MA-yit.
I don't know what he understands.

Я спрошу, где комната.
YA spra-SHU gd'e KOM-nə-tə.
I'll ask where the room is.

Я не знаю, что нужно.
YA n'i ZNA-yu shto NUZH-nə.
I don't know what is necessary.

Я спрошу, что это такое.
ya spra-SHU shto E-tə ta-KOY-ə.
I'll ask what that is.

Он понимает, что я говорю по-русски.
on pə-n'i-MA-yit shto ya gə-va-R'U pə-RU-sk'i.
He understands what I am saying in Russian. ⎫
He understands that I am speaking Russian. ⎬ *
⎭

Мы возьмём, что нужно.
Mɨ vaz'-M'OM shto NUZH-nə.
We'll take what is necessary.

Он говорит, что он хочет сесть.
ON gə-va-R'IT shto on HO-chit S'EST'.
He says that he wants to sit down.

Мы знаем, что он американец.
mɨ ZNA-yim shto on a-m'i-r'i-KA-n'its.
We know that he is an American.

Мы говорим по-русски потому, что это нужно.
mɨ gə-va-R'IM pə-RU-sk'i pə-ta-MU-shtə E-tə NUZH-nə.
We are speaking Russian because it is necessary.

---

* Depending on intonation что means *what* or *that*.

Так как это нужно, мы говорим по-русски.
tak kak E-tə NUZH-nə mі gə-va-R'IM pa-RU-sk'i.
Since it is necessary, we speak Russian.

Если можно, он возьмёт это.
YE-sl'i MOZH-nə on vaz'-M'OT E-tə.
If possible, he'll take that.

Если он захочет, я поговорю с ним об этом.
YE-sl'i on za-HO-chit, ya pə-gə-va-R'U sn'im a-BE-təm.
If he wishes (*lit.*, if he will want), I'll speak with him about this.

Я американец, который говорит по-русски (*or* говорящий по-русски).
YA a-m'i-r'i-KA-n'its ka-TOR-iy gə-va-R'IT pa-RU-sk'i (or gə-va-R'ASH'-chiy pə-ru-sk'i).
I am an American who speaks Russian (*or lit.*, speaking Russian).

(See Grammar 2.6; 7.2)

The foregoing simple sentences can be expanded into the longer and more expressive sentences of normal, everyday speech by the mere addition of more words:

Adverbs

Я хочу сесть сюда.
YA ha-CHU S'EST' su-DA.
I want to sit here.

Я спрошу, кто там.
ya spra-SHU KTO tam.
I'll ask who's there.

Он хорошо говорит по-русски.
on hə-ra-SHO gə-va-R'IT pa-RU-sk'i.
He speaks Russian well.

Кто тут говорит по-русски?
KTO tut gə-va-R'IT pa-RU-sk'i?
Who speaks Russian here?

Это очень нужно.
E-tə O-chin NUZH-nə.
This is very necessary.

Negatives

Я ничего не понимаю.
ya n'i-chi-VO n'i pə-n'i-MA-yu.
I don't understand anything.

Иван никогда не будет завтракать.
i-VAN n'i-kag-DA n'i BU-d'it ZAF-trə-kət'.
John is never going to have breakfast.

Мы ничего не возьмём.
mі n'i-chi-VO n'i vaz'-M'OM.
We won't take anything.

Object pronouns

Я его понимаю.
YA yi-VO pə-n'i-MA-yu.
I understand him.

Это мне нужно.
E-tə mn'e NUZH-nə.
I need that (*lit.*, that is necessary to me).

Вы заказали её.
V'ɨ zə-ka-ZA-l'i yi-YO.
You ordered it (*lit., her,* referring to *room* [fem.]).

Он знает меня.
on ZNA-yit m'i-N'A.
He knows me.

Infinitives

Это нужно знать.
E-tə NUZH-nə ZNAT'.
That is necessary to know.

Как можно пройти туда?
KAK MOZH-nə pray-T'I tu-DA?
How can one get there?

Как можно узнать?
KAK MOZH-nə uz-NAT'?
How can one find out? (*lit.,* How is it possible to find out?)

PREPOSITIONAL PHRASES

(See Grammar 1.2-6)

With nouns

Иван будет завтракать в гостинице.
i-VAN BU-d'it ZAF-trə-kət' vga-ST'I-n'itsi.
John is going to have breakfast in the hotel.

Он говорит по-русски с Иваном.
on gə-va-R'IT pa-RU-sk'i si-VA-nəm.
He is speaking Russian with John.

Я хочу сесть у окна.
YA ha-CHU S'EST' u ak-NA.
I want to sit by the window.

Как можно пройти на вокзал?
KAK MOZH-nə pray-T'I nə-vag-ZAL?
How can one get to the railroad station?

With pronouns

Я поговорю с ним.
ya pə-gə-va-R'U sn'im.
I'll speak with him.

Я поговорю с ним об этом.
ya pə-gə-va-R'U sn'im a-BE-təm.
I'll speak with him about that.

Мы возьмём это с собой.
mi̇ vaz'-M'OM E-tə ssa-BOY.
We'll take this with us (*lit.*, with self).

Я спрошу у него карандаш.
YA spra-SHU u n'i-VO kə-ran-DASH.
I'll ask him for a pencil (*lit.*, I'll ask by him a pencil).

FORMS OF THE VERB БЫТЬ (TO BE)
(See Grammar 6.1)

As shown earlier, Russian does not have forms for the meanings of *is, am* and *are*, but it does have such words as *to be, was, were, will be,* and *there is, are.* The normal way of saying *I have, you have,* etc., is *by me there is, by you there is,* etc.

Он был англичанин.
ON bil an-gl'i-CHA-n'in.
He was an Englishman.

Суп был пересолен.
SUB bil p'i-r'i-SO-l'in.
The soup was oversalted.

Его фамилия была Петров.
yi-VO fa-M'IL'-yə bi-LA p'i-TROF.
His surname was Petrov.

Это будет нужно.
E-tə BU-d'it NUZH-nə.
That will be necessary.

У меня есть спички.
u m'i-N'A yest' SP'ICH-k'i
I have matches (*lit.*, by me there are matches).

Есть у вас словарь?
YEST' u vas sla-VAR'?
Do you have a dictionary?

WORD ORDER IN RUSSIAN SENTENCES

Word order in Russian is not so strict as in English because there is little possibility of misinterpreting the function or meaning of a word, regardless of its position in the sentence. Since each function is marked by a special ending of some sort, Russian words may be either strung out in an order that is not very different from that of English or they may be transposed in various ways to produce important stylistic effects or emphases.

ELLIPSIS

In familiar Russian conversation, subject and object pronouns, certain impersonal forms and even certain verbs are put in or left out of sentences at the speaker's option.

The following examples illustrate both transposition of words and ellipsis:

"*Normal*"	*Modified*

Я не говорю по-русски.
ya n'i gə-va-R'U pa-RU-sk'i.
I don't speak Russian.

По-русски не говорю.
pa-RU-sk'i n'i go-va-R'U.

Я хочу сесть.
YA ha-CHU S'EST.
I want to sit down.

Сесть хочу.
S'EST ha-CHU.

Как мне нужно итти?
KAK mn'e NUZH-nə i-T'I?
How should I go?

Как нужно итти? ⎫
Как мне итти? ⎬
KAK [NUZH-nə] [mn'e] i-T'I?

In some cases, the "normal" example is simply more common than the "modified" one, and requirements of emphasis and intonation determine which one is used at a particular moment:

У вас есть словарь?
u VAS yest' sla-VAR'?
Do you have a dictionary?

Есть у вас словарь?
YEST' u vas sla-VAR'?

Он меня знает.
on m'i-N'A ZNA-yit.
He knows me.

Он знает меня.
on ZNA-yit m'i-N'A.

Как можно туда пройти?
kak MOZH-nə tu-DA pray-T'I?
How can one get there?

Как можно пройти туда?
Как туда пройти?
KAK MOZH-nə pray-T'I tu-DA?
KAK tu-DA pray-T'I?

BASIC QUESTIONS AND ANSWERS
(See Grammar 2.3-5; 4.3)

Он понимает по-русски?
on pə-n'i-MA-yit pa-RU-sk'i?
Does he understand Russian?

Да, понимает.
DA, pə-n'i-MA-yit.
Yes, he does.

Не говорит ли он по-русски?
n'i gə-va-R'IT l'i on pa-RU-sk'i?
Doesn't he speak Russian?

Нет, не говорит.
N'ET, n'i gə-va-R'IT.
No, he doesn't.

Что вы возьмёте с собой?
SHTO vi vaz'-M'O-t'i ssa-BOY?
What will you take with you?

Возьмём эти вещи.
vaz'-M'OM E-t'i V'ESH-chi.
We'll take these things.

Куда хотите сесть?
ku-DA ḥa-T'I-t'i S'EST'?
Where do you want to sit down?

Где комната?
GD'E KOM-nə-tə?
Where is the room?

Это нужно?
E-tə NUZH-nə?
Is that necessary?

Как ваша фамилия?
KAK VA-shə fa-M'IL'-yə?
What is your surname?

Кто он такой?
KTO on ta-KOY?
Who is he?

Есть у вас словарь?
YEST' u vas sla-VAR'?
Do you have a dictionary?

Я хочу сесть сюда.
YA ḥa-CHU S'EST' su-DA.
I want to sit down here.

Комната там.
KOM-nə-tə TAM.
The room is there.

Это очень нужно.
E-tə O-chin' NUZH-nə.
It is very necessary.

Моя фамилия Петров.
ma-YA fa-M'IL'ye p'i-TROF.
My name is Petrov.

Он американец.
on a-m'i-r'i-KA-n'its.
He is an American.

Да, у меня есть.
DA, u m'i-N'A YEST'.
Yes, I have one.

EVERYDAY CONVERSATIONS

BASIC EXPRESSIONS

Да.
DA.
Yes.

Нет.
N'ET.
No.

Хорошо.
hə-ra-SHO.
All right.

Это.
E-tə.
This one.

Нет, не это.
N'ET, n'i E-tə.
No, not this one.

Вот он.
VOT ON.
Here he is.

Вот она.
VOT a-NA.
Here she is

Вот оно.
VOT a-NO.
Here it is.

Когда?
kag-DA?
When?

Где?
GD'E?
Where?

Который?
ka-TOR-iy?
Which?

Почему?
pə-chi-MU?
Why?

Что это такое?
SHTO E-tə ta-KOY-ə?
What is this?

Вы готовы?
vi ga-TO-vi?
Are you ready?

Поспешите!
pə-sp'i-SHŁ-t'i!
Hurry!

Это всё?
E-təf-S'O?
Is that all?

Сколько?
SKOL'-kə?
How much?

Я американец.
ya a-m'i-r'i-KA-n'its.
I am an American. (masc.)

Я американка.
ya a-m'i-r'i-KAN-kə.
I am an American. (fem.)

Я англичанин.
ya an-gl'i-CHA-n'in.
I am an Englishman.

Я англичанка.
ya an-gl'i-CHAN-kə.
I am an Englishwoman.

Я иностранец.
ya i-na-STRA-n'its.
I am a foreigner. (masc.)

Я иностранка.
ya- i-na-STRAN-kə.
I am a foreigner. (fem)

Я из Нью Йорка.
ya iz n'yu YOR-kə.
I am from New York

По-русски не говорю.
pə-RU-sk'i n'i gə-va-R'U.
I don't speak Russian.

33

Как ваша фамилия?
kak VA-shə fa-M'IL'-yə?
What is your name?

Моя фамилия . . .
ma-YA fa-M'IL'-yə . . .
My name is . . .

Вот мой паспорт.
vot moy PAS-pərt.
Here is my passport.

Я живу в Нью Йорке.
ya zhi-VU vn'yu YOR-k'i.
I live in New York.

Кто тут говорит по-английски?
KTO tut gə-va-R'IT pə-an-GL'IY-sk'i?
Who speaks English here?

Я в затруднении.
yav-zə-trud-N'E-n'i-i.
I am in trouble.

Я бы хотел кое что об'яснить вам.
ya-bi-ha-T'EL KOY-ə-shtə ab-jis-N'IT' vam.
I would like to explain something to you.

Как это называется по-русски?
KAK E-tə nə-zi-VA-yit-sə pa RU-sk'i?
What is that called in Russian?

Я понимаю.
ya pə-n'i-MA-yu.
I understand.

Я не понимаю.
ya n'i-pə-n'i-MA-yu.
I don't understand.

Понимаете?
pə-n'i-MA-yi-t'i?
Do you understand?

Доброе утро.
DO-brə-yə U-trə.
Good morning.

Добрый день.
DO-briy D'EN'.
Good afternoon.

Добрый вечер.
DO-bri-y V'E-chir.
Good evening.

Спокойной ночи.
spa-KOY-nəy NO-chi.
Good night.

До свидания.
də-s'v'i-DA-n'i-yə.
Good bye.

Как поживаете?
kak pə-zhi-VA-yi-t'i?
How are you?

Благодарю вас, хорошо.
blə-gə-da-R'U-vas, hə-ra-SHO.
Very well, thanks.

С удовольствием.
su-da-VOL'-s'-t'v'i-im.
With pleasure.

Извините.
iz'-v'i-N'I-t'i.
Excuse me.

Пожалуйста.
pa-ZHA-lə-stə.
Please.

Большое спасибо.
bal'-SHOY-ə spa-S'I-bə.
Thank you very much.

Вы очень любезны.
vi O-chin l'u-B'EZ-ni.
You are very kind.

Ничего!
n'i-chi-VO!
It does not matter.

Это очень неприятно.
E-tə O-chin n'i-pr'i-YAT-nə.
It's very annoying.

Я выхожу.
ya-vi-ha-ZHU.
I am about to go out.

Идите скорее.
i-D'I-t'i ska-R'EY-ə.
Go at once.

Помогите мне.
pə-ma-G'I-t'i mn'e.
Help me.

Принесите мне...
pr'i-n'i-S'I-t'i mn'e...
Bring me...

Дайте мне...
DAY-t'i mn'e...
Give me...

Несите это.
n'i-S'I-t'i E-tə.
Carry this.

Идите за мной.
i-D'I-t'i za-MNOY.
Follow me.

GETTING TO KNOW YOU

Можно вас познакомить с гражданином Петровым?
MOZH-nə vas pəz-na-KO-m'it' zgrazh-da-N'I-nəm p'i-TRO-vim?
May I introduce you to Citizen Petrov?

Это моя жена.
E-tə ma-YA zhi-NA.
This is my wife.

А это мой сын (моя дочка).
a E-tə moy SƗN (ma-YA DOCH-kə).
This is my son (my daughter).

Вы, повидимому, говорите по-русски.
vi, pa-V'I-d'i-mə-mu, go-va-R'I-t'i pa-RU-sk'i.
You speak Russian, I see.

Да, немножко.
DA, n'im-NOSH-kə.
Yes, a little.

Вы очень скромны.
vi O-chin SKROM-ni.
You're very modest.

Это ваша первая поездка в Советский Союз?
E-tə VA-shə P'ER-və-yə pa-YEST-kə fsa-V'ET-sk'iy sa-YUS?
Is this your first trip to the Soviet Union?

Вы довольны своей поездкой?
vi da-VOL'-ni sva-YEY pa-YEST-kəy?
Are you enjoying your trip?

Очень, ваша страна мне очень нравится.
O-chin, VA-shə stra-NA mn'e O-chin NRA-v'it-sə.
Very much, I like your country very much.

Где вы живёте в Соединённых Штатах?
gd'ə vi zhi-V'O-t'i fsə-yi-d'i-N'ON-nih SHTA-təh?
Where do you live in the United States?

Я живу в Нью Йорке.
YA zhi-VU vn'yu YOR-k'i.
I live in New York.

Ах так, это очень интересно.
ah TAK, E-ta O-chin in-t'i-R'ES-nə.
Oh, is that so? That's very interesting.

Да, вы должны обязательно нас навестить когда вы будете в Америке.
Da, vi dalzh-NƗ ab'i-ZA-t'il-nə nas nə-v'i-ST'IT' kag-DA vi BU-d'i-t'i va-M'E-r'i-k'i.
Yes, you must visit us when you come to America.

Очень мило с вашей стороны.
O-chin M'I-lə sVA-shəy stə-ra-NÍ.
That's very nice of you.

Непременно зайдём к вам когда мы будем в Нью Йорке.
n'i-pr'i-M'EN-nə zay-D'OM kvam kag-DA mí BU-d'im vn'yu YOR-k'i.
We'll certainly drop by to see you when we're in New York.

COUNTING

Cardinal Numbers

один *a-D'IN* one	**шесть** *SHES'T'* six	**одиннадцать** *a-D'I-nət-sət'* eleven
два *DVA* two	**семь** *S'EM'* seven	**двенадцать** *dv'i-NAT-sət'* twelve
три *TR'I* three	**восемь** *VO-s'im'* eight	**тринадцать** *tr'i-NAT-sət'* thirteen
четыре *chi-TŦ-r'ə* four	**девять** *D'E-v'it'* nine	**четырнадцать** *chi-TŦR-nət-sət'* fourteen
пять *P'AT'* five	**десять** *D'E-s'it'* ten	**пятнадцать** *p'it-NAT-sət'* fifteen
шестнадцать *shís-NAT-sət'* sixteen	**двадцать один** *DVAT-sət' a-D'IN* twenty-one	**пятьдесят** *p'i-d'i-S'AT* fifty
семнадцать *s'im-NAT-sət'* seventeen	**двадцать два** *DVAT-səd' DVA* twenty-two	**шестьдесят** *shiz-d'i-S'AT* sixty
восемнадцать *və-s'im-NAT-sət'* eighteen	**двадцать три** *DVAT-sət' TR'I* twenty-three	**семьдесят** *S'EM'-d'i-s'it* seventy
девятнадцать *d'i-v'it-NAT-sət'* nineteen	**тридцать** *TR'IT-sət'* thirty	**восемьдесят** *VO-s'im'-d'i-s'it* eighty
двадцать *DVAT-sət'* twenty	**сорок** *SO-rək* forty	**девяносто** *d'i-v'i-NO-stə* ninety

сто
STO
a hundred

миллион
m'i-l'i-ON
a million

тысяча
Tɫ-s'i-chə
a thousand

сто тридцать пять
STO TR'IT-sət' P'AT'
one hundred and thirty-five

.

Ordinal Numbers

первый
P'ER-viy
the first

шестой
shi-STOY
the sixth

одиннадцатый
a-D'I-nəts-tiy
the eleventh

3/4

второй
fta-ROY
the second

1/3

седьмой
s'id'-MOY
the seventh

двенадцатый
d'v'i-NATS-tiy
the twelfth

третий
TR'E-t'iy
the third

1/4

восьмой
vas'-MOY
the eighth

1/8

тринадцатый
tr'i-NATS-tiy
the thirteenth

четвёртый
chit-V'OR-tiy
the fourth

девятый
d'i-V'A-tiy
the ninth

четырнадцатый
chi-TɪR-nəts-tiy
the fourteenth

пятый
P'A-tiy
the fifth

десятый
d'i-S'A-tiy
the tenth

пятнадцатый
p'it-NATS-tiy
the fifteenth

1/5

шестнадцатый
shis-NATS-tiy
the sixteenth

двадцать первый
DVAT-sət' P'ER-viy
the twenty-first

пятидесятый
p'i-t'i-d'i-S'A-tiy
the fiftieth

семнадцатый
s'im-NATS-tiy
the seventeenth

двадцать второй
DVAT-sət' fta-ROY
the twenty-second

шестидесятый
shɪ-s't'd'i-S'A-t:y
the sixtieth

восемнадцатый
və-s'im-NATS-tiy
the eighteenth

двадцать третий
DVAT-sət' TR'E-t'iy
the twenty-third

семидесятый
s'i-m'i-d'i-S'A-tiy
the seventieth

девятнадцатый
d'i-v'it-NATS-tiy
the nineteenth

тридцатый
tr'it-SA-tiy
the thirtieth

восьмидесятый
və-s'm'i-d'i-S'A-tiy
the eightieth

двадцатый
dvat-SA-t:y
the twentieth

сороковой
sə-rə-ka-VOY
the fortieth

девяностый
d'i-v'i-NO-st:y
the ninetieth

сотый
SO-tiy
the one hundredth

миллионный
m'i-l'i-ON-niy
the one millionth

тысячный
Tɬ-s'ich-niy
the one thousandth

сто тридцать пятый
STO TR'IT-sət' P'A-tiy
the one hundred and thirty-fifth

Collective and Fractional Numbers

один раз
a-D'IN RAS
once

два раза
DVA RA-zə
twice

три раза
TR'I RA-zə
thrice

четыре раза
chi-Tɬ-r'i RA-zə
four times

пара
PA-rə
a couple, a pair

один
a-D'IN
single

двойной
dvay-NOY
double

дюжина
D'U-zhi-nə
a dozen

двадцать
DVAT-sət'
a score

четверть
CHET-v'ir't'
a quarter

половина
pə-la-V'I-nə
a half

третья часть
TR'ET'-yə CHAS'T'
a third

пятая часть
P'A-tə-yə CHAS'T'
a fifth

восьмая часть
vas'-MA-yə CHAS'T'
an eighth

THE CLOCK AND THE CALENDAR

Который час?
ka-TOR-iy CHAS?
What's the time?

час
CHAS
One o'clock

два часа
DVA chi-SA
Two o'clock

три часа
TR'I chi-SA
Three o'clock

четыре часа
chi-Tɬ-r'i chi-SA
Four o'clock

пять часов
P'AT' chi-SOF
Five o'clock

шесть часов
SHES'T' chi-SOF
Six o'clock

семь часов
S'EM' chi-SOF
Seven o'clock

восемь часов
VO-s'im' chi-SOF
Eight o'clock

девять часов
D'E-v'it' chi-SOF
Nine o'clock

десять часов
D'E-s'it' chi-SOF
Ten o'clock

одиннадцать часов
a-D'I-nət-sət' chi-SOF
Eleven o'clock

двенадцать часов
d' v'i-NAT-sət' chi-SOF
Twelve o'clock

В котором часу?
fka-TO-rəm chi-SU?
At what time?

В три десять
f-TR'I D'E-s'it'
At 3:10

В три пятнадцать
f-TR'I p'it-NAT-sət'
At 3:15

В три двадцать
f-TR'I DVAT-sət'
At 3:20

В три тридцать
f-TR'I TR'IT-sət'
At 3:30

В три пятьдесят
f-TR'I p'i-d'i-S'AT
At 3:50

В четыре пятьдесят
f-chi-Tɫ-r'i p'i-d'i-S'AT
At 4:50

В восемь пятьдесят
v-VO-s'im' p'i-d'i-S'AT
At 8:50

Утром
U-trəm
In the morning

Днём
DN'OM
In the afternoon

Вечером
V'E-chi-rəm
In the evening

Ночью
NOCH-yu
At night

Days of the week

Какой сегодня день?
ka-KOY s'i-VOD'-n'ə D'EN?
What day is today?

Воскресенье
və-skr'i-S'EN'-yə
Sunday

Понедельник
pə-n'i-D'EL'-n'ik
Monday

Вторник
FTOR-n'ik
Tuesday

Среда
sr'i-DA
Wednesday

Четверг
chit-V'ERK
Thursday

Пятница
P'AT-n'it-sə
Friday

Суббота
su-BO-tə
Saturday

Выходной день
v'i-had-NOY D'EN'
Off-day; day off

Months

Январь
yin-VAR'
January

Февраль
f'iv-RAL'
February

Март
MART
March

Апрель
a-PR'EL'
April

Май
MAY
May

Июнь
i-YUN'
June

Июль
i-YUL'
July

Август
AV-gust
August

Сентябрь
s'in-T'A-br'
September

Октябрь
ak-T'A-br'
October

Ноябрь
na-YA-br'
November

Декабрь
d'i-KA-br'
December

STRANGER IN TOWN

Я американец (*masc.*), **англичанин** (*masc.*).
ya a-m'i-r'i-KA-n'its, an-gl'i-CHA-n'in.
I am an American, Englishman.

Я американка (*femin.*), **англичанка** (*femin.*).
ya a-m'i-r'i-KAN-kə, an-gl'i-CHAN-kə.
I am an American, an Englishwoman.

Далеко отсюда Тверская улица?
də-l'i-KO at-SU-də tv'ir-SKA-yə U-l'itsə?
Is Tversky street far from here?

Как ближе пройти на Тверскую Улицу?
kak BL'I-zhə pray-T'I nə tv'ir-SKU-yu U-l'itsu?
Kindly tell me the shortest way to Tversky Street.

Это Красная Площадь?
E-tə KRAS-nə-yə PLOSH'-chit'?
Is this Red Square?

Извините, как пройти к Кремлю?
iz-v'i-N'I-t'i, kak pray-T'I kkr'im-L'U?
Pardon me, which is the way to the Kremlin?

Куда мне итти направо или налево?
ku-DA mn'e i-T'I, na-PRA-və I-l'i na-L'E-və?
Must I turn to the right or to the left?

Идите прямо.
i-D'I-t'i PR'A-mə.
Go straight ahead.

Второй поворот направо (налево).
fta-ROY pə-va-ROT na-PRA-və (na-L'E-və).
It is the second turn to the right (left).

Каким трамваем (автобусом) мне проехать на Кузнецкий Мост?
ka-K'IM tram-VA-yim (af-TO-bu-səm) mn'e pra-YE-hət' na kuz-N'ETsk'iy MOST?
What streetcar (bus) will take me to Kuznetsky street (lit. bridge)?

Я заблудился (*masc.*), **заблудилась** (*fem.*).
ya zə-blu-D'IL-sə, zə-blu-D'I-ləs.
I have lost my way.

На какой улице находится Третьяковская галерея?
nə ka-KOY U-l'it-si na-HO-d'it-sə tr'it'-yi-KOF-skə-yə gə-l'i-R'EY-ə?
On what street is the Tretyakov Gallery?

Куда ведёт эта дорога?
ku-DA v'i-D'OT E-tə da-RO-gə?
Where does this road lead to?

Там?
TAM?
Over there?

Дайте мне адрес, пожалуйста.
DAY-t'i mn'e A-dr'is, pa-ZHA-lə-stə.
Will you please give me the address?

Здесь живёт ..?
ZD'ES' zhi-V'OT ...?
Does... live here?

Проводите меня до ближайшей почты.
prə-va-D'I-t'i m'i-N'A də-bl'i-ZHAY-shəy POCH-ti.
Take me to the nearest post office.

Проводите меня в Госбанк.
prə-va-D'I-t'i m'i-N'A vgoz-BANK.
Take me to the State Bank.

Хочу пройти на Ленинский Стадион.
ha-CHU pray-T'I na L'E-n'in-sk'iy stə-d'i-ON.
I want to go to the Lenin Stadium.

Где ближайшая стоянка такси?
gd'e bl'i-ZHAY-shə-yə sta-YAN-kə tak-S'I?
Where is the nearest taxi stand?

Я потерял ключ.
ya pə-t'i-R'AL KL'UCH.
I have lost my key.

Не могу найти свой паспорт.
n'i-ma-GU nay-T'I svoy PAS-pərt.
I can't find my passport.

Это очень странно.
E-tə O-chin STRAN-nə.
It's very strange.

Утром я его здесь видел.
U-trəm ya yi-VO z'd'es' V'I-d'il.
I saw it here this morning.

Час тому назад он был у меня в руках.
CHAS ta-MU na-ZAT on BIL u-m'i-N'A v-ru-KAH.
I had it an hour ago.

Нашёл! (нашла! *fem.*)
na-SHOL! (nash-LA!)
I've found it!

Идите вперёд.
i-D'I-t'i fp'i-R'OT.
Lead the way.

Позовите такси.
pə-za-V'I-t'i tak-S'I.
Call a taxi.

Откройте дверь.
at-KROY-t'i DV'ER'.
Open the door.

Закройте дверь.
za-KROY-t'i DV'ER'.
Close the door.

Откройте окно.
at-KROY-t'i ak-NO.
Open the window.

Закройте окно.
za-KROY-t'i ak-NO.
Close the window.

Запишите.
zə-p'i-SHÏ-t'i.
Write it down.

Войдите.
vay-D'I-t'i.
Come in.

Садитесь, пожалуйста.
sa-D'I-t'is, pa-ZHA-lə-stə.
Please sit down.

Спасибо.
spa-S'I-bə.
Thank you.

Пожалуйста.
pa-ZHA-lə-stə.
You are welcome.

Где находится Интурист?
gd'e na-ḤO-d'it-sə in-tu-R'IST?
Where is Intourist?

В этом доме находится Интурист?
vE-təm DO-m'i na-ḤO-d'it-sə in-tu-R'IST?
Is Intourist in this building?

Эту контору я ищу.
E-tu kan-TO-ru ya ish'-CHU.
This is the office I am looking for.

Прочтите это пожалуйста.
prach-T'I-t'i E-tə pa-ZHA-lə-stə.
Would you mind reading this for me, please?

Пожалуйста, проводите меня в метро.
pa-ZHA-lə-stə, prə-va-D'I-t'i m'i-N'A vm'i-TRO
Would you please show me the way to the subway?

Где вход?
GD'E f-ḤOT?
Where is the entrance?

Здесь вход на выставку?
ZD'ES' f-ḤOT na V'i-stəf-ku?
Is this the entrance to the exhibition?

Где бюро пропусков?
gd'e b'u-RO prə-pu-SKOF?
Where do they give out the admission passes?

Где справочный отдел?
gd'e SPRA-vəch-nïy ad-D'EL?
Where is the information desk?

Где я могу получить справку?
gd'e ya ma-GU pə-lu-CHIT' SPRAF-ku?
Where can I have an inquiry answered?

Где можно получить пропуск?
gd'e MOZH-nə pə-lu-CHIT' PRO-pusk?
Where do you get a pass?

Я не говорю по-русски.
ya ni-gə-va-R'U pa-RU-sk'i.
I don't speak Russian.

Я иностранец.
ya i-na-STRA-n'its.
I am a foreigner. (masc.)

Я американец.
ya a-m'i-ri-KA-n'its.
I am an American. (masc.)

Я хочу подняться на шестой этаж.
ya ḥa-CHU pad-N'AT-sə nə shi-STOY i-TASH.
I want to go to the 6th floor.

Где лифт?
gd'e L'IFT?
Where is the elevator?

Мне нужно видеть директора.
mn'e NUZH-nə V'I-d'it' d'i-REK-tə-rə.
I want to see the manager.

Мне нужен секретарь.
mn'e NU-zhin s'i-kr'i-TAR'.
I want the secretary.

Мне нужен управляющий делами.
mn'e NU-zhin u-prav-L'A-yush'-chiy d'i-LA-m'i.
I want the business manager.

Мне нужен заведующий отделом.
mn'e NU-zhin za-V'E-du-yush'-chiy ad-D'E-ləm.
I want the department chief.

Мне нужно иностранное бюро.
mn'e NUZH-nə i-na-STRAN-nə-yə b'u-RO.
I want the foreign section.

Кто здесь говорит по английски?
KTO zd'es' gə-va-R'IT pə-an-GL'IY-sk'i?
Does anyone here speak English?

Мне нужен английский переводчик.
mn'e NU-zhin an-GL'IY-sk'iy p'i-r'i-VOT'-chik.
I need an English interpreter.

ABOARD SHIP

Где моя каюта?
GD'E ma-YA ka-YU-tə?
Where is my cabin?

Где первый класс?
gd'e P'ER-viy KLAS?
Where is the first class?

Где второй класс?
gd'e fta-ROY KLAS?
Where is the second class?

Где ресторан?
gd'e r'i-sta-RAN?
Where is the dining-room?

Где курительная?
gd'e ku-R'I-t'il'-nə-yə?
Where is the smoking room?

Хочу поговорить с капитаном.
ha-CHU pə-gə-va-R'IT' skə-p'i-TA-nəm.
I want to speak to the captain.

Принесите мне чаю в каюту.
pr'i-n'i-S'I-t'i mn'e CHA-yu fka-YU-tu.
Bring me some tea to my cabin.

Принесите мне горячей воды.
pr'i-n'i-S'I-t'i mn'e ga-R'A-chəy va-DÏ.
Bring me some hot water:

Где зал?
gd'e ZAL?
Where is the lounge?

Это зал первого класса?
E-tə ZAL P'ER-və-və KLA-sə?
Is this the first-class lounge?

Когда здесь обеды?
kag-DA zd'es' a-BE-di?
At what time is dinner served?

Когда здесь ужины?
kag-DA zd'es' U-zhi-ni?
At what time is supper served?

Когда отход?
kag-DA at-ḤOT?
When do we start?

Поставьте багаж сюда.
pa-STAF'-t'i ba-GASH su-DA.
Put my baggage here.

Откройте окно.
at-KROY-t'i ak-NO.
Open the window.

Закройте окно.
za-KROY-t'i ak-NO.
Close the window.

Принесите постельное бельё и полотенца.
pr'i-n'i-S'I-t'i pa-ST'EL'-nə-yə b'il'-YO i pə-la-T'ENT-sə.
Fetch me bedding and towels.

Дайте мне ключ от моей каюты.
DAY-t'i mn'e KL'UCH at ma-YEY ka-YU-ti.
Give me the key to my cabin.

Сколько мы здесь стоим?
SKOL'-kə mi zd'es' sta-YIM?
How long do we stay here?

Когда отходит пароход?
kag-DA at-ḤO-d'it pə-ra-ḤOT?
When does the boat sail?

Можно пройти на верхнюю палубу?
MOZH-nə pray-T'I na V'ERḤ-n'i-yu PA-lu-bu?
Are passengers permitted on the upper deck?

Хочу пройти на верхнюю палубу.
ha-CHU pray-T'I na V'ERḤ-n'i-yu PA-lu-bu.
I want to go to the upper deck.

Можно взять этот стул?
MOZH-nə VZ'AT' E-tət STUL?
May I take this chair?

Когда мы будем в Сталинграде?
kag-DA mi BU-d'im fstа-l'in-GRA-d'i?
When will we be in Stalingrad?

Как называется это место?
KAK nə-zi-VA-yit-sə E-tə M'E-stə?
What is the name of this place?

Это Самара?
E-tə sa-MA-rə?
Is this Samara?

Когда мы проедем Саратов?
kag-DA mi pra-YE-d'im sa-RA-təf?
At what time will we pass Saratov?

Пароход опаздывает?
pə-ra-ḤOT a-PAZ-di-və-yit?
Is our boat late?

Где расписание?
gd'e rəs-p'i-SAN'-yə?
Where is the timetable?

Смотрите путеводитель по Волге.
sma-TR'I-t'i pu-t'i-va-D'I-t'il' pa VOL-g'i.
See Volga itinerary.

PLANE TRAVEL

Есть-ли аэроплан на Ленинград?
YEST'-l'i ay-ra-PLAN nə l'i-n'in-GRAT?
Is there a plane for Leningrad?

В котором часу улетает?
fka-TOR-əm chi-SU u-l'i-TA-yit?
What time does it leave?

Сколько стоит билет?
SKOL'-kə STOY-it b'i-L'ET?
What is the fare?

Сколько времени займёт полёт?
SKOL'-kə VR'E-m'i-n'i zay-M'OT pa-L'OT?
How long is the flight?

Дайте пожалуйста место у окна.
DAY-t'i pa-ZHA-lə-stə M'E-stə u ak-NA.
A window seat, please.

Будет-ли обед в этом полёте?
BU-d'it-l'i a-B'ET vE-təm pa-L'O-t'i?
Will lunch be served on this flight?

Сколько весит мой багаж?
SKOL'-kə V'E-s'it moy ba-GASH?
How much does my baggage weigh?

Ваш багаж весит пять фунтов сверх нормы.
vash ba-GASH V'E-s'it P'AT' FUN-təf sv'erh NOR-mi.
Your baggage is five pounds overweight.

Как проехать на аэродром?
KAK pra-YE hət' nə ay-ra-DROM?
How do I get to the airport?

Покажите ваш билет пожалуйста.
pə-ka-ZHÍ-t'i vash b'i-L'ET pa-ZHA-lə-stə.
Show me your ticket, please.

Ваше место номер тридцать.
VA-sha M'E-stə NO-m'ir TR'IT-sət'.
You have seat number 30.

Аэроплан прибудет по расписанию?
ay-ra-PLAN pr'i-BU-d'it pə rəs-p'i-SAN'-yu?
Will the plane arrive on schedule?

По расписанию мы должны быть в Ленинграде через час.
pə-rəs-p'i-SAN'-yu mi dalzh-NÍ bit' vl'i-n'in-GRA-d'i chi-r'is-CHAS.
We are scheduled to arrive in Leningrad in one hour.

ALL ABOARD

Это Ярославский вокзал?
E-tə yi-ra-SLAF-sk'iy vag-ZAL?
Is this the Yaroslavsky station?

Позовите носильщика.
pə-za-V'I-t'i na-S'IL'-sh'chi-kə.
Call a porter.

Носильщик!
na-S'IL'-sh'chik!
Porter!

Снимите эти вещи.
sn'i-M'I-t'i E-t'i V'ESH'-chi.
Take these things down.

Здесь не все вещи.
zd'es' n'i-FS'E V'ESH'-chi.
Not all the things are here.

Поставьте багаж сюда.
pa-STAF'-t'i ba-GASH su-DA.
Put my baggage here.

Когда отходит поезд в Загорск?
kag-DA at-ḤO-d'it POY-ist vza-GORSK?
When does the train for Zagorsk leave?

Это скорый поезд?
E-ta SKO-rəy POY-ist?
Is it a fast train?

Это беспересадочный поезд?
E-tə b'is-p'i-r'i-SA-dach-niy POY-ist?
Is it a through train?

Есть-ли в этом поезде вагон-ресторан?
YES'T-l'i v-E-təm POY-iz-d'i va-GON r'i-sta-RAN?
Is there a dining-car on this train?

Где касса?
GD'E KAS-sə?
Where is the ticket window?

Дайте мне билет первого класса.
DAY-t'i mn'e b'i-L'ET P'ER-və-və KLAS-sə.
Give me a first class ticket.

Билет второго класса.
b'i-L'ET fta-RO-və KLAS-sə.
A second class ticket.

Хочу взять билет в Ленинград.
ha-CHU VZ'AT' b'i-L'ET vl'i-n'in-GRAT.
I want to take a ticket for Leningrad.

Хочу получить место в спальном вагоне.
ha-CHU pə-lu-CHIT' M'E-stə f-SPAL'-nəm va-GO-n'i.
I want to have a berth in a sleeping car.

Сколько стоит спальное место?
SKOL'-kə STOY-it SPAL'nə-yə M'E-stə?
What is the charge for a sleeping berth?

Есть-ли в этом поезде спальный вагон?
YES'T'-l'i v-E-təm POY-iz-d'i SPAL'-niy va-GON?
Is there a sleeping car in this train?

Я хочу это сдать в багаж.
ya ha-CHU E-tə ZDAT' vba-GASH.
I want these registered.

Сколько мне платить за излишек багажа?
SKOL'kə mn'e pla-T'IT' za iz-L'I-shik bə-ga-ZHA?
How much must I pay for excess baggage?

Когда поезд отходит?
kag-DA POY-ist at-ḤO-d'it?
When will the train leave?

Снесите это в камеру хранения.
sn'i-S'I-t'i E-tə f KA-m'i-ru hra-N'EN'-yə.
Put these in the baggage room.

Какой номер моего вагона?
ka-KOY NO-m'ir mə-yi-VO va-GO-nə?
What is the number of my car?

Какой номер моего места?
ka-KOY NO-m'ir mə-yi-VO M'E-stə?
What is the number of my berth?

С какой платформы отходит поезд в Ленинград?
ska-KOY plat-FOR-mi at-ḤO-d'it POY-ist vl'i-n'in-GRAT?
From which platform will the train leave for Leningrad?

Мне нужен вагон для (не)курящих.
mn'e NU-zhin va-GON dl'ə (n'i)ku-R'ASH'-chih.
I want a (non-)smoker.

Поставьте это в мое купэ.
pa-STAF'-t'i E-tə v-ma-YO ku-PE.
Put these in my compartment.

Возьмите этот багаж.
vaz'-M'I-t'i E-tət ba-GASH.
Take this baggage, please.

Несите осторожно.
n'i-S'I-t'i a-sta-ROZH-nə.
Handle it carefully.

Поставьте эти вещи в мой вагон.
pa-STAF'-t'i E-t'i V'ESH'-chi vmoy va-GON.
Put these things into my car.

Когда мы прибудем?
kag-DA mi pr'i-BU-d'im?
What time shall we arrive?

Это купе для курящих?
E-tə ku-PE dl'ə-ku-R'ASH'-chih?
Is this a smoking compartment?

Мне нужно постельное бельё.
mn'e NUZH-nə pa-ST'EL'-nə-yə b'il'-YO.
I want to have bedding.

Приготовьте постель.
pr'i-ga-TOF'-t'i pa-ST'EL'.
Fix up my bed for me, please.

Пожалуйста, принесите чаю.
pa-ZHA-la-stə pr'i-n'i-S'I-t'i CHA-yu.
Please get me some tea.

Извините, это мое место.
iz-v'i-N'I-t'i, E-tə ma-YO M'E-stə.
Excuse me, this is my seat.

Как называется это место?
kak nə-zi-VA-yit-sə E-tə M'E-stə?
What is the name of this place?

Сколько мы здесь стоим?
SKOL'-kə mi z'd'es' sta-YIM?
How long do we stop here?

Много остановок будет по дороге?
MNO-gə a-sta-NO-vək BU-d'it pə da-RO-g'i?
Are there many stops on the road?

Успею сойти?
u-SP'E-yu say-T'I?
Have I time to get out?

Какая ближайшая большая станция?
ka-KA-yə bl'i-ZHAY-shə-yə bal'-SHA-yə STANTsi-yə?
What is the next big stop?

Что это за фабрика?
SHTO E-tə za FA-br'i-kə?
What factory is that?

Что здесь сеют?
SHTO z'd'es' S'E-yut?
What do they cultivate here?

Где пересадка?
gd'e p'i-r'i-SAT-kə?
Where shall we have to change?

Когда мы будем в Минске?
kag-DA mi BU-d'im vM'IN-sk'i?
When shall we be at Minsk?

Можно получить немного кипячёной воды?
MOZH-nə pə-lu-CHIT' n'im-NO-gə k'i-p'i-CHO-nəy va-Dɨ?
May I have some boiled water?

Где уборная?
GD'E u-BOR-nə-yə?
Where is the toilet?

Дайте, пожалуйста, подушку.
DAY-t'i, pa-ZHA-lə-stə, pa-DUSH-ku.
Will you get me a pillow, please.

Закройте, пожалуйста, окно.
za-KROY-t'i, pa-ZHA-lə-stə, ak-NO.
Please close the window.

Покажите ваш билет.
pə-ka-ZHÍ-t'i vash bi-L'ET.
Show me your ticket, please.

Ваш билет на этот поезд не годится.
vash bi-L'ET na E-tət POY-ist n'i-ga-D'IT-sə.
Your ticket is not good for this train.

Вы не на тот поезд сели.
vi n'i na TOT POY-ist S'E-l'i.
You are on the wrong train.

Как мне попасть на поезд в Минск?
KAK mn'e pa-PAS'T' na POY-ist vM'INSK?
How am I to get to the Minsk train?

Где мне слезть?
gd'e mn'e SL'ES'T'?
Where do I get out?

На какой станции?
nə-ka-KOY STANTsiy?
At what station?

Пожалуйста, откройте окно.
pa-ZHA-lə-stə at-KROY-t'i ak-NO.
Please open the window.

Где проводник?
GD'E prə-vad-N'IK?
Where is the porter?

Я хочу нижнее спальное место.
ya ha-CHU N'IZH-n'i-yə SPAL'-nə-yə M'E-stə.
I want to have a lower sleeping berth.

Это мое купе?
E-tə ma-YO ku-PE?
Is this my compartment?

Это мое место?
E-tə ma-YO M'E-stə?
Is this my berth?

GOING THROUGH CUSTOMS

Где таможня?
gd'e ta-MOZH-n'ə?
Where is the Customs House?

Где осматривают багаж?
gd'e a-SMA-tr'i-və-yut ba-GASH?
Where do they examine the baggage?

Будете осматривать мой багаж?
BU-d'i-t'i a-SMA-tr'i-vət' moy ba-GASH?
Will you examine my baggage?

Что у вас подлежит оплате?
SHTO u-VAS pəd-ľi-ZHĬT a-PLA-ťi?
Have you anything to declare?

У меня нет инчего подлежащего оплате.
u-m'i-N'A N'ET n'i-chi-VO pəd-ľi-ZHASH'-chi-və a-PLA-ťi.
I have nothing to declare.

Да, у меня есть.
DA, u m'i-N'A YEST'.
Yes, I have...

Вот мой багаж.
VOT moy ba-GASH.
That is my baggage.

Нужно ли открыть этот чемодан?
NUZH-nə-ľi at-KRĬT E-tət chi-ma-DAN?
Must I open this trunk?

За это взимается пошлина?
za E-tə vz'i-MA-yit-sə POSH-ľi-nə?
Is this dutiable?

Это для собственного потребления.
E-tə dľa SOPST'-v'i-nə-və pa-tr'i-BL'EN'-yə.
These articles are for my own use.

Носильщик, отнесите багаж в камеру хранения.
na-S'IL'-sh'chik, at-n'i-S'I-ťi ba-GASH fKA-m'i-ru ḥra-N'EN'-yə.
Porter, put my luggage in the cloakroom.

Носильщик!
na-S'IL'-sh'chik!
Porter!

Вот мой багаж.
VOT moy ba-GASH.
Here is my baggage.

Несите осторожно.
n'i-S'I-ťi ə-sta-ROZH-nə.
Handle them carefully.

Не ставьте на землю.
n'i-STAF'-ťi na Z'EM-ľu.
Do not put them on the ground.

Снесите это в такси.
sn'i-S'I-ťi E-tə ftak-S'I.
Take this bag to a taxi.

Позовите такси.
pə-za-V'I-ťi tak-S'I.
Call a taxi.

Покажите мне как пройти.
pə-ka-ZHĬ-ťi mn'e kak pray-T'I.
Show me how to get there.

Я возьму эти вещи с собой.
ya vaz'-MU E-ťi V'ESH'-chi s sa-BOY.
I will take these packages with me.

Поезжайте в гостиницу „Метрополь".
pə-yizh'-ZHAY-ťi vga-ST'I-n'itsu m'i-tra-POL'.
Take me to the Metropole hotel.

Сколько вам следует?
SKOL'-kə vam SL'E-du-yit?
How much do I owe you?

Везите меня в Интурист.
v'i-Z'I-ťi m'i-N'A vin-tu-R'IST.
Take me to the Intourist Office.

Я американский турист.
ya a-m'i-r'i-KAN-sk'iy tu-R'IST.
I am an American tourist.

Я английский турист.
ya an-GL'IY-sk'iy tu-R'IST.
I am an English tourist.

Мне нужен носильщик.
mn'e NU-zhɨn na-S'IL'-sh'chik.
I want a porter.

Это не мои вещи.
E-tə n'i-ma-YI V'ESH'-chi.
These are not mine.

Подождите немного.
pə-dazh-D'I-t'i n'im-NO-gə.
Wait a bit.

Снимите этот багаж.
sn'i-M'I-t'i E-tət ba-GASH.
Get this baggage down.

Вот мой чемодан на полке над дверью.
VOT moy chi-ma-DAN na POL-k'i nad D'V'ER'-yu.
There is my trunk, above the door, on the shelf.

Там остался ещё один чемодан.
tam a-STAL-sə yish'-CHO a-D'IN chi-ma-DAN.
There is still one trunk up there.

Возьмите это.
vaz'-M'I-t'i E-tə.
Take this.

Сколько времени будем ехать до гостиницы?
SKOL'-kə VR'E-m'i-n'i BU-d'im YE-hət' də ga-ST'I-n'i-tsɨ?
How long will it take to the hotel?

Сколько возьмёте?
SKOL'-kə vaz'-M'O-t'i?
How much will you charge?

Положите багаж сюда.
pə-la-ZHɨ-t'i ba-GASH su-DA.
Put my baggage here.

Хочу сесть сюда.
ha-CHU S'ES'T' su-DA.
I want to sit here.

STREETCAR AND BUS

Куда идёт этот трамвай (автобус)?
ku-DA i-D'OT E-tət tram-VAY (af-TO-bus)?
Where does this streetcar (bus) go?

Где конечная станция этой линии?
GD'E ka-N'ECH-nə-yə STANTsi-yɑ E-təy L'I-n'i-i?
Where is the last stop of the line?

Автобус № 4 идёт от площади Свердлова до Серебряного Бора.
af-TO-bus NO-m'ir chi-Tɨ-r'i i-D'OT at PLOSH'-chi-d'i sv'ird-LO-və də-s'i-R'E-br'i-nə-və BO-rə.
The No. 4 bus route begins at Sverdlov Square and ends at Silver Wood.

Я хочу проехать в Большой Театр.
ya ha-CHU pra-YE-hət' vbal'-SHOY t'i-AT-r.
I want to go to the Bolshoi Theater.

Какой автобус идёт в центр города.
ka-KOY af-TO-bus i-D'OT fTSENT-r GOR-ə-də?
What bus do we take to get to the center of the city?

Сколько стоит билет?
SKOL'-kə STOY-it b'i-L'ET?
What is the fare?

Когда начинается трамвайное движение?
kag-DA nə-chi-NA-yit-sə tram-VAY-nə-yə dv'i-ZHEN'-yə?
When do the cars start running?

В шесть часов утра и до двенадцать часов ночи.
fSHEST' chi-SOF u-TRA i də dv'i-NAT-sət chi-SOF NO-chi.
At 6 o'clock in the morning and until 12 o'clock midnight.

Вход только с задней площадки.
f-HOT TOL'-kə zZAD-n'iy plash'-CHAT-k'i.
Remember to enter only through the rear door.

Выход только с передней площадки.
Vɪ-hət TOL'kə sp'i-R'ED'-n'iy plash'-CHAT-k'i.
Always get off through the front door.

На ходу не входить.
nə-ha-DU n'if-ha-D'IT'.
Don't jump on the car while it is moving.

Не высовывайтесь.	**Не плевать.**	**Место кондуктора.**
n'i-vɪ-SO-vɪ-vəy-t'is.	*n'i pl'i-VAT'.*	*M'E-stə kan-DUK-tə-rə.*
Don't lean out.	No spitting.	Conductor's seat.

Где можно узнать о вещах, потерянных в трамвае?
GD'E MOZH-nə uz-NAT' ə v'ish'-CHAÇ pa-T'E-r'i-nɪh ftram-VA-yə?
What is the address of the Lost and Found Office?

Всё что кондуктор находит остаётся на хранении на конечной станции в течение одного дня.
FS'O shtə kan-DUK-tər na-HO-d'it a-sta-YOT-sə nə-hra-N'EN'-yi nə-ka-N'ECH-nəy STANTsi-i ft'i-CHEN'-yi ad-na-VO DN'A.
Anything found by the conductor remains at the office of the terminus station the first day.

После этого срока надо обратиться в контору.
PO-sl'i E-tə-və SRO-kə NA-də a-bra-T'IT'-sə fkan-TO-ru.
If you inquire later, you must apply at the office.

Вы здесь сходите?	**Пропустите, пожалуйста.**
vi Z'D'ES' s-HO-d'i-t'i?	*prə-pu-S'T'I-t'i, pa-ZHA-lə-stə.*
Do you get off here?	Please let me pass.

Я схожу.	**Я еду в Сокольники.**
ya s-ha-ZHU.	*ya YE-du fsa-KOL'-n'i-k'i.*
I am getting off.	I'm going to Sokolniki Park.

Где пересадка?
GD'E p'i-r'i-SAT-ka?
Where should I change?

Сколько отсюда езды до финского вокзала?
SKOL'-kə at-SU-də yiz-DÍ da F'IN-skə-və vag-ZA-lə?
How much does it take to get to the Finnish station?

Мы проедем Красную площадь?
mi pra-YE-d'im KRAS-nu-yu PLOSH'-chit'?
Will we pass Red Square?

Что это?
SHTO E-tə?
What is that?

Садитесь, пожалуйста.
sa-D'I-t'is, pa-ZHA-lə-stə.
Sit down, please.

Дайте мне сесть.
DAY-t'i mn'e S'ES'T'.
Let me sit down.

Вы сходите, да?
vi s-HO-d'i-t'i, DA?
You are getting off, aren't you?

Как проехать на финский вокзал?
KAK pra-YE-hət' na F'IN-sk'iy vag-ZAL?
How do I get to the Finnish station?

AT THE HOTEL

Я заказал по телеграфу одну комнату.
ya zə-ka-ZAL pə t'i-l'i-GRA-fu ad-NU KOM-nə-tu.
I have reserved one room by telegraph.

...Две комнаты...
...d'v'e KOM-nə-ti...
...two rooms...

Мне нужна комната.
mn'e nuzh-NA KOM-nə-tə.
I want to reserve a room.

Номер из двух комнат.
NO-m'ir iz DVUH KOM-nət.
Two connecting rooms.

Мне нужна большая комната.
mn'e nuzh-NA bal'-SHA-yə KOM-nə-tə.
I require a large room.

Мне нужен номер с ванной.
mn'e NU-zhin NO-m'ir sl'AN-nəy.
I want a room with a private bath.

Этот номер слишком мал.
E-tət NO-m'ir SL'ISH-kəm MAL.
This room is too small.

Покажите другой номер.
po-ka-ZHÍ-t'i dru-GOY NO-m'ir.
Show me another room.

Номер с двумя кроватями.
NO-m'ir z dvu-M'A kra-VA-t'i-m'i.
A room with two beds.

Мне нужен номер поменьше.
mn'e NU-zhin NO-m'ir pa-M'EN'-shə.
A smaller room will suit me.

Сколько стоит в день (неделю, месяц)?
SKOL'-kə STOY-it vD'EN' (vn'i-D'E-l'u, vM'E-s'its)?
What is the charge per day (week, month)?

Это включает услуги?
E-ta fkl'u-CHA-yit u-SLU-g'i?
Does it include service?

...Эти номера.
...E-t'i nə-m'i-RA.
...these rooms.

Я возьму этот номер.
ya vaz-MU E-tət NO-m'ir.
I will take this room.

Где лифт?
gd'e L'IFT?
Where is the elevator?

Пожалуйста, пришлите багаж.
pa-ZHA-lə-stə pr'ish-L'I-t'i ba-GASH.
Please have my baggage sent up.

Поставьте багаж в мой номер.
pa-STAF'-t'i ba-GASH v moy NO-m'ir.
Put this baggage into my room.

Какой номер моей комнаты?
ka-KOY NO-m'ir ma-YEY KOM-nə-ti?
What is the number of my room?

Я не буду столоваться в гостинице.
ya n'i-BU-du stə-la-VAT-sə vga-ST'I-n'it-si.
I will eat out.

Я буду завтракать в гостинице.
ya BU-du ZAF-trə-kət' vga-ST'I-nit-si.
I will take breakfast at the hotel.

Я буду обедать.
ya BU-du a-B'E-dət'.
I will take dinner.

Я буду ужинать.
ya BU-du U-zhi-nət'.
I will take supper.

Подайте завтрак ко мне в номер.
pa-DAY-t'i ZAF-trək kam-N'E vNO-m'ir.
I will have breakfast served in my room.

Можно получить завтрак в десять часов?
MOZH-nə pə-lu-CHIT' ZAF-trək vD'E-s'it' chi-SOF?
Can I get breakfast at 10 o'clock?

Где ресторан?
gd'e r'i-sta-RAN?
Where is the restaurant?

Я хочу поговорить с заведующим.
ya ḥa-CHU pə-gə-va-R'IT' zza-V'E-du-jush'-chim.
I want to speak to the manager.

У кого можно оставить ценные бумаги на хранение?
u-ka-VO MOZH-nə a-STA-v'it' TSEN-ni-yə bu-MA-g'i nə-ḥra-N'EN-yə.
Where can I deposit my valuable papers?

Часы, кольцо.
chi-Sŧ, kal't-SO.
Watch, ring.

Могу я сдать это вам?
ma-GU ya ZDAT' E-tə vam?
Can I put this in your charge?

Вы мне дадите квитанцию?
vɨ mn'e da-D'I-t'i kv'i-TANTsi-yu?
Will you give me a receipt for this?

Дайте мне ключ от номера.
DAY-t'i mn'e KL'UCH at NO-m'i-rə.
Give me the key to my room.

Почистите мне одежду (пальто).
pa-CHI-st'i-t'i mn'e a-D'EZH-du (pal'-TO).
Brush my clothes (overcoat).

Когда пулучу это обратно?
kag-DA pə-lu-CHU E-tə a-BRAT-nə?
When can I have them back?

Мне это нужно через три дня.
mn'e E-tə NUZH-nə chi-r'is TR'I DN'A.
I must have them in three days.

Мне это нужно завтра утром.
mn'e E-tə NUZH-nə ZAF-trə U-trəm.
I want them tomorrow morning.

Хочу отдать бельё в стирку.
ha-CHU ad-DAT' b'il'-YO f ST'IR-ku.
I want my linen washed.

Где ванная комната?
gd'e VAN-nə-yə KOM-nə-tə?
Where is the bathroom?

Приготовьте мне тёплую ванну.
pr'i-ga-TOF'-t'i mn'e T'O-plu-yu VAN-nu.
I want a warm bath.

Принесите мыло и полотенце.
pr'i-n'i-S'I-t'i MЫ-lə i pə-la-T'ENTsə.
Bring me some soap and towels.

Принесите воды для питья.
pr'i-n'i-S'I-t'i va-DЫ dl'a p'it'-YA.
Get me some drinking water.

Поставьте здесь (там).
pa-STAF'-t'i Z'D'ES' (TAM).
Put it here (there).

Кровать очень жесткая.
kra-l'AT' O-chin ZHOST-kə-yə.
My bed is hard.

Дайте белую нитку.
DAY-t'i B'E-lu-yu N'IT-ku.
Give me white thread.

Вот мой паспорт.
VOT moy PAS-pərt.
Here is my passport.

Почистите мне башмаки?
pa-CHI-st'i-t'i mn'e bəsh-ma-K'I.
Will you polish my boots?

Погладьте одежду.
pa-GLAT'-t'i a-D'EZH-du.
Press my clothes.

Принесите горячей воды.
pr'i-n'i-S'I-t'i ga-R'A-chəy va-DЫ.
Bring me hot water.

Дайте другое одеяло.
DAY-t'i dru-GOY-ə a'-d'i-YA-lə.
Give me another blanket.

Дайте иголку с ниткой.
DAY-t'i i-GOL-ku sN'IT-kəy.
Give me a needle and thread.

Дайте чёрную нитку.
DAY-t'i CHOR-nu-yu N'IT-ku.
Give me black thread.

Принесите бумагу, чернила и перо.
pr'i-n'i-S'I-t'i bu-MA-gu, chir-N'I-lə i p'i-RO.
Bring me paper, ink, and pen.

Мне нужны марки на эти письма.
mn'e nuzh-Nł MAR-k'i na E-t'i P'IS'mə.
I need stamps for these letters.

Отправьте эти письма.
at-PRAF'-t'i E-t'i P'IS'-mə.
Mail these letters.

Где парикмахер?
gd'e pə-r'ik-MA-h'ir?
Where is the hairdresser?

Пришлите парикмахера в мой номер.
pr'ish-L'I-t'i pə-r'ik-MA-h'i-rə v moy NO-m'ir.
Send the barber to my room.

Принесите мне чай (кофе, шоколад).
pr'i-n'i-S'I-t'i mn'e CHAY (KO-f'i, shə-ka-LAT).
Bring me tea (coffee, chocolate).

Где ресторан?
GD'E r'i-sta-RAN?
Where is the restaurant?

Разбудите меня в восемь часов.
raz-bu-D'I-t'i m'i-N'A vVO-s'im' chi-SOF.
Call me at 8 o'clock.

Я буду есть у себя в комнате.
ya BU-du YES'T' u-s'i-B'A fKOM-nə-t'i.
I will eat in my room.

Принесите меню.
pr'i-n'i-S'I-t'i m'i-N'U.
Bring me the menu.

Пошлите за доктором.
pash-L'I-t'i za-DOK-tə-rəm.
Send for a doctor.

Пусть сделают это лекарство.
pus't' ZD'E-lə-yut E-tə l'i-KARST-və.
Get this prescription made up.

Не беспокойтесь.
n'i-b'i-spa-KOY-t'is.
Don't trouble yourself.

Никто меня не спрашивал?
n'ik-TO m'i-N'A n'i-SPRA-shi-vəl?
Has anyone called me?

Я жду одного гражданина *(masc.)*
ya ZHDU ad-na-VO grəzh-da-N'I-nə.
I am expecting a visitor *(lit., citizen).*

Как ваша фамилия?
kak VA-shə fa-M'IL'-yə?
What is your name?

Мне не здоровится.
mn'e n'iz-da-RO-v'it-sə.
I don't feel well.

Пошлите в аптеку.
pash-L'I-t'i vap-T'E-ku.
Send to the pharmacy.

Нет ли мне писем?
N'ET-l'i-mn'e P'I-s'im?
Have you any mail for me?

Я жду одну гражданку (*fem.*).
ya ZHDU ad-NU grazh-DAN-ku.
I am expecting a visitor.

Если кто меня спросит, скажите, что я буду обратно в шесть часов.
YES'-ł'i KTO m'i-N'A SPRO-s'it, ska-ZHŁ-t'i shtə ya BU-du a-BRAT-nə fSHES'T' chi-SOF.
If anyone calls for me say that I will be back at 6 o'clock.

Попросите его (её) подождать.
pə-pra-S'I-t'i yi-VO (yi-YO) pə-dazh-DAT'.
Ask him (her) to wait.

Я сейчас буду внизу.
ya s'i-CHAS BU-du vn'i-ZU.
I will be down right away.

Пошлите его (её) наверх.
pash-L'I-t'i yi-VO (yi-YO) na-V'ERH.
Send him (her) up.

Он (она) не сказал(а) своего имени?
on (a-NA) n'i-ska-ZAL(a) svə-yi-VO I-m'i-n'i?
Did he (she) give his (her) name?

Он (она) оставил(а) записку?
on (a-NA) a-STA-v'i-l(ə) za-P'I-sku?
Did he (she) leave a note?

В котором часу он (она) приходил(а)?
fka-TOR-əm chi-SU on pr'i-ha-D'IL?
At what time did he (she) come?

Я уезжаю сегодня (завтра).
ya u-yizh'-ZH'A-yu s'i-VOD'-n'ə.
I am leaving today (tomorrow).

Поездом.
POY-iz-dəm.
By train.

Дайте счёт, пожалуйста.
DAY-t'i SH'CH'OT, pa-ZHA-lə-stə.
Please have my bill made out.

Здесь ошибка в счёте.
Z'D'ES' a-SHŁP-kə f-SH'CH'O-t'i.
Here is an error in my bill.

Можете вы мне рекомендовать гостиницу?
MO-zhi-t'i vi mn'e r'i-kə-m'in-da-VAT' ga-ST'I-n'it-su?
Can you recommend a hotel to me?

Письма на мое имя отправляйте по этому адресу.
P'IS'-mə nə-ma-YO I-m'ə at-prav-L'AY-t'i pə E-tə-mu A-dr'i-su.
Please forward my mail to this address.

Когда отходит поезд на Кавказ?
kag-DA at-HO-d'it POY-ist nə kaf-KAS?
When does the train leave for the Caucasus?

Я хочу побывать в Крыму.
ya ha-CHU pə-bi-VAT' fkri-MU.
I want to visit the Crimea.

Какая лучшая гостиница в этом городе?
ka-KA-yə LUCH-shə-yə ga-STI-nit-sə vE-təm GOR-ə-d'i?
Which is the best hotel in this town?

Сколько времени туда ехать?
SKOL'-kə VR'E-m'i-n'i tu-DA YE-hət'?
How long does it take to get there?

Покажите на карте где Ялта.
pə-ka-ZHI-t'i na KAR-t'i gd'e YAL-tə.
Show me on the map where Yalta is.

Сколько времени нужно ехать от Москвы?
SKOL'-kə VR'E-m'i-n'i NUZH-nə YE-hət' at mask-Vɫ?
How long does it take to go from Moscow?

Где это место?
GD'E E-tə M'E-stə?
Where is the place?

Хочу получить место в спальном вагоне.
ha-CHU pə-lu-CHIT' M'E-stə fSPAL'-nəm va-GO-n'i.
I want to have a berth in a sleeping car.

С какого вокзала мне ехать на Кавказ?
ska-KO-və vag-ZA-lə mn'e YE-hət' na kaf-KAS?
From what station must I leave for the Caucasus?

Как лучше проехать на Курский вокзал?
KAK LUCH-shə pra-YE-hət' na KUR-sk'iy vag-ZAL?
Which is the best way to the Kursk station?

По дороге в Крым я хочу провести несколько дней в Харькове.
pə da-RO-g'i fKRɫM ya ha-CHU prə-v'i-STI N'E-skəl'-kə DN'EY fHAR'-kə-v'i.
On my way to the Crimea I want to spend some days in Kharkov.

Позовите такси.
pə-za-V'I-t'i tak-S'I.
Call a taxi.

Принесите мой багаж.
pr'i-N'I-s'i-t'i moy ba-GASH.
Will you fetch my baggage?

Одно место вы оставили в номере.
ad-NO M'E-stə vi a-STA-v'i-l'i vNO-m'i-r'i.
You have left a piece of luggage in the room.

Принесите скорей.
pr'i-n'i-S'I-t'i ska-R'EY.
Fetch it quickly.

Снимите эти вещи.
sn'i-M'I-t'i E-t'i V'ESH'-chi.
Take these things down.

Мне нужно такси.
mn'e NUZH-nə tak-S'I.
I want a taxi.

Такси готово?
tak-S'I ga-TO-və?
Is the taxi ready?

Лучше быть раньше.
LUCH-shə bit' RAN'-shə.
I want to be ahead of time.

Несите этот багаж осторожно.
n'i-S'I-t'i E-tət ba-GASH a-sta-ROZH-nə.
Handle this baggage carefully.

Везите меня на Курский вокзал.
v'i-Z'I-t'i m'i-N'A na KUR-sk'iy vag-ZAL.
Take me to Kursk station.

Скажите шофёру на какой вокзал ехать.
ska-ZHÍ-t'i sha-F'OR-u nə-ka-KOY vag-ZAL YE-hət'.
Tell the chauffeur the name of the station.

Поезжайте тише.
pə-yizh'-ZH'AY-t'i T'I-shə.
Do not go so fast.

Пожалуйста, поскорее.
pa-ZHA-lə-sta pə-ska-R'EY-ə.
Hurry, please.

Поезжайте скорей.
pə-yizh'-ZH'AY-t'i ska-R'EY.
Go more quickly.

MAKING AN APPOINTMENT

Вы свободны сегодня вечером (сегодня днём)?
vi sva-BOD-ni s'i-VOD'-n'ə V'E-chi-rəm (s'i-VOD'-n'ə DN'OM)?
Do you happen to be free this evening (this afternoon)?

Когда можно вас видеть?
kag-DA MOZH-nə vas V'I-d'it'?
At what time can I see you?

Дайте мне знать, когда освободитесь.
DAY-t'i mn'e ZNAT' kag-DA a-sva-ba-D'I-t'is.
Let me know when you're free.

Я зайду к семи часам.
ya zay-DU k-s'i-M'I chi-SAM.
I'll come around at 7 o'clock.

Я буду здесь около девяти часов.
ya BU-du Z'D'ES' O-kə-lə d'i-v'i-T'I chi-SOF.
I shall be here at 9 o'clock.

Не можете ли прийти в восемь?
n'i MO-zhi-t'i-l'i pr'i-T'I vVO-s'im'?
I wish you could come at 8.

Дайте мне ваш адрес.
DAY-t'i mn'e vash A-dr'is.
Give me your address.

Когда мне прийти?
kag-DA mn'e pr'i-T'I?
When shall I call?

DINING OUT

Где хороший ресторан?
GD'E ha-RO-shiy r'i-sta-RAN?
Where is a good restaurant?

Пожалуйста, столик на двоих.
pa-ZHA-lə-stə, STO-l'ik na dva-YIH.
I want a table for two.

Пожалуйста, другой стол.
pa-ZHA-lə-stə, dru-GOY STOL.
I want another table.

Пожалуйста, стол около окна.
pa-ZHA-lə-stə, STOL O-kə-lə ak-NA.
I want the table at the window.

Здесь сквозняк.
Z'D'ES' skvaz'-N'AK.
There is a draft here.

Принесите меню.
pr'i-n'i-S'I-t'i m'i-N'U.
Bring me the menu.

Дайте завтрак.
DAY-t'i ZAF-trək.
Serve breakfast.

Дайте обед.
DAY-t'i a-B'ET.
Serve dinner.

Дайте ужин.
DAY-t'i U-zhin.
Serve supper.

Принесите карту вин.
pr'i-n'i-S'I-t'i KAR-tu V'IN.
Bring me the wine list.

Принесите бутылку (полбутылки).
pr'i-n'i-S'I-t'i bu-TIL-ku. (pəl-bu-TIL-k'i).
Bring me a bottle (a half bottle).

Принесите минеральной воды.
pr'i-n'i-S'I-t'i m'i-n'i-RAL'-nəy va-DI.
Bring me some mineral water.

Принесите чайник крепкого чаю.
pr'i-n'i-S'I-t'i CHAY-n'ik KR'EP-kə-və CHA-yu.
Bring me a pot of strong tea.

Принесите чашку черного кофе.
pr'i-n'i-S'I-t'i CHASH-ku CHOR-nə-və KO-f'i.
I want a cup of black coffee.

Пожалуйста, передайте стакан.
pa-ZHA-lə-stə p'i-r'i-DAY-t'i sta-KAN.
Kindly pass the glass.

Принесите острый нож.
pr'i-n'i-S'I-ti O-striy NOSH.
Bring me a sharp knife.

Передайте хлеб.
p'i-r'i-DAY-t'i HL'EP.
Pass me some bread.

Дайте горячей воды.
DAY-t'i ga-R'A-chəy va-DÏ.
Bring me some hot water.

Дайте воды со льдом.
DAY-t'i va-DÏ sal'-DOM.
Bring me some ice water.

Принесите бутылку со льда.
pr'i-n'i-S'I-t'i bu-TÏL-ku sal'-DA.
Bring me a bottle off the ice.

Вино тёплое, поставьте на лёд.
v'i-NO T'O-plə-yə, pa-STAF'-t'i na L'OT.
This wine is warm; put it on the ice.

Уберите.
u-b'i-R'I-t'i.
Take this away.

Я это не заказывал.
ya E-tə n'i-zə-KA-zi-vəl.
I did not order this.

Я заказал другое блюдо.
ya za-ka-ZAL dru-GOY-ə BL'U-də.
I ordered a different dish.

Это холодное.
E-tə hа-LOD-nə-yə.
This is cold.

Это не свежее.
E-tə n'i-SV'E-zhi-yə.
This is not fresh.

Пережарено.
p'i-r'i-ZHA-r'i-nə.
This is overdone.

Недожарено.
n'i-da-ZHA-r'i-nə.
This is underdone.

Слишком жестко.
SL'ISH-kəm ZHOST-kə.
This is too tough.

Слишком сладко.
SL'ISH-kəm SLAT-kə.
This is too sweet.

Слишком кисло.
SL'ISH-kom K'I-slə.
This is too sour.

Суп пересолен.
SUP p'i-r'i-SO-l'in.
There is too much salt in the soup.

Суп недосолен.
SUP n'i-da-SO-l'in.
There is too little salt in the soup.

Подождите минуту.
pə-dazh-D'I-t'i m'i-NU-tu.
Wait a moment.

Позовите старшего официанта.
pə-za-V'I-t'i STAR-shə-və a-f'itsi-AN-tə.
Call the headwaiter.

Не хотите ли кофе?
n'i-ha-T'I-t'i-l'i KO-f'i?
Let me help you to a cup of coffee.

Нет, спасибо.
N'ET, spa-S'I-bə.
No, thank you.

Я кончил.
ya KON'-chil.
I have finished.

Дайте мне счёт.
DAY-t'i mn'e SH'CH'OT.
Give me the bill.

Это неправильно.
E-to n'i-PRA-v'il'-nə.
This is not correct.

Правильно.
PRA-v'il'-nə.
All right.

У вас есть сдачи?
u VAS yes't' ZDA-chi?
Have you got change?

Сколько стоит?
SKOL'-kə STOY-it?
How much is it?

Спасибо, суп не нужен.
spa-S'I-bə, sup n'i-NU-zhin.
Thank you, no soup.

Подайте пожалуйста поскорей.
pa-DAY-t'i pa-ZHA-lə-stə pə-ska-R'EY.
Serve it more quickly.

Когда здесь обеды?
kag-DA z'd'es' a-B'E-di?
At what time do you serve dinners?

Когда здесь ужины?
kag-DA z'd'es' U-zhi-ni?
At what time do you serve suppers?

Когда здесь завтраки?
kag-DA z'd'es' ZAF-trə-k'i?
At what time do you serve breakfasts?

Дайте клубники.
DAY-t'i klub-N'I-k'i.
Give me some (garden) strawberries.

Ещё, пожалуйста.
yish'-CHO, pa-ZHA-lə-stə.
Give me some more, please.

Дайте спички.
DAY-t'i SP'ICH-k'i.
Give me some matches.

FOODS

яблоки *YA-blə-k'i* apples	**фасоль** *fa-SOL'* beans	**борщ** *BORSH'ch* beet soup
хлеб *HL'EP* bread	**масло** *MA-slə* butter	**щи** *SH'CHI* cabbage soup
торт *TORT* cake	**икра** *i-KRA* caviar	**сыр** *SIR* cheese
вишни *V'ISH-n'i* cherries	**курица** *KU-r'i-tsə* chicken	**шоколад** *shə-ka-LAT* chocolate
кофе *KO-f'i* coffee	**виноград** *v'i-na-GRAT* grapes	**каша** *KA-shə* groats

ветчина
v'it-chi-NA
ham

яйца
YAYTsə
eggs

мороженое
ma-RO-zhi-nə-yə
ice cream

салат
sa-LAT
lettuce

молоко
mə-la-KO
milk

перец
P'E-r'its
pepper

рис
R'IS
rice

соль
SOL'
salt

суп
SUP
soup

чай
CHAY
tea

сладкое
SLAT-kə-yə
dessert

рыба
Rɨ-bə
fish

квас
KVAS
kvass (a drink)

печёнка
p'i-CHON-kə
liver

горчица
gar-CHITsə
mustard

пирог
p'i-ROK
pie

ростбиф
ROZD'-b'if
roast beef

сандвич
sand-V'ICH
sandwich

бифштекс
b'if-SHTEKS
steak

индейка
in-D'EY-kə
turkey

утка
UT-kə
duck

селедка
s'i-L'OT-kə
herring

лимон
l'i-MON
lemon

мясо
M'A-sə
meat

апельсин
a-p'il'-S'IN
orange

картофель
kar-TO-f'il'
potatoes

салат
sa-LAT
salad

сосиски
sa-S'I-sk'i
sausages

сахар
SA-hər
sugar

SIGHTSEEING

Где находится Музей Изящных Искусств?
GD'E na-ḤO-d'it-sə mu-Z'EY i-Z'ASH'-nih is-KUSTF?
Where is the Museum of Fine Arts?

На какой улице?
nə-ka-KOY U-l'it-si?
What street is it on?

Как туда доехать?
KAK tu-DA da-YE-hət'?
How can you get there?

Какой трамвай идёт туда?
ka-KOY tram-VAY i-D'OT tu-DA?
What streetcar goes there?

Какой автобус?
ka-KOY af-TO-bus?
What bus?

В какую сторону?
fka-KU-yu STOR-ə-nu?
In what direction?

Где остановка трамвая (автобуса)?
GD'E a-sta-NOF-kə tram-VA-yə (af-TO-bu-sə)?
Where is the streetcar (bus) stop?

По каким дням он открыт?
pə-ka-K'IM DN'AM on at-KRİT?
On what days is it open?

От которого часа?
at ka-TOR-ə-və CHA-sə?
From what time?

До которого часа?
də ka-TOR-ə-və CHA-sə?
To what time?

Где касса?
GD'E KAS-sə?
Where do you pay?

Сколько стоит вход?
SKOL'-kə STOY-it fHOT?
What is the admission?

Где вход?
GD'E fHOT?
Where is the entrance?

Нужно - ли раздеваться?
NUZH-nə-l'i rəz-d'i-VAT-sə?
Must you take off your things?

Дайте мне номерок.
DAY-t'i mn'e nə-m'i-ROK.
Give me a tag (check), please.

Я хочу получить руководителя.
ya ha-CHU pə-lu-CHIT' ru-kə-va-D'I-t'i-l'ə.
I want to get a guide.

Я хочу получить переводчика.
ya ha-CHU pə-lu-CHIT' p'i-r'i-VOT'-chi-kə.
I want an interpreter.

Где купить каталог музея?
GD'E ku-P'IT' kə-ta-LOK mu-Z'EY-ə?
Where can you buy the museum catalog?

План музея?
PLAN mu-Z'EY-ə?
A map of the museum?

Хочу купить путеводитель.
ha-CHU ku-P'IT' pu-t'i-va-D'I-t'il'.
I want to buy a guidebook.

Когда был основан этот музей?
kag-DA bil a-SNO-vən E-tət mu-Z'EY?
When was this museum founded?

Что выставлено на этом этаже?
SHTO Vİ-stəv-l'i-nə na E-təm i-ta-ZHE?
What is shown on this floor?

Есть-ли скульптура?
YES'T'-l'i skul'p-TU-rə?
Are there any sculptures?

Есть-ли картины?
YES'T'-l'i kar-T'I-ni?
Are there any pictures?

Есть-ли документы?
YES'T'-l'i də-ku-M'EN-ti?
Are there any documents?

К какой эпохе это относится?
kka-KOY i-PO-h'i E-tə at-NO-s'it-sə?
What period does this belong to?

Как имя художника?
KAK I-m'ə hu-DOZH-n'i-kə?
What is the artist's name?

Имя скульптора?
I-m'ə SKUL'P-tə-rə?
The sculptor's name?

Это современная картина (скульптура, вещь)?
E-tə sə-vr'i-M'EN-nə-yə kar-T'I-nə (skul'p-TU-rə, V'ESHCH)?
Is that a modern picture (piece of sculpture, object)?

К какой школе она относится?
kka-KOY SHKO-l'i a-NA at-NO-s'it-sə?
What school does it belong to?

Это старинная?
E-tə sta-R'IN-nə-yə?
Is this old?

Какого века?
ka-KO-və V'E-kə?
Of what century is it?

Во всех-ли музеях новая экспозиция?
vaf-S'EH-l'i mu-Z'EY-əh NO-və-yə ik-spa-Z'ITsi-yə?
Do they have this new method of exhibition in all museums?

Есть-ли ещё другие залы?
YES'T'-l'i yish'-CH'O dru-G'I-yə ZA-li?
Are there any other (exhibition) rooms?

Есть-ли филиалы этого музея в других городах?
YES'T'-l'i fi-l'i-A-li E-tə-və mu-Z'EY-ə vdru-G'IX gə-ra-DAH?
Are there any branches of this museum in other cities?

Ну, мне пора итти.
NU, MN'E pa-RA i-T'I.
Well, it's time I went.

Хочу купить открытки и альбом музея.
ha-CHU ku-P'IT' at-KRÏT-k'i i al'-BOM mu-Z'EY-ə
I want to buy some postcards and an album of the museum.

Где выход?
GD'E VÏ-hət?
Where is the exit?

Когда бывают экскурсии в Кремль
kag-DA bi-VA-yut ik-SKUR-s'i-i f KR'EML'?
When are there trips to the Kremlin?

Часто ли бывают туда экскурсии?
CHA-stə-l'i bi-VA-yut tu-DA ik-SKUR-s'i-i?
Are there frequent excursions there?

Кто устраивает эти экскурсии?
KTO u-STRA-i-və-it E-t'i ik-SKUR-s'i-i?
Who arranges these excursions?

У кого записаться?
u ka-VO zə-p'i-SAT-sə?
To whom do we give our names?

Я хочу участвовать в этой экскурсии.
YA ha-CHU u-CHAST-və-vət' VE-təy ik-SKUR-s'i-i.
I want to go on this excursion.

Могу-ли я получить у вас руководителя (переводчика)?
ma-GU-l'i ya pə-lu-CHIT u vas ru-kə-va-D'I-t'i-lə (p'i-r'i-VOT'-chi-kə)?
Can I get a guide (interpreter) through you?

Какая плата?
ka-KA-yə PLA-tə?
What must I pay?

Можно-ли осмотреть Кремль?
MOZH-nə-l'i a-sma-TR'ET' KR'EML'?
Can the Kremlin be visited?

Как получить разрешение?
KAK pə-lu-CHIT' rəz-r'i-SHEN'-yə?
How do you get a permit?

Можно-ли снимать?
MOZH-nə-l'i sn'i-MAT'?
Can you take pictures?

Что нельзя снимать?
SHTO n'il'-Z'A sn'i-MAT'?
What mustn't be photographed?

Хочу осмотреть автомобильный завод.
ha-CHU a-sma-TR'ET' af-tə-ma-B'IL'-nıy za-VOD.
I want to visit an automobile factory.

Запишите меня.
zə-p'i-SHŁ-t'i m'i-N'A.
Put my name down, will you?

В котором часу соберётся группа?
fka-TOR-əm chi-SU sə-b'i-R'OT-sə GRU-pə?
At what time does the group meet?

Куда мне притти?	**Куда?**	**До свидания!**
ku-DA mn'e pr'i-T'I?	*ku-DA?*	*də-sv'i-DAN'-yə!*
Where do I have to go?	Where to?	So long!

SNAPSHOTS FOR REMEMBRANCE

Позвольте мне снять вас.
paz-VOL'-t'i mn'e SN'AT' vas.
Would you mind letting me take your picture?

Продолжайте ваши занятия.
prə-dal-ZHAY-t'i VA-shi za-N'A-t'i-yə.
Just continue your work.

Не смотрите в аппарат.
n'i sma-TR'I-t'i və-pa-RAT.
Don't look into the camera.

Повернитесь пожалуйста в эту сторону.
pə-v'ir-N'I-t'is pa-ZHA-lə-stə VE-tu STOR-ə-nu.
Turn this way, please.

Извините за беспокойство.
iz-v'i-N'I-t'i zə b'is-pa-KOYST-və.
Excuse me for having disturbed you.

Мне нужна плёнка.
mn'e nuzh-NA PL'ON-kə.
I need a roll of film.

Есть-ли у вас каталог фотоплёнок?
YEST'-l'i u VAS kə-ta-LOK fo-ta-PL'O-nək?
Do you have a film catalog?

У вас есть цветная плёнка?
u VAS yest' tsv'it-NA-yə PL'ON-kə?
Do you have color film?

Пожалуйста зарядите мне аппарат.
pa-ZHA-lə-stə zə-r'i-D'I-t'i mn'e a-pa-RAT.
Will you load the camera for me, please?

Затвор заел. Поправьте пожалуйста.
za-TVOR za-YEL. pa-PRAF'-t'i pa-ZHA-lə-stə.
The shutter is stuck. Can you fix it?

Почему моя плёнка всегда поцарапана?
pə-chi-MU ma-YA PL'ON-kə fs'ig-DA pət-sa-RA-pə-nə?
Why is my film always scratched?

Думаете-ли вы нужен мне фильтр?
DU-mə-yi-t'i-l'i vi NU-zhin mn'e F'IL'-tr?
Do you think I should use a filter?

Проявите эту плёнку пожалуйста.
prə-yi-V'I-t'i E-tu PL'ON-ku pa-ZHA-lə-stə.
Please develop this roll.

Сделайте один отпечаток с каждого негатива.
ZD'E-ləy-t'i a-D'IN at-p'i-CHA-tək sKAZH-də-və n'i-ga-T'I-və.
Please make one print of each negative.

Когда они будут готовы?
kag-DA a-N'I BU-dut ga-TO-vi?
When will they be ready?

Вы продаёте фотовспышки?
vi prə-da-YO-t'i fə-taf-SP'ISH-k'i?
Do you sell flashbulbs?

SHOPPING

Где Универмаг?
GD'E u-n'i-v'ir-MAK?
Where is the department store?

Петровка, дом номер два.
p'i-TROF-kə, DOM NO-m'ir DVA.
On Petrovka No. 2.

Где магазин кустарных изделий?
GD'E mə-ga-Z'IN ku-STAR-niḥ iz-D'E-l'iy?
Where is the peasant craft shop?

Леонтьевский переулок, дом семь.
l'i-ONT'-yif-sk'iy p'i-r'i-U-lək, DOM S'EM'.
On Leontievsky No. 7.

Где магазин „Международная Книга"?
GD'E mə-ga-Z'IN m'ezh-du-na-ROD-nə-yə KN'I-gə?
Where is the International Bookshop?

Кузнецкий мост, 18.
kuz-N'ET-sk'iy MOST, və-s'im-NAT-sət'.
At 18 Kuznetsky Most.

Где ближайший рынок?
GD'E bl'i-ZHAY-shiy Rɫ-nək?
Where is the nearest market?

Проводите меня по этому адресу.
prə-va-D'I-t'i m'i-N'A pa E-tə-mu A-dr'i-su.
Take me to this address.

Дайте мне хороший путеводитель на английском языке.
DAY-t'i mn'e ḥa-RO-shiy pu-t'i-va-D'I-t'il' nə an-GL'IY-skəm yi-zi-K'E
Give me a good guidebook in English.

Дайте мне эту книгу.
DAY-t'i mn'e E-tu KN'I-gu.
Give me that book.

Здесь говорят по английски?
Z'D'ES' gə-va-R'AT pə an-GL'IY-sk'i?
Do they speak English here?

Дайте мне (английские) газеты.
DAY-t'i mn'e (an-GL'IY-sk'i-yə) ga-Z'E-ti.
Give me some (English)newspapers.

Сколько всё это стоит?
SKOL'-kə FS'O E-tə STOY-it?
How much will the lot cost?

Хочу купить старые книги.
ḥa-CHU ku-P'IT' STA-ri-yə KN'I-g'i.
I'd like to buy some old books.

Хочу купить старые рукописи.
ḥa-CHU ku-P'IT' STA-ri-yə RU-kə-p'i-s'i.
I'd like to buy some old manuscripts.

Хочу купить открытки.
ḥa-CHU ku-P'IT' at-KRɫT-k'i.
I'd like to buy some postal cards.

Хочу купить старинные картины.
ha-CHU ku-P'IT' sta-R'IN-ni-yə kar-T'I-ni.
I'd like to buy some old pictures.

Дайте мне англо-русский словарь.
DAY-t'i mn'e an-gla-RU-sk'iy sla-VAR'.
Give me an English-Russian dictionary.

Русско-английский словарь.
ru-skə-an-GL'IY-sk'iy sla-VAR'.
Russian-English dictionary.

Хочу купить безделушки.
ha-CHU ku-P'IT' b'iz-d'i-LUSH-k'i.
I want to buy some curios.

Хочу купить старинные вещи.
ha-CHU ku-P'IT' sta-R'IN-ni-yə V'ESH'-chi.
I'd like to buy old-fashioned things.

Где Антикварный отдел?
GD'E ant-t'i-KVAR-niy ad'-D'EL?
Where is the antiques department?

Для чего это?
dl'ə chi-VO E-tə?
What is this used for?

Это солонка.
E-tə sa-LON-kə.
It is a salt box.

Где это сделано?
GD'E E-tə Z'D'E-lə-nə?
Where was it made?

Это выделывается в Сибири.
E-tə vi-D'E-li-və-yii-sə fs'i-B'I-r'i.
It is made in Siberia.

Из какого дерева это сделано?
is ka-KO-və D'E-r'i-və E-tə Z'D'E-lə-nə?
What wood is it made of?

дуб.	сосна.	берёза.	ель.
dup.	*sa-SNA.*	*b'i-R'O-zə.*	*yel'.*
oak.	pine.	birch.	fir.

Дайте этот портсигар.
DAY-t'i E-tət pərt-s'i-GAR.
Give me this cigarette box.

Дайте мне эту шаль.
DAY-t'i mn'e E-tu SHAL'
Give me this shawl.

Дайте мне эту русскую рубашку.
DAY-t'i mn'e E-tu RU-sku-yu ru-BASH-ku.
Give me this Russian blouse.

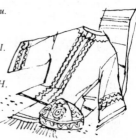

Дайте мне эти татарские сапоги.
DAY-t'i mn'e E-t'i ta-TAR-sk'i-yə sə-pa-G'I.
Give me this pair of Tartar top boots.

Дайте мне эту кавказскую брошь.
DAY-t'i mn'e E-tu kaf-KA-sku-yu BROSH.
Give me this Caucasian brooch.

Это из чистого серебра?
E-tə is CHI-stə-və s'i-r'i-BRA?
Is that made of pure silver?

Покажите мне это украинское платье.
pə-ka-ZHɬ-t'i mn'e E-tə u-kra-IN-skə-yə PLAT'-yə.
Show me this Ukrainian dress.

Покажите мне эту татарскую шапку.
pə-ka-ZHɬ-t'i mn'e E-tu ta-TAR-sku-yu SHAP-ku.
Show me this Tartar cap.

Это ручная вышивка?
E-tə ruch-NA-yə VI-shif-kə?
Is it hand embroidered?

Сколько это стоит?
SKOL'-kə E-tə STOY-it?
What is the price?

Какой это размер?
ka-KOY E-tə raz-M'ER?
What size is this?

Слишком узко.
SL'ISH-kəm U-skə.
This is too narrow.

Слишком широко.
SL'ISH-kəm shi-ra-KO.
That is too wide.

Слишком дорого.
SL'ISH-kəm DOR-ə-gə.
It is too expensive.

Есть у вас что-нибудь получше?
YES'T' u vas SHTO-n'i-but' pa-LUCH-shə?
Have you anything better?

Есть у вас что-нибудь подешевле?
YES'T' u vas SHTO-n'i-but' pə-d'i-SHEV-l'ə?
Have you any cheaper?

Это все мне не нравится.
E-təf-S'O mn'e n'in-RA-v'it-sə.
I don't care for any of these.

Цена одинаковая?
tsi-NA a-d'i-NA-kə-və-yə?
Is the price the same?

Такого же сорта, но большего размера.
ta-KO-və-zhə SOR-tə, nə BOL'-shə-və raz-M'E-rə.
Like this, but larger.

Я куплю это.
ya ku-PL'U E-tə.
I will buy this one.

Что нибудь в этом роде.
SHTO-n'i-but' vE-təm RO-d'i.
I want something like this.

Это не совсем то, что мне нужно.
E-tə n'i saf-S'EM TO, shtə mn'e NUZH-nə.
That is not quite what I want.

Покажите мне что-нибудь другое.
pə-ka-ZHɬ-t'i mn'e SHTO-ni-bud' dru-GOY-ə.
Can you show me anything different?

Нужно-ли чек в кассу?
NUZH-nə-l'i CHEK fKAS-su?
Do I need a check for the cash-desk?

Где касса?
GD'E KAS-sə?
Where is the cash-desk?

Вот там.
VOT TAM.
Over there.

Где выдают покупки?
GD'E vi-da-YUT pa-KUP-k'i?
Where do I get my purchases?

Пожалуйста, запакуйте тщательно.
pa-ZHA-lə-stə, zə-pa-KUY-t'i TSH'CHA-t'il'-nə.
Please pack this carefully.

Пошлите по этому адресу.
pash-L'I-t'i pa E-tə-mu A-dr'i-su.
Send them to this address.

Пошлите это в гостиницу „Метрополь".
pash-L'I-t'i E-tə vga-ST'I-n'itsu m'i-tra-POL'.
Send them to the Metropole Hotel.

Мне это нужно сегодня вечером.
mn'e E-tə NUZH-nə s'i-VOD'-n'ə V'E-chi-rəm.
I must have them tonight.

Я оставлю задаток.
ya a-STAV-l'u za-DA-tək.
I will leave a deposit.

Я возьму это.
ya vaz'-MU E-tə.
I will take it.

Я возьму это с собой.
ya vaz'-MU E-tə ssa-BOY.
I will take them with me.

Будет уплачено при доставке.
BU-d'it u-PLA-chi-nə pr'i da-STAF-k'i.
You will be paid on delivery.

LAUNDRY AND CLEANING

Хочу отдать бельё в стирку.
ha-CHU ad-DAT' b'il'-YO fST'IR-ku
I want to have my laundry washed.

Мне это нужно как можно скорее.
mn'e E-tə NUZH-nə kak MOZH-nə ska-R'EY-ə.
I want it as soon as possible.

Когда можно получить обратно?
kag-DA MOZH-nə pə-lu-CHIT' a-BRAT-nə?
When can I have it back?

Просмотрите список.
prə-sma-TR'I-t'i SP'I-sək.
Look over the list.

Верно ли записано?
V'ER-nə-l'i za-P'I-sə-nə?
Is it correct?

Всего десять штук.
fs'i-VO D'E-s'it' SHTUK.
There are 10 pieces altogether.

Это не крахмальте.
E-tə n'i-krah-MAL'-t'i.
Don't put any starch in this.

Это не мое.
E-tə n'i-ma-YO.
This is not mine.

Плохо выстирано.
PLO-hə VÏ-st'i-rə-nə.
They are very badly done.

пожалуйста погладьте воротники и рубашки.
pa-ZHA-ə-stə pa-GLAT'-t'i və-rət-n'i-K'I i ru-BASH-k'i.
Please iron my collars and shirts.

Эти воротники и рубашки недостаточно накрахмалены.
E-t'i və-rət-n'i-K'I i ru-BASH-k'i n'i-da-STA-tach-nə nə-krah-MA-l'i-ni.
These collars and shirts do not have enough starch in them.

Несколько штук пропало.
N'E-skəl'-kə SHTUK pra-PA-lə.
There are some pieces missing.

HAIRDRESSER AND BARBER

Где дамский зал (косметический кабинет)?
GD'E DAM-sk'iy ZAL (kəs-m'i-T'I-chi-sk'iy kə-b'i-N'ET)?
Where is the ladies' hairdresser (the beauty parlor)?

Подстригите мне волосы.
pət-str'i-G'I-t'i mn'e VO-lə-si.
I want my hair cut.

Завейте мне волосы.
za-l''EY-t'i mn'e VO-lə-si.
I want my hair waved.

Хочу сделать маникюр.
ha-CHU Z'D'E-lət' mə-n'i-K'UR.
I want to have a manicure.

Сделайте мне массаж лица.
Z'D'E-ləy-t'i mn'e ma-SASH l'itSA.
I want a face massage.

Дайте немного пудры.
DAY-t'i n'im-NO-gə PU-drï.
Bring me a little powder.

Не слишком коротко.
n'i-SL'ISH-kəm KOR-ət-kə.
Not too short.

Дайте шампунь.
DAY-t'i sham-PUN'.
Give me a shampoo.

Скажите, пожалуйста, где находится парикмахерская?
ska-ZHÏ-t'i, pa-ZHA-lə-stə, GD'E na-ḤO-d'it-sə pə-r'ik-MA-h'ir-skə-yə?
Can you tell me where the barber shop is, please?

Подстригите немного сзади и с боков.
pət-str'i-G'I-t'i n'im-NO-gə ZZA-d'i i zba-KOF.
Just trim round the back and ears.

Снимите немного здесь.
sn'i-M'I-t'i n'im-NO-gə Z'D'ES'.
Take a little off here.

Побрейте меня.
pa-BR'EY-t'i m'i-N'A.
Shave me, please.

Один раз будет достаточно.
a-D'IN RAS BU-d'it da-STA-təch-nə.
Once over will be sufficient.

Подстригите бороду.
pət-str'i-G'I-t'i BOR-ə-du.
Trim my beard.

Положите немного крема на волосы.
pə-la-ZHĪ-t'i n'im-NO-gə KR'E-mə na VO-lə-si.
Put on a little hair dressing.

Сделайте мне маникюр.
Z'D'E-ləy-t'i mn'e mə-n'i-K'UR.
Give me a manicure.

Подстригите усы.
pət-str'i-G'I-t'i u-Sĭ.
Trim my moustache.

Прекрасно!
pr'i-KRA-snə!
Yes, that's all right.

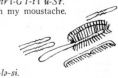

GOING TO THE THEATER

Где театр Революции?
GD'E t'i-A-tr r'i-va-L'U-tsi-i?
Where is the Theater of the Revolution?

Где Художественный театр?
GD'E hu-DO-zhist-v'in-niy t'i-A-tr?
Where is the Art Theater?

Где оперный театр (балет)?
GD'E O-p'ir-niy t'i-A-tr (ba-L'ET)?
Where is the Opera House (ballet)?

Когда начало спектакля?
kag-DA na-CHA-lə sp'ik-TAK-l'ə?
When does the performance begin?

Что идёт сегодня?
SHTO i-D'OT s'i-VOD'-n'ə?
What is on today?

Где вход?
GD'E fHOT?
Where is the entrance?

Где касса?
GD'E KAS-sə?
Where is the box office?

Сколько стоят билеты?
SKOL'-kə STOY-ət b'i-L'E-ti?
What are the prices?

Сколько стоят места в партере?
SKOL'-kə STOY-it m'i-STA fpar-TE-r'i?
What are the prices in the orchestra?

Сколько стоит место в первом ярусе?
SKOL'-kə STOY-it M'E-stə fP'ER-vəm YA-ru-s'i?
What are the prices in the first balcony (dress circle)?

Сколько стоит место на балконе?
SKOL'-kə STOY-it M'E-stə nə-bal-KO-n'i?
What are the prices in the balcony?

Сколько стоит место во втором ярусе?
SKOL'-kə STOY-it M'E-stə vaf-ta-ROM YA-ru-s'i?
What are the prices in the upper circle (second balcony)?

Дайте мне один билет на сегодня.
DAY-t'i mn'e a-D'IN b'i-L'ET nə-s'i-VOD'-n'ə.
Let me have one ticket for tonight's performance.

Два билета.
dva b'i-L'E-tə.
Two tickets.

В десятом ряду.
vd'i-S'A-təm r'i-DU.
In the 10th row.

Где гардероб?
GD'E gər-d'i-ROP?
Where is the cloakroom?

Дайте мне номерок.
DAY-t'i mn'e nə-m'i-ROK.
Give me the cloaktag.

Дайте программу.
DAY-t'i pra-GRAM-mu.
Give me a program.

Где можно достать бинокль?
GD'E MOZH-nə da-STAT' b'i-NO-kl'?
Where can I rent opera glasses?

Пропустите, пожалуйста.
prə-pu-ST'I-t'i, pa-ZHA-lə-stə.
Please allow me to pass.

Извините, это мое место.
iz-v'i-N'I-t'i, E-tə ma-YO M'E-stə.
Pardon me, this is my seat.

Где буфет?
GD'E bu-F'ET?
Where is the refreshment room?

Сколько всего действий?
SKOL'-kə fs'i-VO D'EYST-v'iy?
How many acts are there?

В котором часу пьеса окончится?
fka-TOR-əm chi-SU p'YE-sə a-KON'-chit-sə?
At what hour is the performance over?

Здесь не курят.
Z'D'ES' n'i-KU-r'ət.
Smoking forbidden.

Запасной выход.
zə-pas-NOY VÏ-hət.
Emergency exit.

Где курительная комната?
GD'E ku-R'I-t'il'-nə-yə KOM-nə-tə?
Where is the smoking room?

EXCHANGING MONEY

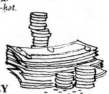

Где можно обменять американские деньги?
GD'E MOZH-nə ab-m'i-N'AT' a-m'i-r'i-KAN-sk'i-yə D'EN'-g'i?
Where can I get American money changed?

Английские деньги?
an-GL'IY-sk'i-yə D'EN'-g'i?
English money?

Где Государственный банк (Госбанк)?
GD'E gə-su-DARST'-vin-niy BANK (goz-BANK)?
Where is the State Bank?

Где ближайшее отделение Государственного банка?
GD'E bl'i-ZHAY-shə-yə ad'-d'i-L'EN-yə goz-BAN-kə?
Where is the nearest branch of the State Bank?

Можно ли обменять деньги в Интуристе?
MOZH-nə-l'i ab-m'i-N'AT' D'EN'-g'i vin-tu-R'I-st'i?
Can I change money at the Intourist Office?

Можете обменять американские деньги?
MO-zhi-t'i ab-m'i-N'AT' a-m'i-r'i-KAN-sk'i-yə D'EN'-g'i?
Can you change American money?

Каков курс?
ka-KOF KURS?
What is the rate of exchange?

Оплатите этот чек.
a-pla-T'I-t'i E-tət CHEK.
Cash this check.

Дайте мелкие кредитки.
DAY-t'i M'EL-k'i-yə kr'i-D'IT-k'i.
Give me bills of a smaller denomination.

Дайте чек, я должен расписаться.
DAY-t'i CHEK, ya DOL-zhin rə-sp'i-SAT-sə.
Give me the check, I must endorse it.

Вот аккредитив от моего банка.
VOT a-kr'i-d'i-T'IF at mə-yi-VO BAN-kə
Here is the letter of credit from my bank.

Где расписаться?
GD'E rə-sp'i-SAT-sə?
Where should I sign?

COMMUNICATIONS

Mail, Telegrams and Cables

Где ближайшая почта?
GD'E bl'i-ZHAY-shə-yə POCH-tə?
Where is the nearest post office?

Где ближайший телеграф?
GD'E bl'i-ZHAY-shəy t'i-l'i-GRAF?
Where is the nearest telegraph office?

Как туда пройти?
KAK tu-DA pray-T'I?
How do I get there?

Проводите меня до ближайшей почты.
prə-va-D'I-t'i m'i-N'A də-bl'i-ZHAY-shəy POCH-ti.
Take me to the nearest post office.

Каким трамваем нужно туда ехать?
ka-K'IM tram-VA-yim NUZH-nə tu-DA YE-hət'
What streetcar should I take to get there?

Как мне итти? Прямо?
KAK mn'e i-T'I? PR'A-mə?
Should I go straight ahead?

Как мне итти? Направо?
KAK mn'e i-T'I? na-PRA-və?
Should I turn to the right?

Как мне итти? Налево?
KAK mn'e i-T'I? na-L'E-və?
Should I turn to the left?

Где получают письма до востребования?
GD'E pə-lu-CHA-yut P'IS'-mə də-vas-TR'E-bə-vən'-yə?
Where is the General Delivery counter?

Моя фамилия Петров.
ma-YA fa-M'IL'-yə p'i-TROF.
My name is Petrov.

Нет ли мне писем?
N'ET-l'i mn'e P'I-s'im?
Are there any letters for me?

Нет ли мне посылки?
N'ET-l'i mn'e pa-SƗL-k'i?
Are there any parcels for me?

Вот мой паспорт.
VOT moy PAS-pərt.
Here is my passport.

Где можно достать марки?
GD'E MOZH-nə da-STAT' MAR-k'i?
Where can I get stamps?

Дайте мне одну марку (марки).
DAY-t'i mn'e ad-NU MAR-ku (MAR-k'i).
Give me a stamp (stamps).

Дайте мне семь конвертов.
DAY-t'i mn'e S'EM' kan-V'ER-təf
Give me seven envelopes.

Дайте мне писчую бумагу.
DAY-t'i mn'e P'ISH-chu-yu bu-MA-gu.
Give me writing paper.

Какие марки на письмо в Чикаго?
ka-K'I-yə MAR-k'i nə p'is'-MO fchi-KA-gə?
What is the postage for this letter to Chicago?

Пошлите это письмо заказным.
pash-L'I-t'i Eto p'is'-MO zə-kaz-NƗM.
Please register this letter.

Сколько стоят эти открытки?
SKOL'-kə STOY-ət E-t'i at-KRƗT-k'i?
What is the price of these post cards?

Где ближайший почтовый ящик?
GD'E bl'i-ZHAY-shəy pach-TO-viy YASH'-chik.
Where is the nearest mail box?

Дайте мне виды города.
DAY-t'i mn'e V'I-di GOR-ə-də.
I want to have some views of the town.

Хочу послать телеграмму.
ha-CHU pa-SLAT' t'i-l'i-GRA-mu.
I want to send a telegram.

Дайте телеграфный бланк.
DAY-t'i t'i-l'i-GRAF-niy BLANK.
Give me a telegraph form.

Сколько стоит слово?
SKOL'-kə STOY-it SLO-və?
What is the charge per word?

Сколько нужно платить?
SKOL'-kə NUZH-nə pla-T'IT'?
What is the charge?

Сколько стоит эта телеграмма?
SKOL'-kə STOY-it E-tə t'i-l'i-GRA-mə?
How much will this telegram cost?

Telephoning

Где телефон?
GD'E t'i-l'i-FON?
Where is the phone?

Можно позвонить?
MOZH-nə pəz-va-N'IT'?
May I use your phone?

Дайте телефонную книжку.
DAY-t'i t'i-l'i-FON-nu-yu KN'ISH-ku.
Give me the telephone directory.

Позвоните по этому номеру.
pəz-va-N'I-t'i pa E-tə-mu NO-m'i-ru.
Please get me this number.

Дайте город (Центральную).
DAY-t'i GOR-ət (tsin-TRAL'-nu-yu).
Give me an outside line.

1-64-62, один шестьдесят четыре, шестьдесят два.
a-D'IN shiz-d'i-S'AT chi-T‡-r'i shiz-d'i-S'AD DVA.
1-64-62.

Алло! Это Иван?
a-LO! E-tə i-VAN?
Hello. Is that John?

Попросите его к телефону.
pə-pra-S'I-t'i yi-VO kt'i-l'i-FO-nu.
Ask him to come to the phone.

Говорит Марья.
gə-va-R'IT MAR'-ya.
Mary speaking.

Попросите его позвонить когда вернётся.
pə-pra-S'I-t'i yi-VO pəz-va-N'IT' kag-DA v'ir-N'OT-sə.
Ask him to phone me when he returns.

Запишите мой номер.
zə-p'i-SH‡-t'i moy NO-m'ir.
Take my number.

Позовите кого-нибудь кто говорит по-английски.
pə-za-V'I-t'i ka-VO-n'i-but' kto gə-va-R'IT pə an-GL'IY-sk'i.
Call someone who can speak English.

Не кладите трубку.
n'i kla-D'I-t'i TRUP-ku.
Hold the line.

Алло! Нас разъединили.
a-LO! nas rəz-yi-d'i-N'I-l'i.
Hello. They have cut us off.

Говорите громче.
gə-va-R'I-t'i GROM-chə.
Speak louder.

Я вас плохо слышу.
ya vas PLO-hə SLɨ-shu.
I can't hear you very well.

Я позвоню позже.
ya pəz-va-N'U POZH'-zhə.
I'll ring up later.

YOUR HEALTH ABROAD

Проводите меня в аптеку.
prə-va-D'I-t'i m'i-N'A vap-T'E-ku.
Take me to a drugstore.

Приготовьте это лекарство.
pr'i-ga-TOF'-t'i E-tə l'i-KARST-və.
Make up this medicine.

Я нездоров.
YA n'iz-da-ROF.
I am ill.

Пошлите за доктором.
pash-L'I-t'i za DOK-tə-rəm.
Send for the doctor.

Где ближайшая больница?
GD'E bl'i-ZHAY-shə-yə bal'-N'I-tsa?
Where is the nearest hospital?

Здесь болит.
Z'D'ES' ba-L'IT.
I have pain here.

Я заболел (заболела *fem.***) по дороге.**
ya zə-ba-L'EL (zə-ba-L'E-lə) pə-da-RO-g'i.
I was ill on my journey.

Я простудился (простудилась *fem.***).**
YA prə-stu-D'IL-sə (prə-stu-D'I-ləs).
I have caught a cold.

У меня боль в желудке.
u-m'i-N'A BOL' vzhi-LUT-k'i.
I've a pain in my stomach.

Пошлите в аптеку; закажите этот рецепт.
pash-L'I-t'i vap-T'E-ku; zə-ka-ZH-t'i E-tət r'it-SEPT.
Send to a drugstore; get this prescription made up.

Сейчас мне лучше.
s'i-CHAS mn'e LUCH-shə.
I feel better now.

VISAS

Где можно продлить выездную визу?
GD'E MOZH-nə prad-L'IT' vi-yiz-NU-yu V'I-zu?
Where can I extend my exit visa?

Где можно получить выездную визу?
GD'E MOZH-nə pə-lu-CHIT' vi-yiz-NU-yu V'I-zu?
Where does one get the exit visa?

Где Административный Отдел Совета?
GD'E ad-m'i-n'i-stra-T'IV'-niy ad'-D'EL sa-V'E-tə?
Where is the City Council's Administrative Section?

Где иностранный отдел?
GD'E i-na-STRAN-niy ad'-D'EL?
Where is the Foreign Department?

На какой улице?
nə-ka-KOY U-l'itsi?
What street is it on?

Здесь иностранный отдел?
Z'D'ES' i-na-STRAN-niy ad-D'EL?
Is this the Foreign Department?

Я иностранец.
ya i-na-STRA-n'its.
I am a foreigner (m.).

Я иностранка.
ya i-na-STRAN-kə.
I am a foreigner (f.).

Я американец.
YA a-m'i-r'i-KA-n'its.
I am an American (m.).

Я американка.
YA a-m'i-r'i-KAN-kə.
I am an American (f.).

Я англичанин.
YA an-gl'i-CHA-n'in.
I am an Englishman.

Я англичанка.
YA an-gl'i-CHAN-kə.
I am an Englishwoman.

Я не говорю по-русски.
YA n'i-gə-va-R'U pa-RU-sk'i.
I don't speak Russian.

Кто здесь говорит по-английски?
KTO z'd'es' gə-va-R'IT pə-an-GL'IY-sk'i?
Does anyone here speak English?

Что мне нужно для получения выездной визы?
SHTO mn'e NUZH-nə dl'ə pə-lu-CHEN'-yə vi-yiz-NOY V'I-zi?
What have I to do to get my exit visa?

Что мне нужно для продления визы?
SHTO mn'e NUHZ-nə dl'ə prad-L'EN'-yə V'I-zi?
What must I do to extend my visa?

Я хочу продлить визу на две недели.
ya ha-CHU prad-L'IT' V'I-zu na DV'E n'i-D'E-l'i.
I want to extend my visa for 2 weeks.

Где можно получить анкету для заполнения?
GD'E MOZH-nə pə-lu-CHIT' an-K'E-tu dl'ə zə-pal-N'EN'-yə?
Where do I get a questionnaire?

У вас можно получить анкету?
u VAS MOZH-nə pə-lu-CHIT' an-K'E-tu?
Can we get the questionnaire from you?

Благодарю вас.
blə-gə-da-R'U vas.
Thank you.

Сколько фотографических карточек вам нужно?
SKOL'-kə fə-tə-gra-F'I-chi-sk'ih KAR-tə-chik vam NUZH-nə?
How many photographs do you need?

Вот мои фотографические карточки.
VOT ma-YI fə-tə-gra-F'I-chi-sk'iyə KAR-təch-k'i.
Here are my photographs.

Сколько стоит регистрация?
SKOL'-kə STOY-it r'i-g'i-STRATsi-yə?
What is the registration fee?

Где я должен подписаться?
GD'E ya DOL-zhin pət-p'i-SAT-sə?
Where should I sign?

Когда я могу получить свой паспорт с готовой визой?
kag-DA ya ma-GU pə-lu-CHIT' svoy PAS-pərt zga-TO-vəy V'I-zəy?
When can I get my passport with the visa?

У кого я получу свой паспорт?
u-ka-VO ya pə-lu-CHU svoy PAS-pərt?
Where do I get my passport from?

Когда у вас выходной день?
kag-DA u-VAS vi-had-NOY D'EN'?
When is your day off?

От которого часа вы работаете?
at ka-TOR-ə-və CHA-sə vi ra-BO-tə-yi-t'i?
When do you start to work?

До которого часа вы работаете?
də ka-TOR-ə-və CHA-sə vi ra-BO-tə-yi-t'i?
When do you stop working?

Как мне проехать в гостиницу „Метрополь".?
KAK mn'e pra-YE-ħət' vga-ST'I-n'itsu m'i-tra-POL'?
How do I get from here to the Metropole hotel?

Как мне проехать на Киевский вокзал?
KAK mn'e pra-YE-ħət' na K'I-yif-sk'iy vag-ZAL?
How do I get from here to the Kiev station?

SIGNS

Курить воспрещается
ku-R'IT vəs-pr'ish'-CHA-yit-sə
No smoking allowed

Вход воспрещается
FḤOT vəs-pr'ish'-CHA-yit-sə
No admittance

Тяните
t'i-N'I-t'i
Pull

Толкайте
tal-KAY-t'i
Push

Проезд воспрещен
pra-YEST vəs-pr'ish'-CHON
No thoroughfare

Вход
fḤOT
Entrance

Здесь только выход
Z'DES' TOL'-kə VI-ḥət
Exit only

Касса
KAS-sə
Ticket counter (window)

Почта
POCH-tə
Post Office

Камера для хранения багажа
KA-m'i-rə dl'a ḥra-N'EN'-yə bə-ga-ZHA
Baggage room

Буфет
bu-F'ET
Refreshments

Дамская комната
DAM-skə-yə KOM-nə-tə
Ladies waiting room

Курительная
ku-R'I-t'il'-nə-yə
Smoking

Не плевать
n'i pl'i-V'AT'
No spitting

Не высовываться
n'i vi-SO-vi-vət-sə
Don't lean out

На ходу не сходить
no ḥa-DU n'i s-ḥa-D'IT'
Don't get off while car is moving

Держитесь правой стороны
d'ir-ZHI-t'is PRA-vəy stə-ra-NI
Keep to the right

For additional signs, see the Appendix on p. 107.

SPORTS

Tennis

Как мне проехать на теннисные корты?
KAK mn'e pra-YE-ḥət' na TE-n'is-ni-yə KOR-ti?
How do I get to the tennis courts?

К кому обратиться за разрешением на игру?
kka-MU a-bra-T'IT-sə zə rəz-r'i-SHEN'-yəm nə i-GRU?
From whom do I get permission to play?

Можно тут поиграть в теннис?
MOZH-nə tut pə-i-GRAT' fTE-n'is?
May I play tennis here?

У меня есть своя ракетка.
u m'i-N'A yest' sva-YA ra-K'ET-kə.
I have my own racket.

Мне нужны теннисные мячи; где можно их получить?
mn'e nuzh-N‡ TE-n'is-ni-yə m'i-CHI; GD'E MOZH-nə yiḥ pə-lu-CHIT'?
I need tennis balls; where can I get some?

Soccer Match

Я хотел бы посмотреть настоящий русский футбольный матч.
YA ḥa-T'EL-bi pə-ˀsma-TR'ET' nə-sta-YASH'-chiy RU-sk'iy fud-BOL'-
   niy MAT'CH.
I would like to see a real Russian soccer match.

Прекрасно, поедем на Ленинский Стадион.
pr'i-KRAS-nə, pa-YE-d'im na L'E-n'in-sk'iy stə-d'i-ON.
Fine, let's go to Lenin Stadium.

Какие команды играют сегодня?
ka-K'I-yə ka-MAN-di i-GRA-yut s'i-VOD'-nə?
Which teams are playing today?

Сколько стоит вход?
SKOL'-kə STOY-it f-ḤOT?
How much is the admission?

Swimming and Bathing

Поедем купаться.
pa-YE-d'im ku-PAT-sə.
Let's go swimming (lit., bathing).

Где пляж? На реке?
GD'E PL'ASH? nə-r'i-K'E?
Where is the beach? On the river?

Да. Не забудьте принести купальный костюм, полотенце и крем для загара.
DA. n'i za-BUT'-t'i pr'i-n'i-ST'I ku-PAL'-niy ka-ST'UM, pə-la-T'ENTsə i KR'EM dl'ə za-GA-rə.
Yes. Don't forget to bring your bathing suit, a towel, and sun-tan cream.

Мне крем не нужен, я очень хорошо загораю.
MN'E KR'EM n'i NU-zhin. YA O-chin ḥə-ra-SHO zə-ga-RA-yu.
I don't need any cream. I tan very well.

Хотите я принесу одеяло.
ha-T'I-t'i ya pr'i-n'i-SU a-d'i-YA-lə?
Do you want me to bring a blanket?

Нет, не надо. Лучше будем лежать на песке.
N'ET, n'i NA-də. LUCH-shə BU-d'im l'i-ZHAT' nə-p'i-SK'E.
No, that's not necessary. We'll lie on the sand.

Посмотрите какая тихая вода.
pə-sma-TR'I-t'i ka-KA-yə T'I-ḥə-yə va-DA.
Look how still the water is!

Это же река. Если вы хотите большие волны, надо эхать на Чёрное Море.

E-tə-zhə r'i-KA. YE-sl'i vi ha-T'I-t'i bal'-SHɨ-yə VOL-nɨ, NA-də YE-ħət' na-CHOR-nə-yə MO-r'ə.

After all, this is a river. If you want big waves, you have to go down to the Black Sea.

О я люблю и море и реку.

O YA l'u-BL'U I MO-r'ə I r'i-KU.

Oh, I like both the sea and the river.

Fishing

Мне нужны удилище, леска, и крючки.

mn'e nuzh-Nɨ u-D'I-l'ish'-chə, L'E-skə, i kr'uch-K'I.

I need a rod, line and hooks.

Где можно взять напрокат лодку?

GD'E MOZH-nə vz'at' nə-prə-KAT LOT-ku?

Where can I rent a boat?

Какие рыбы водятся в этой реке (в этом озере)?

ka-K'I-yə Rɨ-bɨ VO-d'ət-sə vE-təy r'i-K'E (vE-təm O-z'i-r'i)?

What kind of fish are found in this river (in this lake)?

OUTLINE OF RUSSIAN GRAMMAR

OUTLINE OF RUSSIAN GRAMMAR

Although, for purposes of everyday practical needs, you will be able to get by with some stock of common Russian words and phrases, it is advisable also to have some understanding of the parts of speech and their various forms and uses as well as of the manner in which Russian sentences are constructed. In the following pages we have attempted to present the "highlights" of Russian grammar very concisely, so as to enable you to understand the how and why of the phrases in this book. This survey is of necessity brief, but the main facts for your daily needs have been covered.

1. THE NOUN

1.0. Nouns in Russian are never preceded by a definite or indefinite article because there are no articles in Russian. When translating from Russian into English, *the* and *a* should be supplied to fit the meaning.

1.1. Russian nouns are declined (change endings) for number, gender, and case. There are two numbers (singular and plural) and three genders (masculine, feminine, and neuter). In Russian the gender is grammatical. Although the *meaning* of a word does not usually give a clue to its gender, the gender can generally be determined by the written ending of the *nominative* or first case (see **1.2**) according to the following rules:

Masculine nouns end in a consonant (стол, table); in **й** (чай, tea); and in some cases in **ь** (словáрь, dictionary).

Feminine nouns end in **a** (газéта, newspaper) or **я** (дерéвня, village); the majority of nouns ending in **ь** is also feminine (лóшадь, horse).

Neuter are all words ending in **e** (кóфе, coffee); in **o** (слóво, word); and in **мя** (врéмя, time).

Nouns indicating *animate beings* are generally masculine when they refer to males and feminine when they refer to females. In a few cases, however, nouns with feminine endings are used to refer to male beings and are therefore considered masculine nouns. Thus, дя́дя (uncle) is a masculine noun despite its final -я. Nouns designating *inanimate objects* are masculine, feminine or neuter according to the above rules. See **1.3-6.**

1.2. Russian has six cases. Their basic uses and functions are:

The **nominative** indicates the subject of the sentence.

The **genitive** indicates possession and is usually translated by "of the" or the English possessive case. It is also used with some prepositions, the most common of which are: **бе́з** (without), **для** (for), **до** (up to), **из** (out of), **круго́м** (around), **о́коло** (near, about), **от** (from), **по́сле** (after) and **у** (at, with, by).

It is important to remember that in Russian the meaning of *to have* is idiomatically expressed by the preposition **у** followed by the genitive of a noun or pronoun: **у меня́ есть до́м** is the normal way of saying "I have a house" (literally: With me there is [a] house).

The **dative** is used to indicate the indirect object, so that it usually can be translated with "to the" or "for the." It is also used after the prepositions **к** (to) and **по** (along, according to).

The **accusative** indicates the direct object of the verb and is also used after the prepositions **в** (to, into), **за** (behind), **на** (to, into, on), **под** (under), **про** (about) and **че́рез** (through).

The **instrumental** is used to indicate the agent of action or the instrument (means) with which the action described by the verb is performed. It is usually translated with "by means of," "by (the)" or "with (the)." It is also used after the prepositions **с** or **со** (with), **ме́жду** (between, among), **пе́ред** (in front of), **над** (over), **под** (under) and **за** (behind).

The **prepositional** or **locative** indicates either location or the subject of discourse. It is governed by the prepositions **в** (in), **на** (on), **о, об** or **о́бо** (about, concerning), **при** (in the presence of).

The case to be used with a preposition naturally depends on the meaning of the sentence: **в го́роде** (*in* the city: prepositional); **в го́род** (*to* the city: accusative).

1.3. THE FIRST DECLENSION

Nouns ending in **a** or **я** belong to the first declension. These nouns are *feminine*.

Nouns ending in **a**

Nom.	газе́та	the newspaper	газе́ты	the newspapers
Gen.	газе́ты	of the newspaper	газе́т	of the newspapers
Dat.	газе́те	to the newspaper	газе́там	to the newspapers
Acc.	газе́ту	the newspaper	газе́ты	the newspapers
Instr.	газе́той *	with (by means of) the newspaper	газе́тами	with (by means of) the newspapers
Prep.	о газе́те	about the newspaper	о газе́тах	about the newspapers

Nouns ending in **я**

	Singular		Plural	
Nom.	простыня́	the sheet	про́стыни	the sheets
Gen.	простыни́		просты́нь	
Dat.	простыне́		простыня́м	
Acc.	простыню́		про́стыни	
Instr.	простынёй *		простыня́ми	
Prep.	о простыне́		о простыня́х	

Nouns in which the ending **я** is preceded by another vowel are declined as follows:

	Singular		Plural
Nom.	тео́рия	theory	тео́рии
Gen.	тео́рии		тео́рий
Dat.	тео́рии		тео́риям
Acc.	тео́рию		тео́рии
Instr.	тео́рией *		тео́риями
Prep.	о тео́рии		о тео́риях

1.4. THE SECOND DECLENSION

Nouns ending in a plain or "hard" consonant or in **й** belong to the second declension. They are always masculine. To the same declension belong some of the masculine nouns which end in **ь**.

Nouns ending in **о** or **е** also belong to the second declension. The gender of these nouns is *neuter*.

---

* Feminine instrumental forms in -ою or -ёю are not used in normal speech, but constitute literary and poetic usage.

Nouns ending in hard consonants

	Singular		Plural
Nom.	стол	table	столы́
Gen.	стола́		столо́в
Dat.	столу́		стола́м
Acc.	стол		столы́
Instr.	столо́м		стола́ми
Prep.	о столе́		о стола́х

Nouns ending in **ь**

	Singular		Plural
Nom.	слова́рь	dictionary	словари́
Gen.	словаря́		словаре́й
Dat.	словарю́		словаря́м
Acc.	слова́рь		словари́
Instr.	словарём		словаря́ми
Prep.	о словаре́		о словаря́х

Nouns ending in **й**

	Singular		Plural
Nom.	слу́чай	case, occasion	слу́чаи
Gen.	слу́чая		слу́чаев
Dat.	слу́чаю		слу́чаям
Acc.	слу́чай		слу́чаи
Instr.	слу́чаем		слу́чаями
Prep.	о слу́чае		о спу́чаях

Nouns ending in **о**

	Singular		Plural
Nom.	сло́во	word	слова́
Gen.	сло́ва		слов
Dat.	сло́ву		слова́м
Acc.	сло́во		слова́
Instr.	сло́вом		слова́ми
Prep.	о сло́ве		о слова́х

Nouns ending in **е**

	Singular		Plural
Nom.	по́ле	field	поля́
Gen.	по́ля		поле́й
Dat.	по́лю		поля́м
Acc.	по́ле		поля́
Instr.	по́лем		поля́ми
Prep.	о по́ле		о поля́х

1.5. THE THIRD DECLENSION

Feminine nouns ending in **ь** belong to the third declension.

	Singular		*Plural*
Nom.	дверь	door	две́ри
Gen.	две́ри		двере́й
Dat.	две́ри		дверя́м
Acc.	дверь		две́ри
Instr.	две́рью		дверя́ми
Prep.	о две́ри		о дверя́х

1.6. Masculine nouns in both singular and plural, and feminine nouns in the plural only, have identical endings in the nominative and accusative when they designate *inanimate* objects, and in the genitive and accusative when they designate *animate* beings. Examples: Nominative and accusative singular заво́д (factory), nom. and acc. pl. заво́ды; nom. singular оте́ц (father), gen. and acc. singular отца́, nom. pl. отцы́, gen. and acc. pl. отцо́в.

1.7. Contrary to the general rule, the final **a** or **я** of the *genitive singular* of some masculine nouns is often replaced by **y**, especially in a partitive sense: ча́шка ча́ю (a cup of tea), са́хару (some sugar), фунт табаку́ (a pound of tobacco).

Also, the *prepositional singular* of some monosyllabic masculine nouns ends in stressed **y** (instead of **e**), but only after в (in) and на (on): в саду́ (in the garden), в снегу́ (in the snow), на полу́ (on the floor).

The *nominative plural* of a number of masculine nouns ending in a consonant terminates in stressed **a** (instead of **ы** or **и**): дома́ (houses), города́ (cities), глаза́ (eyes), леса́ (forests). A few nouns of foreign origin also have this irregular case ending: доктора́ (doctors), профессора́ (professors).

1.8. Russian names and patronymics. In Russian it is common practice to address adult persons by their first name and the patronymic:

Никола́й Ива́нович	Nikolai, son of Ivan
Ви́ктор Никола́евич	Victor, son of Nikolai
Мари́я Ива́новна	Maria, daughter of Ivan
Ве́ра Никола́евна	Vera, daughter of Nikolai

The patronymic is derived from the first name of the father. Whenever that name ends in a hard consonant, the suffix -ович (for persons of the male sex) or the suffix -овна́ (for persons of the female sex) is added:

$$\text{Ива́н} \quad \left\{ \begin{array}{l} + \text{ович} = \text{Ива́нович } (m.) \\ + \text{овна} = \text{Ива́новна } (f.) \end{array} \right.$$

In all other cases, the suffixes -евич (for males) and -евна (for females) are used:

$$\text{Никола́й} \quad \left\{ \begin{array}{l} + \text{евич} = \text{Никола́евич } (m.) \\ + \text{евна} = \text{Никола́евна } (f.) \end{array} \right.$$

2. THE ADJECTIVE

2.0. In Russian, the adjectives agree with the noun they modify in number, gender and case. This includes the cases where the masculine genitive singular and the feminine genitive plural are used as accusative forms of animate beings (see **1.6**).

2.1. *Hard* adjectives, in the nominative singular, end in **ый** or **ой** when they govern masculine nouns; in **ая** when they govern feminine nouns; and in **ое** when they govern neuter nouns. Examples: большо́й дом (a large house); твёрдый каранда́ш (a hard pencil); больша́я ко́мната (a large room); большо́е окно́ (a large window).

2.2. *Soft* adjectives, in the nominative singular, end in **ий** when they govern masculine nouns; in **яя** when they govern feminine nouns; and in **ее** when they govern neuter nouns. Examples: си́ний каранда́ш (a blue pencil); си́няя кни́га (a blue book); си́нее стекло́ (a blue glass).

2.3. DECLENSION OF ADJECTIVES

Hard, ending in **ый, ая, ое**

Singular

	Masculine		*Feminine*	*Neuter*
Nom.	но́вый	new	но́вая	но́вое
Gen.	но́вого		но́вой	но́вого
Dat.	но́вому		но́вой	но́вому
Acc.	но́вый		но́вую	но́вое
Instr.	но́вым		но́вой	но́вым
Prep.	о но́вом		о но́вой	о но́вом

Plural

	Masculine	*Feminine*	*Neuter*
Nom.	но́вые	но́вые	но́вые
Gen.	но́вых	но́вых	но́вых
Dat.	но́вым	но́вым	но́вым
Acc.	но́вые	но́вые	но́вые
Instr.	но́выми	но́выми	но́выми
Prep.	о но́вых	о но́вых	о но́вых

Hard, ending in **ой, ая, ое**

Nom.	густо́й	thick	густа́я	густо́е
Gen.	густо́го		густо́й	густо́го
Dat.	густо́му		густо́й	густо́му
Acc.	густо́й		густу́ю	густо́е
Instr.	густы́м		густо́й	густы́м
Prep.	о густо́м		о густо́й	о густо́м

The plural of hard adjectives ending in **ой, ая, ое** is formed like that of the other hard adjectives.

Hard adjectives, when used predicatively, are sometimes shortened: дом но́вый or дом нов (the house [is] new). The shortened forms are more common in literature than in conversational speech. However, there are some adjectives which are always short in predicative position: он бо́лен (he is sick), она́ больна́ (she is sick); э́то ну́жно (this is necessary). The "long" forms of these two adjectives are больно́й and ну́жный.

Soft, ending in **ий, яя, ее**
Singular

	Masc.		*Fem.*	*Neut.*
Nom.	си́ний	blue	си́няя	си́нее
Gen.	си́него		си́ней	си́него
Dat.	си́нему		си́ней	си́нему
Acc.	си́ний		си́нюю	си́нее
Instr.	си́ним		си́ней	си́ним
Prep.	о си́нем		о си́ней	о си́нем

Plural

Nom.	си́ние	си́ние	си́ние
Gen.	си́них	си́них	си́них
Dat.	си́ним	си́ним	си́ним
Acc.	си́ние	си́ние	си́ние
Instr.	си́ними	си́ними	си́ними
Prep.	о си́них	о си́них	о си́них

Adjectives having a stem in **ж, ц, ш, щ**
Singular

	Masc.		*Fem.*	*Neut.*
Nom.	све́жий	fresh	све́жая	све́жее
Gen.	све́жего		све́жей	све́жего
Dat.	све́жему		све́жей	све́жему

Acc.	свéжий	свéжую	свéжее
Instr.	свéжим	свéжей	свéжим
Prep.	о свéжем	о свéжей	о свéжем

The plural is formed like синий, above.

2.4. THE COMPARATIVE DEGREE

The comparative degree in many cases is formed by placing the word **бóлее** (more) before the adjective: интерéсный (interesting), бóлее интерéсный (more interesting); дорогóй (expensive or dear), бóлее дорогóй (more expensive or dearer). There is another form of the comparative degree which has the same meaning and is produced by adding **e** or **ee** to the stem of the adjective: интерéсн(ый) (interesting), интерéснее (more interesting).

2.4.1. The comparative degree of some important adjectives is formed irregularly:

хорóший	good	лýчше	better
плохóй	bad	хýже	worse
широкий	wide	шире	wider
ýзкий	narrow, tight	ýже	narrower, tighter
высóкий	high	выше	higher
низкий	low	ниже	lower
дорогóй	expensive	дорóже	more expensive
дешёвый	cheap	дешéвле	cheaper

2.5. THE SUPERLATIVE DEGREE

The superlative degree is formed by placing the word **сáмый, -ая, -ое,** which is declined like an adjective, before the adjective:

плохóй	bad (m.)	сáмый плохóй	the worst
плохáя	bad (f.)	сáмая плохáя	the worst
плохóе	bad (n.)	сáмое плохóе	the worst

The endings **-áйший** and **-éйший** are sometimes used to form superlatives. Examples: ближáйший, nearest (from близкий, near); новéйший, latest, newest (from нóвый, new).

2.6. Many adverbs are derived from adjectives by adding the letter **o** to the stem of the adjective: хорóш(ий) (good), хорошó (well); плох(óй) (bad), плóхо (badly).

2.7. Adverbs of time, like ле́том (in summer), зимо́й (in winter), у́тром (in the morning), днём (during the daytime), ра́но (early) and пото́м (then, later), denote the time when an action is performed or takes place. These forms actually are the instrumentals of the respective nouns (see **1.2**). Compare:

Nouns		*Adverbs*	
у́тро	morning	у́тром	in the morning
день	day	днём	in the daytime
ве́чер	evening	ве́чером	in the evening
ночь	night	но́чью	at night, in the night

3. THE NUMERALS

3.0. The cardinal numbers are listed on page 36.

3.1. The numeral оди́н (one) agrees in gender and case with the noun it qualifies: оди́н стул (one chair), одна́ ко́мната (one room), одно́ окно́ (one window). Оди́н is declined as follows:

		Singular		*Plural*
	Masc.	*Fem.*	*Neut.*	(*all genders*)
Nom.	оди́н	одна́	одно́	одни́
Gen.	одного́	одно́й	одного́	одни́х
Dat.	одному́	одно́й	одному́	одни́м
Acc.	оди́н or одного́	одну́	одно́	одни́
Instr.	одни́м	одно́й	одни́м	одни́ми
Prep.	об одно́м	об одно́й	об одно́м	об одни́х

The plural form is used with nouns which have no singular form: одни́ часы́ (one watch) and одни́ но́жницы (one pair of scissors).

3.2. The numbers 2, 3 and 4 are followed by the genitive singular of the noun they qualify when they are in the nominative or accusative. All other numbers are followed by the genitive plural when they are in the nominative or accusative: два, три, четы́ре окна́ (two, three, four windows); пять, шесть око́н (five, six windows), etc.

Два (two) and о́ба (both) are masculine and neuter forms. Their feminine counterparts are две and о́бе. The other numerals make no such differentiation between genders.

	Masc. & neut.	*Fem.*	*All genders*
Nom.	два (2)	две (2)	три (3)
Gen.	двух	двух	трёх
Dat.	двум	двум	трём
Acc.	два	две	три
Instr.	двумя	двумя	тремя
Prep.	о двух	о двух	о трёх

	All genders	*Masc. & neut.*	*Fem.*
Nom.	четыре (4)	оба (both)	обе (both)
Gen.	четырёх	обоих	обеих
Dat.	четырём	обоим	обеим
Acc.	четыре	оба	обе
Instr.	четырьмя	обоими	обеими
Prep.	о четырёх	об обоих	об обеих

3.3. The numbers from 5 to 20 and the number 30 are declined like feminine nouns in **-ь**. The declensions of the cardinal numbers from 5 to 10 are given below:

Nom.	пять (5)	шесть (6)	семь (7)
Gen.	пяти	шести	семи
Dat.	пяти	шести	семи
Acc.	пять	шесть	семь
Instr.	пятью	шестью	семью
Prep.	о пяти	о шести	о семи

Nom.	восемь (8)	девять (9)	десять (10)
Gen.	восьми	девяти	десяти
Dat.	восьми	девяти	десяти
Acc.	восемь	девять	десять
Instr.	восемью	девятью	десятью
Prep.	о восьми	о девяти	о десяти

3.4. The numbers 40, 90 and 100 have only two declensional forms, one for the nominative and accusative and one for all the other cases. They are: сорок, сорока; девяносто, девяноста; сто, ста.

Both parts of the compound numerals 50, 60, 70, 80 and the number for hundreds from 200 to 900 are declined.

3.5. The ordinal numbers are listed on page 37. They are declined like regular adjectives.

3.6. Ordinal numerals used in dates appear in the neuter gender: десятое февраля (February 10th), десятого февраля (*on* February 10th).

3.7. In fractions, a cardinal number is used for the numerator and an ordinal for the denominator in the genitive plural: три восьмы́х (three eighths).

4. THE PRONOUN

4.1. The **personal pronouns** are:

Singular

	1st person	2nd person
Nom.	я (I)	ты (you)
Gen.	меня́ (of me)	тебя́
Dat.	мне (to me)	тебе́
Acc.	меня́ (me)	тебя́
Instr.	мной (by me)	тобо́й
Prep.	обо мне́ (about me)	о тебе́

3rd person

	Masc.	*Fem.*	*Neut.*
Nom.	он (he)	она́ (she)	оно́ (it)
Gen.	(н)его́	(н)её	(н)его́
Dat.	(н)ему́	(н)ей	(н)ему́
Acc.	(н)его́	(н)её	(н)его́
Instr.	(н)им	(н)ей	(н)им
Prep.	о нём	о ней	о нём

Plural

Nom.	мы (we)	вы (you)	они́ (they)
Gen.	нас (of us)	вас (of you)	(н)их (of them)
Dat.	нам (to us)	вам (to you)	(н)им (to them)
Acc.	нас (us)	вас (you)	(н)их (them)
Instr.	на́ми (by us)	ва́ми (by you)	(н)и́ми (by them)
Prep.	о нас (about us)	о вас (about you)	о них (about them)

The two forms of the third person (его́ and него́; её and неё, etc.) are not interchangeable. The forms with н- are used when the pronoun is governed by a preposition.

Note that "you" can be expressed in two ways in Russian:

a) The familiar or ты-form, which is used in addressing close friends, relatives, children and pets.

b) The polite or вы-form, which is used in addressing mere acquaintances, strangers, older persons and superiors.

Ты and вы correspond in form and usage to French *tu* and
vous.

4.2. The **reflexive pronouns** are себя and сам.

Себя (self) may refer to any person in the singular or plural,
and corresponds to the English pronouns myself, yourself, himself, herself, itself, ourselves,.. yourselves, themselves. It has no
nominative. The form себя is used for the genitive and accusative; себе for the dative; собой for the instrumental; and
о себе for the prepositional. This word is used when no special
emphasis is desired: он думает о себе (he thinks about
himself).

Сам, which is used to express the idea of myself, yourself,
himself, etc., in an emphatical manner, follows the pronoun immediately, but generally precedes the noun: он сам (he himself); сам директор (the manager himself). The declension of
сам is as follows:

| | *Singular* | | | *Plural* |
	Masc.	*Fem.*	*Neut.*	*All genders*
Nom.	сам	сама	само	сами
Gen.	самого	самой	самого	самих
Dat.	самому	самой	самому	самим
Acc.	самого	самоё	само	самих
Instr.	самим	самой	самим	самими
Prep.	о самом	о самой	о самом	о самих

4.3. The **possessive adjectives** and **pronouns** are:

Singular

		Masc.	*Fem.*	*Neut.*
1st person		мой (my)	моя	моё
2nd person		твой (your)	твоя	твоё
3rd person	*masc.*	его (his)	его	его
	fem.	её (her)	её	её
	neut.	его (its)	его	его

Plural

1st person	наш (our)	наша	наше
2nd person	ваш (your)	ваша	ваше
3rd person	их (their)	их	их

The possessive pronouns of the third person plural do not
change for gender, number, and case. They have only one form.

Мой (my), твой (your, sing.), свой (one's own, their own) are declined in the same way, as follows:

| | *Singular* | | | *Plural* |
	Masc.	*Fem.*	*Neut.*	*All genders*
Nom.	мой	моя́	моё	мои́
Gen.	моего́	мое́й	моего́	мои́х
Dat.	моему́	мое́й	моему́	мои́м
Acc.	мой	мою́	моё	мои́
Instr.	мои́м	мое́й	мои́м	мои́ми
Prep.	о моём	о мое́й	о моём	о мои́х

The declensions of наш (our) and ваш (your: plural and/or polite) are identical, so that any declined form of ваш can be determined simply by substituting в for н.

| | *Singular* | | | *Plural* |
	Masc.	*Fem.*	*Neut.*	*All genders*
Nom.	наш	на́ша	на́ше	на́ши
Gen.	на́шего	на́шей	на́шего	на́ших
Dat.	на́шему	на́шей	на́шему	на́шим
Acc.	наш	на́шу	наш	на́ши
Instr.	на́шим	на́шей	на́шим	на́шими
Prep.	о на́шем	о на́шей	о на́шем	о на́ших

The possessive pronouns мой, твой, наш, ваш agree in gender, number, and case with the noun they qualify: моё письмо́ (my letter), твоего́ словаря́ (of your dictionary), на́ши кни́ги (our books).

As explained in **1.6**, when two forms are shown for the accusative, the fact whether an inanimate object or an animate being is designated determines if the accusative has the form of the nominative or of the genitive.

4.4. The most common **demonstrative adjectives** and **pronouns** in Russian are э́тот (this *or* that) and тот (that, contrasting with *this*). They are declined as follows:

| | *Singular* | | | | | |
	Masc.	*Fem.*	*Neut.*	*Masc.*	*Fem.*	*Neut.*
Nom.	э́тот	э́та	э́то	тот	та	то
Gen.	э́того	э́той	э́того	того́	той	того́
Dat.	э́тому	э́той	э́тому	тому́	той	тому́
Acc.	э́тот	э́ту	э́то	тот	ту	то
Instr.	э́тим	э́той	э́тим	тем	той	тем
Prep.	об э́том	об э́той	об э́том	о то́м	о той	о то́м

Plural

All genders

Nom.	э́ти		те
Gen.	э́тих		тех
Dat.	э́тим		тем
Acc.	э́ти		те
Instr.	э́тими		те́ми
Prep.	·об э́тих		о тех

4.5. The **interrogative adjectives** and **pronouns** are:

Кото́рый, -ая, -ое, -ые (who *or* which; *also* that *when used as a relative pronoun*).

Како́й, -ая, -ое, -ые (what kind of).

Both кото́рый and како́й are declined as regular adjectives.

Чей, чья, чьё, чьи (whose), which has the same declension as мой.

Кто (who) and **что** (what, which), which are also used as relative pronouns. They are declined as follows:

Nom.	кто	(who)	что	(what)
Gen.	кого́	(of whom)	чего́	(of what, which)
Dat.	кому́	(to whom)	чему́	(to what, which)
Acc.	кого́	(whom)	что	(what, which)
Instr.	кем	(by whom)	чем	(by what, which)
Prep.	о ком	(about whom)	о чём	(about what, which)

4.6. The **indefinite pronouns** and **adjectives**, declined as regular adjectives, are:

Masc.		*Fem.*	*Neut.*	*Plur.*
вся́кий	(any)	вся́кая	вся́кое	вся́кие
любо́й	(anyone)	люба́я	любо́е	любы́е
ка́ждый	(every, each)	ка́ждая	ка́ждое	ка́ждые
друго́й	(other)	друга́я	друго́е	други́е
тако́й	(such)	така́я	тако́е	таки́е

The particles **-то** and **-нибудь** are added to кто, что and other interrogative words to form compounds of *any* and *some*: кто́-то (someone); кто́-нибудь (anyone); что́-то (something); что́-нибудь (anything); где́-то (somewhere); где́-нибудь (anywhere).

The adjective and pronoun **весь** (all) is declined as follows:

| | *Singular* | | | *Plural* |
	Masc.	*Fem.*	*Neut.*	*All genders*
Nom.	весь	вся	всё	все
Gen.	всего	всей	всего	всех
Dat.	всему	всей	всему	всем
Acc.	весь	всю	всё	все
Instr.	всем	всей	всем	всёми
Prep.	обо всём	обо всей	обо всём	обо всёх

5. THE CONJUNCTION

5.1. *Coordinating* conjunctions join sentences, clauses, phrases, and words of equal rank. The most common ones are: **и** (and), **а** (and, but), **но** (but), **и...и** (both...and), **йли** (or), **йли...йли** (either...or), **ни...ни** (neither...nor).

5.2. *Subordinating* conjunctions introduce dependent clauses. The most common ones are: **éсли** (if), **когда** (when), **как** (as), **потому что** (because).

6. THE VERB

6.1. The verb быть (to be) has no forms for the present tense. The words *am, is* and *are*, therefore, are implied, not expressed: я инженéр (I am an engineer); он студéнт (he [is a] student); мы друзья (we [are] friends); они коммерсáнты (they [are] businessmen).

The future of быть is: я бýду, ты бýдешь, он (онá, онó) бýдет, мы бýдем, вы бýдете, они бýдут (I shall *or* will be, you will be, etc.).

The past of быть has the following forms: был (1st, 2nd and 3rd person masc. sing.), былá (1st, 2nd and 3rd person fem. sing.), бýло (1st, 2nd and 3rd person neut. sing.), были (1st, 2nd and 3rd person plural for all three genders).

The word есть, which is the third person singular of быть, is most generally used in the meaning of *there is* or *there are*. In combination with у меня, у тебé, у негó, у неё, у нас, у вас and у них, it forms the common Russian idiom for *I have, you have*, etc. (lit.: "with me, you, etc., there is"): У вас есть карандáш? (have you [got] a pencil?); у меня есть два билéта (I have two tickets); есть у негó дéньги? (does he have [any] money?). The negative form requires the use of the genitive: у меня нет книги (I do not have the book *or* I have no book).

6.2. ASPECTS

Most Russian verbs have two kinds of forms which are called "aspects" because they have to do with two ways of expressing actions or processes.

The *imperfective* aspect is used to describe an action in progress or one which is repeated or habitual without reference to the completion of the action.

The *perfective* aspect, on the other hand, is used to express the fact of the completion of the action. Consequently, there can be no present tense in this aspect.

Examples:

Я хочу́ чита́ть	I want to read (in general).
Я хочу́ писа́ть	I want to write (in general).
Я хочу́ прочита́ть э́ту кни́гу	I want to read this book through.
Я хочу́ написа́ть э́то письмо́	I want to write this letter (and finish it).

The infinitive of the perfective aspect is derived from the infinitive of the imperfective in various manners:

a) By prefixing prepositions to the infinitive of the imperfective:

чита́ть to read	прочита́ть to read through
писа́ть to write	написа́ть to write (and finish writing)

b) By changing the vowel which connects the stem with the infinitive ending -ть:

получа́ть to get (in general)   получи́ть to get (one particular thing)

c) By using a verb of a different stem:

говори́ть to speak   сказа́ть to say

6.3. CONJUGATIONS

The Russian verb is changed according to person, number and tense. This change is known as conjugation. There are two conjugations in Russian. The *first conjugation* is characterized by the vowel **e** which is predominant in the personal endings of the present tense. The *second conjugation* is characterized by the vowel **и** which predominates the personal endings of the present tense.

6.4. THE IMPERFECTIVE ASPECT

Infinitive

чита́ть to read   стро́ить to build

Present

FIRST CONJUGATION

Singular		*Plural*	
Я чита́ю	I read	мы чита́ем	we read
ты чита́ешь	you read	вы чита́ете	you read
он $\}$ чита́ет	he $\}$ reads	они́ чита́ют	they read
она́	she		

Imperative

чита́й! read! (familiar)   чита́йте! read! (plural or polite)

SECOND CONJUGATION

Singular		*Plural*	
я стро́ю	I build	мы стро́им	we build
ты стро́ишь	you build	вы стро́ите	you build
он $\}$ стро́ит	he $\}$ builds	они́ стро́ят	they build
она́	she		

Imperative

стро́й! build! (familiar)   стро́йте! build! (plural or polite)

Future

The future is formed by adding the future of the verb быть (to be) to the infinitive:

я бу́ду чита́ть	I shall be reading
ты бу́дешь чита́ть	you will be reading
он $\}$	he $\}$
она́ $\}$ бу́дет чита́ть	she $\}$ will be reading
оно́ $\}$	it $\}$
мы бу́дем чита́ть	we shall be reading
вы бу́дете чита́ть	you will be reading
они́ бу́дут чита́ть	they will be reading

The imperfective future is generally used to express future meaning with no prediction as to the end of the contemplated action.

Past

The past tense is formed by changing the ending -ть of the infinitive into л, ла, ло:

	Singular			*Plural*	
я	чита́л (*masc.*)	I read	мы чита́ли	we read
я	чита́ла (*fem.*)	I read	вы чита́ли	you read
ты	чита́л (*m.*)	you read	они́ чита́ли	they read
ты	чита́ла (*f.*)	you read		
он	чита́л (*m.*)	he read		
она́	чита́ла (*f.*)	she read		
оно́	чита́ло (*n.*)	it read		

The imperfective past may describe a number of repeated actions or it may describe a single past action or process. In all such cases, this form is used to express interest in the action itself without taking into account its possible completion.

6.5. THE PERFECTIVE ASPECT

Infinitive

| прочита́ть | to read through |
| постро́ить | to build something (and finish it) |

Present

The verbs belonging to the perfective aspect have no present tense.

Future

FIRST CONJUGATION

я прочита́ю I shall read (through)	мы прочита́ем we shall read (through)
ты прочита́ешь you will read	вы прочита́ете you will read
он прочита́ет he will read	они прочита́ют they will read

SECOND CONJUGATION

Я постро́ю I shall build (and finish it)	мы постро́им we shall build
ты постро́ишь you will build	вы постро́ите you will build
он постро́ит he will build	они постро́ят they will build

The perfective future expresses future meaning with the expectation that the contemplated action will be completed.

Past

The past tense is formed by changing the ending -ть of the infinitive into л, ла, ло.

	Singular	*Plural*
я прочитáл (*m.*)	{ I read through	мы прочитáли
	{ I have read	вы прочитáли
	{ I have read through	они́ прочитáли
я прочитáла (*f.*)		
ты прочитáл (*m.*)		
ты прочитáла (*f.*)		
он прочитáл (*m.*)		
онá прочитáла (*f.*)		
оно́ прочитáло (*n.*)		

The perfective past is used to describe a past action or a series of past actions which have been completed. Я прочитáл э́ту кни́гу (I read the book through, I have read the book *or* I have read the book through).

The **conditional** is formed by adding the particle **бы** after the imperfective past: я читáл бы (I would read *or* I would have read).

6.6. The passive voice is frequently expressed by attaching the particle **-ся** (**-сь** after a vowel sound) to all the forms of a transitive verb: стрóит дом (he builds a house); дом стрóится (a house is built).

6.6.1. The particle -ся is also used with reflexive verbs: онá одевáется (she dresses herself *or* she is dressing). Онá одевáет means *she dresses (someone)*; it requires an object to complete its sense.

6.7. A number of verbs are classified as irregular by most grammarians. Actually, they constitute an additional conjugation and share the same endings, which are characterized by the vowel **ё** in the present tense. The most important of these verbs are: **брать** (to take), **вести́** (to lead), **давáть** (to give), **идти́** (to go), **жить** (to live), **звать** (to call), **нести́** (to carry).

Singular	*Plural*	*Singular*	*Plural*
я беру́ I take	мы берём	я даю́ I give	мы даём
ты берёшь	вы берёте	ты даёшь	вы даёте
он берёт	они́ беру́т	он даёт	они даю́т

6.8. VERBS OF MOTION

There are two main groups of verbs of motion in Russian:

I. ходи́ть	е́здить	бега́ть	лета́ть	вози́ть	носи́ть
II. идти́	е́хать	бежа́ть	лете́ть	везти́	нести́
to go, to walk	to ride	to run	to fly	to drive	to carry

Each verb of group I has a corresponding verb in group II. In English both the verb of group I and its corresponding verb in group II are rendered by the same verb.

The verbs of group I denote an action of movement that has taken place repeatedly or during an indefinite period of time. Those of the second group indicate an action of movement that takes place at a definite time and in a definite direction: Ива́н ходи́т в шко́лу (John goes to school [usually or in general]); Ива́н идёт в шко́лу (John is going to school [at this moment]).

In the Dictionary section, verbs of group I are labeled *indefinite* (*ind.*) and those of group II are labeled *definite* (*def.*).

6.9. Russian **participles** usually have the following endings:

a) Present active participle, in	**-щий** : чита́ющий he who reads
b) Past active participle, in	**-вший** : чита́вший he who read
c) Present passive participle, in	**-мый** : чита́емый he that is read
d) Past passive participle, in	**-нный** : чи́танный he that was read

There are two **gerunds** in Russian:

a) Present gerund, in **-я** :	чита́я when reading
b) Past gerund, in **-в** or **-вши** :	чита́вши when having read

7. WORD ORDER

7.1. Word order is not so strict in Russian as it is in English since there is little possibility of misinterpreting the function of a word, regardless of its position. Since each function is characterized by specific word endings, the normal word order often is not different from that of English, but transpositions of subject and verb for stylistic effect are very common. This phenomenon is amply illustrated by the conversational sentences in this book.

7.2. The double negative is required in Russian: я ничего́ не зна́ю or я не зна́ю ничего́ (I don't know anything [*lit.*: "not nothing"]); он никогда́ не идёт or он не идёт никогда́ (he doesn't go anywhere [*lit.*: "not nowhere"]).

APPENDICES

IMPORTANT SIGNS

Билéтная кáсса	Ticket window	Крутóй поворóт	Sharp curve
Внимáние	Attention	Крутóй спуск	Sharp slope
Вокзáл	Railroad station	Курйть воспрещáется	No smoking
Вскáкивать и соскáкивать на ходý стрóго воспрещáется	Getting on or off while car is in motion is strictly forbidden	Мéдленная езда́	Drive slowly
		Мост	Bridge
Вход	Entrance	Мýжская кóмната	Men's room
Вход воспрещáется	No admittance, keep out	Объéзд	Detour
Вы́ход	Exit	Опáсно	Danger
Грунтова́я доро́га	Dirt road	Остано́вка ваго́нов	Streetcar stop
		Осторóжно	Caution
Да́мская кóмната	Ladies' room	Отделéние милйции	Police station
Держáться прáвой (лéвой) стороны́	Keep to the right (left)	Откры́то	Open
Для жéнщин	Women	Перекрёсток	Street crossing, intersection
Для мужчйн	Men	Пересечéние доро́г	Road crossing
Доро́га в плохóм состоя́нии	Road in bad condition	Переходйте ýлицу тóлько на перекрёстках	Cross the street at corners only
Доро́га ремонтйруется	Road under repair	Плева́ть воспрещáется	No spitting
Железнодорóжный переéзд	Railroad crossing	Пожáрная лéстница	Fire escape
Закры́то	Closed	Почтóвое отделéние	Post office
Замéдлить ход	Slow down		

Преде́льная ско́рость 50 км. в час	Speed limit 50 km. per hour	Стой! (стоп!)	Stop!
		Стоя́нка воспреща́ется	No parking
Прое́зд в одну́ сто́рону	One-way traffic	Телегра́ф	Telegraph office
Прое́зд закры́т	Road closed	Ток высо́кого напряже́ния	High tension line
Путь свобо́ден	Road open	Тупи́к	Dead end
Разгова́ривать с вагоновожа́тым стро́го воспреща́ется	Talking to conductor prohibited	Убо́рная	Toilet, washroom
		Ходи́ть и е́здить по путя́м стро́го воспреща́ется	All persons are forbidden to enter or cross the tracks
Сквозно́й прое́зд закры́т	No thoroughfare		
		Ходи́ть по траве́ воспреща́ется	Keep off the grass
Спра́вки	Information bureau		
Ста́нция ско́рой по́мощи	First aid station	Ша́гом	Go slow
		Шоссе́	Paved road

A few more signs will be found on page 81.

COUNTRIES AND PEOPLES

This list, which also contains the names of continents, gives the names of the countries in the first column and the English equivalent in the second column. The third and fourth columns give the corresponding words for the adjectives and inhabitants, respectively. Example: Фра́нция (France), францу́зский (French), францу́з (Frenchman). Note that the adjectives and the words for the inhabitants are not spelled with an initial capital letter.

Name of Country	English Equivalent	Adjective	Inhabitant
Австра́лия	Australia	австрали́йский	австрали́ец
А́встрия	Austria	австри́йский	австри́ец
А́зия	Asia	азиа́тский	азиа́т
Аля́ска	Alaska	аля́скский	—
Аме́рика	America	америка́нский	америка́нец
А́нглия	England	англи́йский	англича́нин
Ара́вия	Arabia	ара́бский	ара́б
Аргенти́на	Argentina	аргенти́нский	аргенти́нец
Афганиста́н	Afghanistan	афга́нский	афга́нец
А́фрика	Africa	африка́нский	африка́нец
Бе́льгия	Belgium	бельги́йский	бельги́ец

Name of Country	English Equivalent	Adjective	Inhabitant
Би́рма	Burma	бирма́нский	бирма́нец
Болга́рия	Bulgaria	болга́рский	болга́рин
Боли́вия	Bolivia	боливи́йский	боливи́ец
Брази́лия	Brazil	брази́льский	бразилья́нец
Великобрита́ния	Great Britain	брита́нский	брита́нец
Ве́нгрия	Hungary	венге́рский	венге́рец
Венецуэ́ла	Venezuela	венецуэ́льский	венецуэ́лец
Герма́ния	Germany	неме́цкий	не́мец
Голла́ндия	Holland	голла́ндский	голла́ндец
Гре́ция	Greece	гре́ческий	грек
Да́ния	Denmark	да́тский	датча́нин
Евро́па	Europe	европе́йский	европе́ец
Еги́пет	Egypt	еги́петский	египтя́нин
Изра́иль	Israel	изра́ильский	изра́илец
Ира́к	Iraq	—	—
Ира́н	Iran, Persia	ира́нский, перси́дский	ира́нец, перс
Ирла́ндия	Ireland	ирла́ндский	ирла́ндец
Исла́ндия	Iceland	исла́ндский	исла́ндец
Испа́ния	Spain	испа́нский	испа́нец
Ита́лия	Italy	италья́нский	италья́нец
Кана́да	Canada	кана́дский	кана́дец
Кита́й	China	кита́йский	кита́ец
Колу́мбия	Colombia	колумби́йский	колумби́ец
Люксембу́рг	Luxemburg	люксембу́ргский	люксембу́ржец
Манчжу́рия	Manchuria	манчжу́рский	манчжу́р
Ме́ксика	Mexico	мексика́нский	мексика́нец
Монго́лия	Mongolia	монго́льский	монго́л
Норве́гия	Norway	норве́жский	норве́жец
Пана́ма	Panama	пана́мский	пана́мец
Парагва́й	Paraguay	парагва́йский	парагва́ец
По́льша	Poland	по́льский	поля́к
Португа́лия	Portugal	португа́льский	португа́лец
Росси́я (СССР)	Russia (USSR)	ру́сский	ру́сский
Румы́ния	Rumania	румы́нский	румы́н
Се́верная Аме́рика	North America	се́веро-америка́нский	—

Name of Country	English Equivalent	Adjective	Inhabitant
Соединённые Шта́ты Аме́рики (США)	United States of America (USA)	америка́нский	америка́нец
Ту́рция	Turkey	туре́цкии	ту́рок
Уругва́й	Uruguay	уругва́йский	уругва́еп
Финля́ндия	Finland	финля́ндский, фи́нский	финля́ндец, финн
Фра́нция	France	францу́зский	францу́з
Центра́льная Аме́рика	Central America	—	—
Чехослова́кия	Czechoslovakia	чехослова́цкий, че́шский	чех
Чи́ли	Chile	чили́йский	чили́ец
Швейца́рия	Switzerland	швейца́рский	швейца́рец
Шве́ция	Sweden	шве́дский	швед
Эквадо́р	Ecuador	эквадо́рский	эквадо́рец
Югосла́вия	Yugoslavia	югосла́вский	—
Ю́жная Аме́рика	South America	южно-америка́нский	—
Япо́ния	Japan	япо́нский	япо́нец

GIVEN NAMES

Male

Full Names	Diminutives	Full Names	Diminutives
Апекса́ндр	Са́ша, Шу́ра, Са́ня	Константи́н	Ко́стя
		Лев	Лёва
Алексе́й	Алёша	Макси́м	—
Андре́й	Андрю́ша	Михаи́л	Ми́ша
Бори́с	Бо́ря	Никола́й	Ко́ля
Васи́лий	Ва́ся	О́сип	О́ся
Влади́мир	Воло́дя, Во́ва	Па́вел	Па́ша, Па́влик
Григо́рий	Гри́ша	Пётр	Пе́тя
Дми́трий	Ми́тя, Ди́ма	Семён	Се́ня
Евге́ний	Же́ня	Серге́й	Серёжа
Его́р	Его́рушка	Степа́н	Стёпа
Ива́н	Ва́ня	Фёдор	Фе́дя
И́горь	Го́ря	Ю́рий	Ю́ра
Илья́	Илью́ша	Яков	Яша
Ио́сиф	О́ся		

Female

Full Names	Diminutives	Full Names	Diminutives
Алекса́ндра	Са́ша, Шу́ра	Ксе́ния	Ксю́ша
Анаста́сия	На́стя	Ли́дия	Ли́да
А́нна	А́ня, Аню́та,	Любо́вь	Лю́ба
	Анну́шка	Людми́ла	Лю́да, Ми́ла
Валенти́на	Ва́ля	Мари́я	Ма́ша, Ма́ня
Варва́ра	Ва́ря	Ма́рфа	Марфу́ша
Ве́ра	—	Наде́жда	На́дя
Гали́на	Га́ля	Ната́лья	Ната́ша, На́та
Да́рья	Да́ша	Ни́на	—
Екатери́на	Ка́тя	О́льга	О́ля
Еле́на	Ле́на, Лёля	Со́фья	Со́ня
Елизаве́та	Ли́за	Тама́ра	—
Ири́на	И́ра	Татья́на	Та́ня
Зинаи́да	Зи́на, И́да		

RUSSIAN MONEY

черво́нец	chervonets (monetary unit of the USSR)
бума́жный черво́нец	paper chervonets (2-dollar bill *)
рубль	ruble (1/10 chervonets)
копе́йка	kopek (1/100 ruble)

Nickel-bronze Coins

копе́йка	(1-kopek piece)	kopek
две копе́йки	(2-kopek piece)	
три копе́йки	(3-kopek piece)	
пятачо́к, пыта́к	(5-kopek piece)	piatachok

Silver Coins

гри́венник	(10-kopek piece)	grivennik
пятна́дцать копе́ек	(15-kopek piece)	
два́дцать копе́ек	(20-kopek piece)	
полти́нник	(50-kopek piece)	poltinnik
рубль	(1-ruble piece)	ruble

Gold Coin

черво́нец	(1-chervonets piece)	chervonets

Paper Money

рублёвая бума́жка	(1-ruble bill)
трёхрублёвка	(3-ruble bill)
пятирублёвка	(5-ruble bill)

* U.S. equivalent.

десятирублёвка	(10-ruble bill)
червонец	(1-chervonets bill)
бумажка в два червонца	(2-chervonets bill)
бумажка в три червонца	(3-chervonets bill)
бумажка в пять червонцев	(5-chervonets bill)
бумажка в десять червонцев	(10-chervonets bill)
бумажка в двадцать пять червонцев	(25-chervonets bill)
бумажка в пятьдесят червонцев	(50-chervonets bill)

RUSSIAN MEASURES

Length

	Metric system		*Old measures still in use*
метр	meter (39.37 inches)	верста	verst (0.66 mile)
сантиметр	centimeter (0.39 inch)	сажень	sazhen (7 feet)
миллиметр	millimeter (0.04 inch)	аршин	arshin (28 inches)
километр	kilometer (0.62 mile)	вершок	vershok (1.75 inches)
		фут	fut (1 foot)
		дюйм	dyuim (1 inch)

Area

	Metric system		*Old measure still in use*
гектар	hectare (2.47 acres)	десятина	desyatina (2.7 acres)

Weight

	Metric system		*Old measures still in use*
килограмм	kilogram (2.2 pounds)	фунт	funt (0.9 pound)
грамм	gram (0.04 ounce)	пуд	pud (36.07 pounds)
тонна	ton (2,204 pounds)		

Liquid

литр	liter (1.05 liquid quarts)	

RUSSIAN-ENGLISH

AND

ENGLISH-RUSSIAN DICTIONARY

ABBREVIATIONS USED IN THE DICTIONARY SECTION

acc.	accusative	*indef.*	indefinite
adj.	adjective	*loc.*	locative
adv.	adverb		(= prepositional)
conj.	conjunction	*m.*	masculine
dat.	dative	*n.*	neuter
def.	definite	*perf.*	perfective
f.	feminine	*pl.*	plural
gen.	genitive	*prep.*	preposition
imp.	imperfective	*pron.*	pronoun
indecl.	indeclinable	*rel.*	relative

RUSSIAN-ENGLISH DICTIONARY

In the Russian-English Dictionary, the following points should be noted:

Nouns are always given with their gender, so that their pattern of declension can be easily located in the Outline of Grammar (**1.3-5**).

Adjectives are listed in their masculine nominative singular form. (For the declension of adjectives, see **2.3** in the Grammar section.) When English words used both as nouns and adjectives function as adjectives, they are marked with (adj.) following the English word.

Verbs: The imperfective and the perfective infinitives are listed as separate entries (when both exist), marked *imp.* and *perf.,* respectively. Those not marked are imperfective in form and/or function, and do not have a perfective counterpart. For verbs of motion, both the indefinite and definite infinitives (see Grammar, **6.8**) are given, marked *indef.* and *def.,* respectively. When the reflexive has the same meaning as the non-reflexive form of the verb, it is marked with (**ся**) or (**сь**) attached to the infinitive of the verb, but when the reflexive has a different meaning it is given as a separate entry.

A

а but; and
абза́ц *m.* paragraph
абрико́с *m.* apricot
а́вгуст *m.* August
автобус *m.* bus
автомоби́ль *m.* automobile
а́втор *m.* author
а́гент *m.* agent
аго́ния *f.* agony
агре́ссия *f.* aggression
ад *m.* hell
адвока́т *m.* lawyer
администра́тор *m.* administrator
администрати́вный administrative
а́дрес *m.* address
аккредити́в *m.* letter of credit
актёр *m.* actor
актри́са *f.* actress
алкого́ль *m.* alcohol
альбо́м *m.* album
алло́! hello! (on telephone)

Аме́рика *f.* America
америка́нский American (adj.)
америка́нец American (masc.)
америка́нка American (fem.)
ана́лиз *m.* analysis
англи́йский English
англича́нин *m.* Englishman
англича́нка *f.* Englishwoman
А́нглия *f.* England
анке́та *f.* questionnaire
антиква́рный antiquarian
аппара́т *m.* apparatus
апре́ль *m.* April
апте́ка *f.* drugstore
арбу́з *m.* watermelon
аргуме́нт *m.* argument
аре́ст *m.* arrest
арифме́тика *f.* arithmetic
а́рмия *f.* army
архите́ктор *m.* architect
ата́ка *f.* attack
атле́т *m.* athlete

а́том *m.* atom
афи́ша *f.* bill, poster
ах! ah!
аэродро́м *m.* airport
аэропла́н *m.* airplane

Б

ба́ба *f.* peasant woman
ба́бочка *f.* butterfly
ба́бушка *f.* grandmother
бага́ж *m.* baggage
ба́за *f.* base, basis
база́р *m.* market
баклажа́н *m.* eggplant
бал *m.* ball, dance
бала́нс *f.* balance
бале́т *m.* ballet
балко́н *m.* balcony
балова́ть *imp.* to spoil, to indulge
бана́н *m.* banana
банк *m.* bank
ба́нка *f.* jar
бара́нина *f.* mutton
бастова́ть *imp.* to (go on) strike
башма́к *m.* shoe
бе́гать *indef.* to run
беда́ *f.* trouble, mishap
бе́дный poor
бежа́ть *def.* to run; to escape
без without
безделу́шка *f.* curio, trifle
бе́лый white
бельё *n.* linen; laundry
бе́рег *m.* shore; coast; bank (of a river)
берёза *f.* birch
бесе́да *f.* conversation, talk
беспереса́дочный express (train)
беспоко́йство *n.* disturbance
беспоко́ить *imp.* to disturb
беспоко́иться *imp.* to worry
биле́т *m.* ticket
бино́кль *m.* binoculars
бискви́т *m.* sponge cake
бить *imp.* to beat; to hit; to strike
бифште́кс *m.* steak
благодари́ть *imp.* to thank
благода́рный thankful, grateful
благодаря́ thanks to
благоро́дный noble
бланк *m.* form
бле́дный pale

блесте́ть *imp.* to glitter; to shine
блестя́щий brilliant
бли́зкий near
бли́зко near
ближа́йший nearest, closest
бли́же nearer, closer
блонди́н *m.* blonde
блонди́нка *f.* blonde
блу́зка *f.* blouse
блю́до *n.* dish
Бог *m.* God
бога́тый rich, wealthy
бо́дрый cheerful
бой *m.* fight, conflict
бо́йкий smart, sharp; glib
бок *m.* side
бо́лее more
боле́знь *f.* illness, sickness
боле́ть *imp.* to hurt, to be sick
болта́ть *imp.* to chatter
боль *f.* pain
бо́льно painful
больно́й sick, ill
бо́льше more, bigger
большинство́ *n.* majority
большо́й big, large, great
борода́ *f.* beard
боро́ться *imp.* to struggle; to wrestle
борщ *m.* borsht, beet soup
борьба́ *f.* fight, struggle
боя́ться *imp.* to be afraid
брат *m.* brother
брать *imp.* to take
брить (ся) *imp.* to shave (oneself)
бровь *f.* eyebrow
броса́ть *imp.* to throw; to give up
бро́сить *perf.* to throw; to give up
брошь *f.* brooch
буди́ть *imp.* to awaken, to wake up
бу́дто as if, as though
бу́дущее *n.* the future
бу́дущий future, next
бульо́н *m.* bouillon, broth
бума́га *f.* paper
буты́лка *f.* bottle
буфе́т *m.* refreshment room
бы *conditional particle*
быва́ть *iter.* to take place
бы́стро fast, quickly
бы́стрый fast, quick
быть to be

B

в in
вагóн *m.* railroad car
вагóн-ресторáн *m.* dining car
вáжный important
вам *dat.* of вы
вáнна *f.* bath
вáнная *f.* bathroom
варúть *imp.* to cook
вас *gen.* and *loc.* of вы
ваш your (*plural and polite form*)
вверх up, upward
ввестú *perf.* to introduce; to lead in
вдоль along, by
вдруг suddenly
ведь well; after all
вездé everywhere
везтú *def.* to convey, to transport
век *m.* century
велéть *imp.* to order, to command
велúкий great
великолéпный splendid
вéна *f.* vein
венчáть *imp.* to marry
вéра *f.* belief, faith
верёвка *f.* cord, rope, string
вéрить *imp.* to believe, to trust
вéрно true, right
вернýть, *perf.* to bring back; to return
вернýться to return
вéрный true, faithful
вероя́тно probably, likely
вертéться *imp.* to turn; to revolve
верх *m.* upper part, top
вéрхний upper
вершúна *f.* top, peak, summit
вес *m.* weight; influence
вéсело gaily, merrily
весёлый gay, cheerful
вéсить *imp.* to weigh
веснá *f.* spring
вестú *def.* to lead
весь all
весьмá very much, exceedingly
вéтер *m.* wind
вéчер *m.* evening
вéчером in the evening
вéчный eternal
вещь *f.* thing
взгляд *m.* glance; view

взгля́дывать *imp.* to throw a glance (at)
взгляну́ть *perf.* to throw a glance at
вздор *m.* nonsense
вздохну́ть *perf.* to sigh
вздыхáть *imp.* to sigh
взимáть to levy (taxes, duties, etc.)
взять *perf.* to take
вид *m.* view
видáть *iter.* to see (now and then)
вúдеть *imp.* to see
вúдимо apparently, evidently
вúдно evidently, apparently
вúдный visible; prominent
вúза *f.* visa
вúлка *f.* fork
винá *f.* fault, guilt
винó *n.* wine
виновáтый guilty; sorry
висéть *imp.* to hang
вúшня *f.* cherry
включáть *imp.* to include
включúть *perf.* to include
вкус *m.* taste
вкýсный tasty
владéть *imp.* to own, to possess; to control
власть *f.* power; authority, rule
влия́ние *n.* influence
влюбúться *perf.* to fall in love
влюбля́ться *imp.* to fall in love
вмéсте together
вмéсто instead of
внача́ле in the beginning, at first
внé outside
внезáпно suddenly
внéшний external
вниз downwards
внизý downstairs; below
внимáние *n.* attention
внимáтельно attentively
вновь anew, over again
внук *m.* grandson
внýтренний inner, internal
внутрú inside, within
во врéмя during
вó-время on time
вóвсе completely, altogether
...нет not at all
во-вторы́х secondly
водá *f.* water

водить *indef.* to lead
водиться to live, to inhabit
водка *f.* vodka
водород *m.* hydrogen
военный military
возвращать *imp.* to bring back; to return
возвращаться to come back, to return
воздух *m.* air
воздушный air-
возле near; beside
возможно possible
возможность *f.* possibility; chance
возможный possible
возникать *imp.* to arise
возникнуть *perf.* to arise
возраст *m.* age
война *f.* war
войско *n.* troops, army
войти *perf.* to go in
вокзал *m.* railroad station
вокруг around, about
волна *f.* wave
волнение *n.* agitation, disturbance
волос *m.* hair
вольность *f.* freedom, liberty
воля *f.* will; freedom
вон there (is); yonder
вообще generally, in general
во-первых in the first place
вопрос *m.* question
ворота *f., pl.* gate, gateway
воротник *m.* collar
восемнадцать eighteen
восемь eight ·
восемьдесят eighty
восемьсот eight hundred
воскликнуть *perf.* to exclaim
восклицать *imp.* to exclaim
воскресенье *n.* Sunday
воспитание *n.* upbringing; education
воспоминание *n.* recollection, reminiscence
воспретить *perf.* to forbid, to prohibit
воспрещать *imp.* to forbid, to prohibit
восток *m.* east
восторг *m.* delight
востребование *n.* claiming

до востребования general delivery (at post office)
восхитительный delightful
восьмой eighth
вот here is, are
впервые the first time
вперёд ahead; forward
впереди ahead (of); in front (of); before
впечатление *n.* impression
вполне completely, entirely, quite
враг *m.* enemy
врать *imp.* to lie, to tell lies
врач *m.* physician
вредно harmful
время *n.* time
всегда always
всё everything
всё-таки nevertheless, still
вскоре shortly, soon (after)
вскакивать *imp.* to jump up
вскочить *perf.* to jump up
вслух aloud
вспоминать *imp.* to remember, to recall
вспомнить *perf.* to remember, to recall
вспышка *f.* outburst; flash bulb
вставать *imp.* to get up, to stand up, to rise
встать *perf.* to get up, to stand up, to rise
встретить *perf.* to meet
встреча *f.* meeting
встречать *imp.* to meet
вступать *imp.* to enter; to join
вступить *perf.* to enter; to join
всюду everywhere
всякий any, every
вторник *m.* Tuesday
второй second
вход *m.* entrance
входить *imp.* to go in
вчера yesterday
вчерашний yesterday's
вы you (*plural and polite*)
выбирать *imp.* to choose; to elect
выбор *m.* choice
выбрать *perf.* choose; to elect
вывести *perf.* to lead out; to conclude

выводи́ть *imp.* to lead out; to conclude

вы́глядеть to look like

выдава́ть *imp.* to distribute; to betray

вы́дать *perf.* to distribute; to betray

вы́держать *perf.* to bear, to stand, to endure

выде́рживать *imp.* to bear, to stand, to endure

вы́езд *n.* departure

вы́ездной exit-

выезжа́ть *imp.* to leave, to depart

вы́ехать *perf.* to leave, to depart

вы́звать *perf.* to call out; to challenge; to provoke

вызыва́ть *imp.* to call out; to challenge; to provoke

вы́йти *perf.* to go out, to get out

вы́нести *perf.* to carry out, to take out

вынима́ть *imp.* to take out, to remove

выноси́ть *imp.* to carry out, to take out

вы́нуть *perf.* to take out, to remove

вы́пить *perf.* to drink up

выпуска́ть *imp.* to let out, to release

вы́пустить *perf.* to let out, to release

выража́ть(ся) *imp.* to express (oneself)

выраже́ние *n.* expression

вы́разить(ся) *perf.* to express (oneself)

выраста́ть *imp.* to grow (up)

вы́расти *perf.* to grow (up)

выставля́ть *imp.* to stick out, to put out

высо́вываться *imp.* to lean out

высо́кий high, tall

высоко́ high

вы́ставить *perf.* to put out, to display

выставля́ть *imp.* to put out, to display

вы́ставка *f.* exhibition

вы́стирать *perf.* to launder, to wash

выступа́ть *imp.* to come forward; to perform

вы́ступить *perf.* to step forward; to break out

вы́шивка *f.* embroidery

вы́ход *m.* exit

выходи́ть *perf.* to go out, to get off

выходно́й день day off

Г

газе́та *f.* newspaper

галере́я *f.* gallery

гало́ша *f.* rubbers

га́лстук *m.* necktie

гара́ж *m.* garage

гаранти́ровать *imp.* to guarantee

гара́нтия *f.* guarantee

гардеро́б *m.* wardrobe

гармо́ния *f.* harmony

где where

где́-то somewhere

генера́л *m.* general

ге́ний *m.* genius

геогра́фия *f.* geography

геоме́трия *f.* geometry

геро́й *m.* hero

ги́бнуть *imp.* to perish

гита́ра *f.* guitar

глава́ *f.* head, chief; chapter

гла́вный main, chief

глаго́л *m.* verb

гла́дить *imp.* to iron

глаз *m.* eye

глота́ть *imp.* to swallow

глубина́ *f.* depth

глубо́кий deep

глубоко́ deeply, profoundly

глу́пый stupid, silly, foolish

глухо́й deaf

гляде́ть *imp.* to look

гнев *m.* anger

гнездо́ *n.* nest

говори́ть *imp.* to speak

говя́дина *f.* beef

год *m.* year

годи́ться *imp.,* to be valid

голова́ *f.* head

го́лод *m.* hunger

голо́дный hungry

го́лос *m.* voice

голу́бка *f.* darling

голубо́й light-blue, sky-blue

голу́бчик *m.* dear
го́лый bare, naked
гора́ *f.* mountain
гора́здо by far; much
горди́ться *imp.* to be proud of
го́рдость *f.* pride
го́рдый proud
го́ре *n.* grief; misfortune
горе́ть *imp.* to burn; to glow
го́рло *n.* throat
го́род *m.* city
городско́й urban, municipal
го́рький bitter
горя́чий hot
го́спиталь *m.* hospital
господи́н *m.* mister, gentleman
госпожа́ *f.* Mrs., lady
гости́ная *f.* living room
гости́ница *f.* hotel
гость *m.* guest
госуда́рственный state-, government-
госуда́рство *n.* state, government
гото́вить *imp.* to prepare, to cook
гото́виться to prepare (oneself)
гото́вый ready
гра́дус *m.* degree
граждани́н *m.* citizen
гражда́нка *f.* citizeness
грани́ца *f.* border
грех *m.* sin
грибы́ *m. pl.* mushrooms
гроза́ *f.* thunderstorm
грози́ть *imp.* to threaten
грома́дный huge, vast
гро́мкий loud
гро́мко aloud, loudly
гро́мче louder
грубый crude, rough, coarse
грудь *f.* breast, chest, bosom
гру́ппа *f.* group
гру́стный sad
гру́ша *f.* pear
гря́зный dirty, muddy, filthy
грязь *f.* dirt, mud, filth
губа́ *f.* lip
гуля́ть *imp.* to take a walk
густо́й thick, dense

Д

да yes
дава́ть *imp.* to give

давно́ long ago
да́же even
да́лее farther, further
далеко́ far
далёкий far; remote
дальне́йший further
да́льний distant
да́льше farther away
да́ма *f.* lady; queen (cards)
да́мский ladies'
дать *perf.* to give
да́ча *f.* country house, cottage
два two
два́дцать twenty
двена́дцать twelve
дверь *f.* door
две́сти two hundred
дви́гатель *m.* motor
дви́гаться *imp.,* to move, to stir
дви́нуться *perf.* to move, to advance
движе́ние *n.* movement, traffic
дво́е two
двойно́й double
двор *m.* back yard, courtyard
де́вочка *f.* little girl
де́вушка *f.* young lady, girl
девятна́дцать nineteen
девяно́сто ninety
девя́тый ninth
де́вять nine
девятьсо́т nine hundred
де́душка *m.* grandfather
де́йствие *n.* act (of a play), action
действи́тельно really, actually
действи́тельность *f.* reality; validity
действи́тельный actual, real, valid
де́йствовать *imp.* to act; to function, to work
декабрь *m.* December
де́лать *imp.* to make, to do
де́латься to become
деле́ние *n.* division
дели́ть *imp.* to divide
де́ло *n.* affair, matter, business
день *m.* day
де́ньги *f. pl.* money
дере́вня *f.* village; country
де́рево *n.* tree
деревя́нный wooden

держа́ть *imp.* to hold; to keep
де́рзкий impudent, insolent
десе́рт *m.* dessert
деся́ток *m.* ten
де́сять ten
деся́тый tenth
дета́ль *f.* detail
де́ти *n. pl.* children
де́тский children's, childish
де́тство *n.* childhood
деше́вле cheaper
дёшево cheaply
дешёвый cheap
де́ятельность *f.* activity
дива́н *m.* divan, sofa
ди́кий wild; savage
дире́ктор *m.* director
дитя́ *n.* child
дли́нный long
для for
дно *n.* bottom
до until, up to, as far as
добива́ться *imp.* to strive (for), to seek
доби́ться *perf.* to get, to obtain
до́брый good, kind
дово́льно enough; rather
дово́льный pleased, satisfied
доезжа́ть *imp.* to ride up to, to reach
дождеви́к *m.* raincoat
дождь *m.* rain
дойти́ *perf.* to reach, to get to
доказа́ть *perf.* to prove
дока́зывать *imp.* to prove
до́ктор *m.* doctor
докуме́нт *m.* document
долг *m.* debt; duty
до́лгий long, prolonged
до́лго for a long time
до́лжен must, have to, ought to
до́лжный due, proper
до́ллар *m.* dollar
до́ля *f.* share; lot, fate
дом *m.* house, home
до́ма at home
дома́шний domestic
домо́й home
допуска́ть *imp.* to admit, to allow
допусти́ть *perf.* to admit, to allow
доро́га *f.* road, way
дорого́й dear, expensive

доска́ *f.* board; plank
достава́ть *imp.* to get; to fetch
доста́вить *perf.* to deliver
доставля́ть *imp.* to deliver
доста́точно enough
доста́точный sufficient
доста́ть *perf.* to get; to reach
достиже́ние *n.* achievement
досто́инство *n.* dignity; quality
досто́йный deserving, worthy
дохо́д *m.* profit
доходи́ть *imp.* to reach, to get to
до́чка *f.* daughter
дочь *f.* daughter
дра́ма *f.* drama
дра́ться *imp.* to fight
дре́вний ancient
дрожа́ть *imp.* to tremble; to shiver
друг *m.* friend
друго́й other
дру́жба *f.* friendship
ду́мать *imp.* to think
ду́ра *f.* fool
дура́к *m.* fool
дурно́й bad, nasty
дуть *imp.* to blow
дух *m.* spirit
духо́вный spiritual
душа́ *f.* soul
душе́вный sincere; mental
ду́шный stuffy
дым *m.* smoke
ды́ня *f.* melon
дыра́ *f.* hole
дыша́ть *imp.* to breathe
дыха́ние *n.* breathing, respiration
дю́жина *f.* dozen
дя́дя *m.* uncle

Е

его́ his; its
еда́ *f.* food
едва́ hardly, scarcely
еди́нственный only
еди́ный single; united
езда́ *f.* drive, ride
е́здить *indef.* to go (by vehicle), to ride
ель *f.* fir tree
е́сли if

есте́ственный natural
есть *imp.* to eat
есть there is, are
е́хать *def.* to go (by vehicle), to ride
ещё still, yet

Ж

жа́дный greedy
жале́ть *imp.* to feel sorry, to regret
жа́лкий miserable, pitiful
жа́лоба *f.* complaint
жа́ловаться *imp.* to complain
жаль *impers.* pity, be sorry
жар *m.* heat; fever
жара́ *m.* heat; hot weather
жа́рить *imp.* to fry, to roast
жа́ркий hot
ждать *imp.* to wait
же *emphatic particle*
жела́ние *n.* wish, desire
жела́ть *imp.* to wish
желе́за *f.* iron
желе́зный iron, ferrous
жёлтый yellow
желу́док *m.* stomach
жена́ *f.* wife
жени́ться *imp. & perf.,* to marry; to get married
же́нский female, feminine
же́нщина *f.* woman
же́ртва *f.* victim
жёсткий stiff, hard
жесто́кий cruel; severe
жи́во lively
живо́й alive; lively
живо́т *m.* abdomen, belly
жизнь *f.* life
жир *m.* fat, grease
жи́рный fat
жить *imp.* to live
журна́л *m.* journal, magazine
журнали́ст *m.* journalist

З

за after, behind
заблуди́ться *perf.* to lose one's way
заблужда́ться *imp.* to lose one's way

забыва́ть *imp.* to forget
забы́ть *perf.* to forget
заве́дующий *m.* manager
завести́ *perf.* to acquire; to start (a motor); to wind up (a watch)
завива́ть *imp.* to wave (hair)
зави́ть *perf.* to wave (hair)
заво́д *m.* factory, plant
за́втра tomorrow
за́втрак *m.* breakfast
за́втракать *imp.* to have breakfast
зага́дка *f.* riddle
зага́р *m.* suntan
за́говор *m.* plot, conspiracy
загля́дывать *imp.* to peep in, to drop in
загляну́ть *perf.* to peep in, to drop in
заговори́ть *perf.* begin to speak
загора́ть *imp.* to tan
загоре́ть *perf.* to tan
зада́ча *f.* problem
зада́ток *m.* deposit, down payment
за́дний back-
заду́маться *perf.* to become thoughtful, pensive
заду́мываться *imp.* to become thoughtful
заеда́ть *imp.* to jam, to get stuck
зае́сть *perf.* to jam, to get stuck
зайти́ *perf.* to drop by
зака́з *m.* order
заказа́ть *perf.* to order
заказно́й registered (letter)
зака́зывать *imp.* to order
заключе́ние *n.* conclusion; imprisonment
зако́н *m.* law
закрича́ть *perf.* to cry out, to scream, to yell
закрыва́ть *imp.* to close, to shut
закры́ть *perf.* to close, to shut
зал *m.* hall, salon
заме́на *f.* replacement, substitution
замени́ть *perf.* to substitute, to replace
заменя́ть *imp.* to substitute, to replace
замерза́ть *imp.* to freeze
замёрзнуть *perf.* to freeze
замести́тель *m.* substitute
заме́тить *perf.* to notice; to remark

заме́тно noticeably
замеча́тельный remarkable
замеча́ть *imp.* to notice
замо́к *m.* lock
занима́ть *imp.* to occupy
заня́тие *n.* occupation; activity
заня́ть *perf.* to occupy; to borrow
за́нятый busy
за́пад *m.* west
за́падный western
запакова́ть *perf.* to pack; to wrap
запако́вывать *imp.* to pack; to wrap
запа́с *m.* fund; supply
запасно́й emergency (door, exit)
за́пах *m.* smell, scent, odor
запере́ть *perf.* to lock
запира́ть *imp.* to lock
записа́ть *perf.* to write down
запи́ска *f.* note
запи́сывать *imp.* to write down
запла́кать *perf.* to start crying
заполне́ние *n.* filling out
запо́лнить *perf.* to fill out
заполня́ть *imp.* to fill out
запрети́ть *perf.* to forbid
запреща́ть *imp.* to forbid
заряди́ть *perf.* to load (a camera)
заряжа́ть *imp.* to load (a camera)
засмея́ться *perf.* to begin to laugh
засну́ть *perf.* to fall asleep
застава́ть *imp.* to find in
заста́вить *perf.* to compel, to force
заставля́ть *imp.* to compel, to force
заста́ть *perf.* to find in
засыпа́ть *imp.* to fall asleep
затво́р *m.* shutter (camera)
зате́м thereupon, subsequently
зато́ whereas; on the other hand
затрудне́ние *n.* trouble, difficulty
захвати́ть *perf.* to seize, to capture
захва́тывать *imp.* to seize, to capture
заходи́ть *imp.* to drop by
захоте́ть *perf.* to want, to feel like
заче́м why, what for
защи́та *f.* defense; protection
заяви́ть *perf.* to declare
заявля́ть *imp.* to declare
звать *imp.* to call
звезда́ *f.* star

зверь *m.* beast
звони́ть *imp.* to call, to ring, to telephone
звук *m.* sound
зда́ние *n.* building
здесь here
здоро́вый well, healthy
здоро́вье *n.* health
зелёный green
зе́лень *f.* greens, vegetables
земля́ *f.* earth, land
земно́й earthly
зе́ркало *n.* mirror
зима́ *f.* winter
зло *n.* evil; harm
зло́ба *f.* malice, wickedness
злой evil, wicked
знак *m.* sign; mark; symbol
знако́мить *imp.* to acquaint; to introduce
знако́миться *imp.* to become acquainted with
знако́мство *n.* acquaintance
знако́мый familiar
знамени́тый famous
зна́ние *n.* knowledge
знато́к *m.* expert
знать *imp.* to know
значе́ние *n.* meaning; significance
зна́чить *imp.* to mean
зо́лото *n.* gold
золото́й golden
зре́ние *n.* (eye)sight, vision
зуб *m.* tooth

И

и and
и . . . и both . . . and
иго́лка *f.* needle
игра́ *f.* playing, game
игра́ть *imp.* to play
игру́шка *f.* toy
иде́я *f.* idea
идти́ *def.* to go, to walk
из out of, from
изве́стный well-known
извини́ть *perf.* to excuse
извини́ться to apologize
извиня́ть *imp.* to excuse
извиня́ться to apologize
изде́лие *n.* manufactured article, ware

из-за from behind; from; because of

изли́шек *m.* excess

из-под from under

изю́м *m.* raisins

изя́щный elegant, refined

икра́ *f.* caviar

и́ли or

и́ли...и́ли either...or

и́менно just, exactly; namely

име́ть to have (used in a very few expressions)

и́мя *n.* first name

ина́че otherwise; else

иногда́ sometimes

иностра́нец *m.* foreigner

иностра́нка *f.* foreigner

иностра́нный foreign

интере́с *m.* interest

интере́сный interesting

интересова́ть *imp.* to interest

интересова́ться to be interested in

инти́мность *f.* intimacy

инти́мный intimate

Интури́ст *m.* intourist

иро́ния *f.* irony

иска́ть *imp.* to look for, to seek

исключе́ние *n.* exception; expulsion

и́скренний sincere

иску́сство *n.* art

испыта́ть *perf.* to try out, to test

испы́тывать *imp.* to try out, to test

исполне́ние *n.* performance; fulfilment

истори́ческий historic(al)

исто́рия *f.* history; story, tale

исчеза́ть *imp.* to disappear

исче́знуть *perf.* to disappear

итти́ or **идти́** *def.* to go (on foot)

их their

ию́ль *m.* July

ию́нь *m.* June

К

к to, toward

кабине́т *m.* study; private office

каблу́к *m.* heel

кавка́зкий Caucasian

ка́ждый each, every

каза́ться *imp.* to seem; to look like

как how, as

как-бу́дто as if, it seems

как-то somehow

како́в how, what, which

како́й what kind, which

како́й-нибудь some; any (kind)

како́й-то some kind of, any

ка́менный stone, of stone

ка́мень *m.* stone

ка́мера *f.* chamber, room

...хране́ния cloak room, luggage room

капита́л *m.* capital

капита́н *m.* captain

ка́пля *f.* drop

капу́ста *f.* cabbage

каранда́ш *m.* pencil

карма́н *m.* pocket

ка́рта *f.* map

карти́на *f.* picture

ка́рточка *f.* card

карто́шка *f.* potato

ка́сса *f.* ticket window, booking office, cashier's window

катало́г *m.* catalog

ка́чество *n.* quality

ка́шель *m.* cough

ка́шлять *imp.* to cough

каю́та *f.* cabin

кварти́ра *f.* apartment

квита́нция *f.* receipt

кино́ *n.* movies

кипяти́ть *imp.* to boil

кислоро́д *m.* oxygen

ки́слый sour

класс *m.* class

класть *imp.* to put

клуб *m.* club

клубни́ка *f.* strawberries

ключ *m.* key

кни́га *f.* book

кни́жка *f.* book(let)

кни́жный book-, bookish

князь *m.* prince

ковёр *m.* rug, carpet

когда́ when

когда́-нибудь ever; sometime or other

когда́-то once, formerly

ко́е-что something

ко́жа *f.* skin, leather

колбаса́ *f.* sausage

коле́но *n.* knee

колесо́ *n.* wheel
коли́чество *n.* quantity; amount
ко́локол *m.* bell
колхо́з *m.* collective farm
колхо́зник *m.* collective farmer
колыбе́ль *f.* cradle
кольцо́ *n.* ring
кома́нда *f.* team
коме́дия *f.* comedy
ко́мната *f.* room
конве́рт *m.* envelope
конду́ктор *m.* conductor
коне́ц *m.* end
коне́чно of course
коне́чный final, last
конто́ра *f.* office
конча́ть(ся) *imp.* to finish, to end
ко́нчить(ся) *perf.* to finish, to end
конья́к *m.* cognac
копе́йка *f.* kopek
ко́рень *m.* root
коридо́р *m.* corridor
корми́ть *imp.* to feed
коро́бка *f.* box
коро́ва *f.* cow
коро́ткий short
ко́ротко briefly
корт *m.* court (tennis)
кость *f.* bone
костю́м *m.* suit
котле́та *f.* cutlet, chop
кото́рый which
ко́фе *n.* coffee
кра́йний extreme, utmost
краси́вый pretty, handsome
кра́ска *f.* paint, dye
кра́сный red
красота́ *f.* beauty
крахма́лить *imp.* to starch
креди́тка *f.* money bill, banknote
крем *m.* cream
кре́пкий strong
кре́пко solidly, strongly, firmly
кре́сло *n.* armchair, easy chair
крест *m.* cross
крестья́нин *m.* peasant
крик *m.* cry, shout
кри́кнуть *perf.* to shout, to cry out
крича́ть *imp.* to shout, to scream
крова́ть *f.* bed
кровь *f.* blood
кро́ме except

круг *m.* circle
кру́глый round; complete
круго́м around
кру́пный large, big
крыло́ *n.* wing, fender
крыльцо́ *n.* doorstep
кры́ша *f.* roof
крючо́к *m.* hook
кто who
кто́-то someone
кто́-нибудь anyone
куда́ where (whereto)
кула́к *m.* fist; rich peasant
купа́льный bathing (adj.)
купа́ть(ся) *imp.* to bathe
купе́ *n.* railroad compartment
купи́ть *imp.* to buy
кури́тельная *f.* smoking car
кури́ть *imp.* to smoke
ку́рица *f.* chicken
курс *m.* course, rate of exchange
куря́щий *m.* smoker
кусо́к *m.* piece, bit
куст *m.* bush
куста́рный handicraft (adj.)
ку́хня *f.* kitchen
ку́ча *f.* heap, lot

Л

ла́дно all right, okay
ладо́нь *f.* palm
ла́зать, ла́зить *indef.* to climb
ла́ска *f.* caress
ласка́ть *imp.* to caress
ла́сково kindly
ла́сковый affectionate
ла́ять *imp.* to bark
лев *m.* lion
ле́вый left
лёгкий light, easy
легко́ lightly, easily
лёд *m.* ice
лежа́ть *imp.* to lie
лезть *def.* to climb
лека́рство *n.* medicine
ле́кция *f.* lecture
лени́вый lazy
ленты́й *m.* lazy person
ленты́йка *f.* lazy person
лес *m.* forest; wood
ле́ска *f.* fishing line

ле́стница *f.* ladder, steps
ле́стничка *f.* little ladder
лета́ть *indef.* to fly
лете́ть *def.* to fly
ле́тний summer-
ле́то *n.* summer
ли *interrogative particle*
лимо́н *m.* lemon
ли́ния *f.* line
лист *m.* leaf, sheet (of paper)
лите́йный заво́д *m.* foundry
литерату́ра *f.* literature
лифт *m.* elevator, lift
ли́фчик *m.* brassiere
лицо́ *n.* face, person
ли́чно personally, in person
ли́чность *f.* personality
ли́чный personal, individual
ли́шний superfluous; unnecessary; spare
лоб *m.* forehead; brow
ло́дка *f.* boat
ложи́ться *imp.* to lie down, to go to bed
ло́жка *f.* spoon
ложь *f.* lie
ло́коть *m.* elbow
лома́ть *imp.* to break
лососи́на *f.* salmon
ло́шадь *f.* horse
луг *m.* meadow
лу́жа *f.* puddle, pool
лужа́йка *f.* lawn
лук *m.* onion
луна́ *f.* moon
луч *m.* ray, beam
лу́чше better
лу́чший better
любе́зный kind, polite
люби́ть *imp.* to love
любо́вь *f.* love
любо́й any, every
любопы́тство *n.* curiosity
любопы́тный curious
лю́ди *m. pl.* people

М

магази́н *m.* store
май *m.* May
ма́ленький small, little
ма́ло little, few

ма́лый small, little
ма́льчик *m.* boy
ма́ма *f.* mama
маникю́р *m.* manicure
ма́рка *f.* stamp
март *m.* March
ма́сло *n.* butter; oil
ма́сса *f.* mass, heap, lot
масса́ж *m.* massage
ма́стер *m.* craftsman; skilled worker; foreman
матема́тика *f.* mathematics
материа́л *m.* material, cloth
матч *m.* match (sports)
мать *f.* mother
маха́ть *imp.* to wave; to wag
махну́ть *perf.* to wave; to wag
маши́на *f.* machine, engine
ме́бель *f.* furniture
мёд *m.* honey
медве́дь *m.* bear
ме́дленно slowly
медсестра́ *f.* nurse
медь *f.* copper
ме́жду between, among
междунаро́дный international
мел *m.* chalk
ме́лкий shallow; fine
ме́лочь *f.* detail, trifle; (small) change
ме́нее less
ме́ньше less
меню́ *n.* menu
меня́ *acc. & gen. of* **я** у ... I have
меня́ть *imp.* to change
ме́ра *f.* measure
ме́стный local
ме́сто *n.* place; seat; piece of luggage
ме́сяц *m* month
мета́лл *m.* metal
метла́ *f.* broom
ме́тод *m.* method
метр *m.* meter
метро́ *n.* subway
меха́ник *m.* mechanic
мечта́ *f.* daydream; ambition
мечта́ть *imp.* to daydream
меша́ть *imp.* to hinder; to disturb
мешо́к *m.* sack, bag
мёртвый dead

миг *m.* instant, moment
миллиа́рд *m.* billion
миллио́н *m.* million
ми́лость *f.* favor, mercy
ми́лый nice, sweet; dear
ми́ля *f.* mile
ми́мо by, past
минда́ль *m.* almond
минера́льный mineral
мину́та *f.* minute
мир *m.* world; peace
мирово́й world-wide, world
мне *dat., loc. of* **я**
мне́ние *n.* opinion
мно́гий many a, numerous (*used mostly in plural*)
мно́го much, many
моги́ла *f.* grave
мо́да *f.* fashion, vogue
мо́жно possible, permissible
мой my
молодёжь *f.* youth, young people
молодо́й young
мо́лодость *f.* youth
молоко́ *n.* milk
молото́к *m.* hammer
мо́лча silently, in silence
молча́ние *n.* silence
молча́ть *imp.* to be silent, to keep quiet
моме́нт *m.* moment
мо́ре *n.* sea
морко́вь *f.* carrot(s)
мост *m.* bridge
мочь to be able
мра́чный dark, gloomy
муж *m.* husband
мужи́к *m.* peasant
мужчи́на *m.* man
музе́й *m.* museum
му́зыка *f.* music
му́ка *f.* torment, torture
мука́ *f.* flour
мураве́й *m.* ant
му́скул *m.* muscle
му́ха *f.* fly
мы we
мы́ло *n.* soap
мысль *f.* thought, idea
мы́ть(ся) *imp.* to wash (oneself)
мышь *f.* mouse
мя́гкий soft; mild

мя́со *n.* meat
мяч *m.* ball (sports)

Н

на on
наблюда́ть to watch, to observe
наве́рно probably; surely
наверху́ upstairs
навести́ть *perf.* to visit
навеща́ть *imp.* to visit
навсегда́ forever, for good
навстре́чу towards
над over, above
надева́ть *imp.* to put on
наде́жда *f.* hope
наде́ть *perf.* to put on
наде́яться *imp.* to hope
на́до it is necessary
надоеда́ть *imp.* to bore, annoy
надое́сть *perf.,* to bore, to annoy
наза́д back; ago
назва́ть *perf.* to call, to name
назнача́ть *imp.* to set; to appoint; to assign
назна́чить *perf.* to set; to appoint; to assign
называ́емый called, named
называ́ть *imp.* to call, to name
называ́ться to be called, to be named
наибо́лее the most
наилу́чший the best
найти́ *perf.* to find
найти́сь to be found, to be located
наконе́ц finally, at last
нале́во to the left
налива́ть *imp.* to pour
нали́ть *perf.* to pour
нало́г *m.* tax
наме́рение *n.* intention, purpose
нанима́ть *imp.* to hire
наня́ть *perf.* to hire
наоборо́т *adv.* on the contrary, just the opposite
написа́ть *perf.* to write
напомина́ть *imp.* to remind
напо́мнить *perf.* to remind
направле́ние *n.* direction; way
напра́во to the right
напра́сно in vain
наприме́р for example, for instance
напрока́т for hire

напро́тив *prep.* across, opposite
наро́д *m.* people; nation
наро́дный national, people's
наро́чно purposely, on purpose
настоя́щий real, genuine
настрое́ние *n.* mood
насчёт about, concerning
нау́ка *f.* science; scholarship
нау́чный scientific; scholarly
находи́ть *imp.* to find
находи́ться to be found, to be located
на́ция *f.* nation
нача́ло *n.* beginning
нача́льник *m.* chief, boss
нача́ть *perf.* to begin, to start
нача́ть(ся) to start, to begin
начина́ть(ся) *imp.* to begin, to start
наш our
нашёл found (masc.)
не not
не́бо *n.* sky; heaven
невозмо́жно impossible
нево́льно involuntarily
негати́в *m.* negative (photography)
неда́вно recently, lately
неде́ля *f.* week
недожа́реный insufficiently fried, roasted (= rare)
недоса́ливать *imp.* not to salt enough
недосоли́ть *perf.* not to salt enough
недоста́точно not enough, insufficiently
не́жный tender; affectionate; delicate
незаме́тно unnoticed
нездоро́виться not to feel well
нездоро́вый not well, sick, ill
незнако́мый unfamiliar, unknown
не́который some, certain
нельзя́ impossible, not permitted
неме́дленно immediately
не́мец *m.* German
не́мка *f.* German
неме́цкий German
немно́го a little, a while
немно́жко a little bit
не́нависть *f.* hatred
необходи́мость *f.* necessity
необходи́мый necessary
необыкнове́нный unusual

неожи́данно unexpectedly; suddenly
неожи́данный unexpected
непоня́тный incomprehensible
непра́вильный not right, incorrect
непреме́нно without fail, certainly
неприя́тный unpleasant
не́сколько several, a few
несмотря́ in spite of
нести́ *def.* to carry
нести́сь to rush (about)
несча́стный unhappy, unfortunate
несча́стье *n.* misfortune; disaster
нет no, there is (are) not
неуже́ли really? indeed?
нечая́нно accidentally
не́что something
ни not
нигде́ nowhere
ни́зкий low
ни́зко low, down
ни́жний lower
ника́к by no means
никогда́ never
никто́ nobody
никуда́ nowhere
ниско́лько not a bit, not at all
ни́тка *f.* thread
ничего́ nothing
ничто́ nothing
но but
но́вость *f.* news
но́вый new
нога́ *f.* foot; leg
нож *m.* knife
но́жницы *f. pl.* scissors
но́мер *m.* number, room (in hotel)
номеро́к *m.* tag (with number), check
но́рма *f.* norm, standard
норма́льно normally
норма́льный normal
нос *m.* nose
носи́льщик *m.* porter
носи́ть *iter.* to carry
носи́ться to wear
носки́ *m. pl.* socks
ночь *f.* night
ночно́й night, nocturnal
но́чью at night
ноя́брь *m.* November
нрав *m.* disposition, temper

нра́виться *imp.* to please
нра́вственный moral
нра́вы *m. pl.* customs; morals
ну well (*exclamation*)
нужда́ *f.* want, need
ну́жно necessary; must
ну́жный necessary
ны́не nowadays
ны́нешний present, modern

O

о about; against
о́ба *m.* both
обе́д *m.* dinner
обе́дать *imp.* to dine; to have dinner
обезья́на *m.* monkey
оберну́ть *perf.* to wrap up
оберну́ться to turn around
обёртывать *imp.* to wrap up
обеща́ть *imp. & perf.* to promise
оби́да *f.* insult; offense
оби́деть(ся) *perf.* to offend
обижа́ть(ся) *imp.* to offend
о́блако *n.* cloud
о́бласть *f.* district, province; domain, field
обме́нивать *imp.* to exchange
обмени́ть or **обменя́ть** *perf.* to exchange
обмени́ться to switch
обора́чивать *imp.* to wrap up
обора́чиваться to turn around
о́браз *m.* image; form; icon
образова́ние *n.* education
образо́ванный (well)-educated
обрати́ть *perf.* to direct; to convert
обрати́ться to apply to; to turn to
обра́тно back (adv.)
обра́тный reverse
обраща́ть *imp.* to direct; to change
обраща́ться to turn to, to apply or appeal to
обстано́вка *f.* furnishings; conditions, atmosphere
обстоя́тельство *n.* circumstance
обще́ственный public, social
о́бщество *n.* society
о́бщий common; general
объяви́ть *perf.* to announce

объясне́ние *n.* explanation
объявля́ть *imp.* to announce
объясни́ть *perf.* to explain
объясня́ть *imp.* to explain
обыкнове́нно usually; generally
обыкнове́нный ordinary
обы́чный usual, ordinary
обя́занность *f.* duty, responsibility
обя́занный obligated, indebted
обяза́тельно obligatory
овладева́ть *imp.* to take possession; to master
овладе́ть *perf.* to take possession; to master
огля́дываться *imp.* to look back (around)
огляну́ться *perf.* to look back (around)
ого́нь *m.* fire
огро́мный huge; tremendous
ограни́чивать *imp.* to limit
ограни́чить *perf.* to limit, to restrict
огуре́ц *m.* cucumber
оде́жда *f.* clothing, clothes
одева́ть(ся) *imp.* to dress (oneself)
оде́тый dressed, clothed
оде́ть(ся) *perf.* to dress (oneself)
одея́ло *n.* blanket
оди́н one
одина́ковый identical
оди́ннадцать eleven
одино́кий lonely; single
одна́жды once
одна́ко however; but
ожере́лье *n.* necklace
ожида́ние *n.* expectation
ожида́ть *imp.* to expect
о́зеро *n.* lake
оказа́ть *perf.* to render
оказа́ться to happen to be; to find oneself
ока́зывать *imp.* to render
ока́зываться to happen to be, to happen, to turn out to be; to find oneself
ока́нчивать(ся) *imp.* to end
око́нчить(ся) *perf.* to end
окно́ *n.* window
о́коло near; about
оконча́тельно absolutely

октя́брь *m.* October
ома́р *m.* lobster
омле́т *m.* omelette
он he
она́ she
они́ they
оно́ it
опа́здывать *imp.* to be late
опа́сность *f.* danger
опа́сный dangerous
о́пера *f.* opera
опера́ция *f.* operation
о́перный opera (adj.)
описа́ние *n.* description
описа́ть *perf.* to describe
опи́сывать *imp.* to describe
опла́та *f.* payment
оплати́ть *perf.* to pay
опла́чивать *imp.* to pay
опозда́ние *n.* delay
опозда́ть *perf.* to be late
определённый definite, certain
определи́ть *perf.* to define, to determine
определя́ть *imp.* to define
опуска́ть *imp.* to lower
опусти́ть *perf.* to lower; to omit
о́пыт *m.* experiment; experience
опя́ть again
организа́ция *f.* organization
орёл *m.* eagle
оре́х *m.* nut
ору́дие *n.* equipment, tool; gun
ору́жие *n.* weapon, arms
освободи́ть *perf.* to liberate; to release
освободи́ться to become vacant
освобожда́ть *imp.* to liberate; to release
освобожда́ться to become vacant
осёл *m.* donkey, ass
о́сень *f.* autumn, fall
осмотре́ть *perf.* to examine, to inspect
осма́тривать *imp.* to examine, to inspect
осмо́тр *m.* inspection; examination
осно́ва *f.* basis
основа́ние *n.* basis, foundation
основа́ть *perf.* to found
основно́й basic, main
осно́вывать *imp.* to found

осо́бенно especially
осо́бенность *f.* peculiarity, feature
осо́бенный particular, peculiar
осо́бый special, extra
остава́ться *imp.* to stay, to remain
оста́вить *perf.* to leave; to abandon
оставля́ть *imp.* to leave
остально́й remaining
останови́ть(ся) *perf.* to stop; to stay
остано́вка *f.* stop
остана́вливать(ся) *imp.* to stop; to stay
оста́ться *perf.* to stay, to remain
осторо́жно carefully
осторо́жный careful
о́стрый sharp
от away from, from
отве́т *m.* answer, reply
отве́тить *perf.* to answer, to reply
отвеча́ть *imp.* to answer; to be responsible
отдава́ть *imp.* to give up; to give back
отда́ть *perf.* to give up; to give back
отде́л *m.* section, department
отделе́ние *n.* department, branch
отде́льный separate
о́тдых *m.* rest, relaxation
оте́ц *m.* father
отказа́ться *perf.* to refuse
отка́зываться *imp.* to refuse
открыва́ть *imp.* to open
откры́тка *f.* postcard
откры́ть *perf.* to open
откры́тый open, outspoken
отку́да whence, where from
отлича́ть *imp.* to distinguish, to tell from
отлича́ться to be different, to stand out
отличи́ть *perf.* to distinguish, to tell from
отличи́ться to distinguish oneself, to excel
отнести́ *perf.* to take or carry to (someone)
отнести́сь to treat
относи́ть *imp.* to take or carry to (someone)
относи́ться to refer; to treat

отношéние *n.* attitude, relation
отойти́ *perf.* to go away, to depart
отпеча́ток *m.* print (photography)
отпра́вить *perf.* to send off, to forward (mail), to dispatch
отпра́виться to betake oneself, to start out
отправля́ть *imp.* to send off, to forward (mail), to dispatch
отправля́тся to betake oneself, to start out
отря́д *m.* outfit, detachment
отсу́тствие *n.* absence
отсю́да from here
оттого́ therefore
отту́да from there
отча́яние *n.* despair
отчего́ why, wherefore
отхо́д *m.* departure
отходи́ть *imp.* to go away, to depart
офице́р *m.* officer
официа́нт *m.* waiter
ох oh! ah!
охо́та *f.* hunt; inclination
очеви́дно obviously, apparently
о́чень very
о́чередь *f.* line, queue; turn
оши́бка *f.* mistake
ощуще́ние *n.* sensation

П

па́дать *imp.* to fall, to drop
па́лец *m.* finger
па́лка *f.* stick, cane
па́луба *f.* deck
пальто́ *n.* coat
па́мять *f.* memory
па́ра *f.* pair, couple
па́рень *m.* fellow, chap
парикма́хер *m.* barber
парохо́д *m.* steamship
парте́р *m.* orchestra (in theater)
па́ртия *f.* party (political)
па́спорт *m.* passport
па́хнуть to smell (of)
пе́рвый first
перебива́ть *imp.* to interrupt
переби́ть *perf.* to interrupt
перевести́ *perf.* to translate
перево́д *m.* translation

переводи́ть *imp.* to translate
перево́дчик *m.* interpreter
пе́ред in front of, before
передава́ть *imp.* to pass, to hand, to transmit
переда́ть *perf.* to pass; to hand
пере́дний front (adj.)
пере́дник *m.* apron
перейти́ *perf.* to get over; to cross
пережа́ренный overfried, over-roasted
переме́на *f.* change, alteration
перемени́ть *perf.* to change
переменя́ть *imp.* to change
переса́дка *f.* change (of train, station)
переса́ливать *imp.* to oversalt
пересоли́ть *perf.* to oversalt
перестава́ть *imp.* to stop
переста́ть *perf.* to stop
переу́лок *m.* alley, lane
переходи́ть *imp.* to get over; to cross
пери́од *m.* period, phase
перо́ *n.* pen
пе́рсик *m.* peach
пе́сня *f.* song
песо́к *m.* sand
петь *imp.* to sing
печа́льный sad, mournful
печа́ть *f.* seal
пи́во *n.* beer
пиро́жное *n.* pastry
писа́тель *m.* writer
писа́ть *imp.* to write
письмо́ *n.* letter
пи́счий writing-
пи́счая бума́га *f.* writing paper
пить *imp.* to drink
питьё *n.* drinking, drink
пла́вать *indef.* to swim
пла́кать *imp.* to weep, to cry
план *m.* plan, chart
пла́та *f.* pay
плати́ть *imp.* to pay
плато́к *m.* handkerchief; shawl
платфо́рма *f.* platform
пла́тье *n.* dress
плова́ть *imp.* to spit
плечо́ *n.* shoulder
плёнка *f.* film, roll of film
пло́хо badly, poorly

плохо́й bad
площа́дка *f.* platform
пло́щадь *f.* square
пляж *m.* beach
по along, according to, in (a language)
побе́да *f.* victory
побежа́ть *perf.* to run
побере́жье *n.* shore, coast
пове́рить *perf.* to believe
поверну́ть(ся) *perf.* to turn
по-ви́димому evidently
по́вод *m.* cause, reason
повора́чивать(ся) *imp.* to turn (around)
поворо́т *m.* turn
повтори́ть *perf.* to repeat
повторя́ть *imp.* to repeat
погиба́ть *imp.* to perish
поги́бнуть *perf.* to perish
поговори́ть *perf.* to talk (over), to chat
под under, below, underneath
подава́ть *imp.* to give, to hand; to serve; to submit
пода́ть *perf.* to give, to hand; to serve; to submit
поддержа́ть *perf.* to support, to maintain
подде́рживать *imp.* to support, to maintain
подлежа́ть *imp.* to be subject to
поднима́ть *imp.* to lift, to raise
подня́ться *imp.* to go up, to come up
подня́ть *perf.* to lift, to raise
подня́ться to go up, to come up
подо́бный similar
подожда́ть *perf.* to wait for
подойти́ *perf.* to approach
подписа́ться *perf.* to sign, to subscribe
подпи́сываться *imp.* to sign, to subscribe
подро́бность *f.* detail
подстрига́ть *imp.* to cut, to trim (hair)
подстри́чь *perf.* to cut, to trim (hair)
поду́мать *perf.* to think (a little, for a while)
поду́шка *f.* pillow, cushion
подходи́ть *imp.* to approach; to fit

по́езд *m.* train
пое́здка *f.* journey, trip
пое́хать *perf.* to depart
пожа́луйста please
пожа́луй perhaps, maybe, possibly
пожива́ть to get along, to live
позва́ть *perf.* to call
позво́лить *perf.* to permit, to allow
позволя́ть *perf.* to permit, to allow
по́здно late
по́зже later
пойти́ *perf.* to go
пока́ while; for the time being; so long!
пока́...не until
показа́ть *perf.* to show
показа́ться to seem, to appear; to show off
пока́зывать *imp.* to show
пока́зываться to show off
поко́й *m.* rest
поко́йный calm, restful
покрыва́ть *imp.* to cover
покры́ть *perf.* to cover
покупа́ть *imp.* to buy
пол *m.* floor; sex
полага́ть *imp.* to suppose, to deem
полбуты́лка *f.* half a bottle
по́ле *n.* field
поле́зный useful; healthful
полёт *m.* flight
поли́тика *f.* politics; policy
полити́ческий political
полк *m.* regiment
по́лка *f.* shelf
по́лный full, complete; stout
полови́на *f.* half
положе́ние *n.* situation, condition
положи́ть *perf.* to put; to suppose
полоса́ *f.* stripe, strip; zone
полоте́нце *n.* towel
получа́ть *imp.* to receive
получе́ние *n.* receiving
получи́ть *perf.* to receive
по́льза *f.* profit; benefit; use
по́льзоваться *imp.* to use
по́мнить *imp.* to remember
помога́ть *imp.* to help
помо́чь *perf.* to help
по́мощь *f.* aid, help
понеде́льник *m.* Monday
понима́ть *imp.* to understand

поня́тие *n.* idea, notion
поня́тный understandable, clear
поня́ть *perf.* to understand
попада́ть *imp.* to hit, to strike; to get (into or to something)
попа́сть *perf.* to hit, to strike; to get (into or to something)
попра́вить *perf.* to correct, to fix
поправля́ть *imp.* to correct, to fix
попре́жнему as before, as usual
попро́бовать *perf.* to try, to taste
попроси́ть *perf.* to ask
попы́тка *f.* attempt
пора́ *f.* time, season
поража́ть *imp.* to amaze
порази́ть *perf.* to amaze
порт *m.* port
портни́ха *f.* dressmaker
портно́й *m.* tailor
портре́т *m.* portrait
портфе́ль *m.* briefcase
портсига́р *m.* cigarette case
поря́док *m.* order
посади́ть *perf.* to seat; to plant; to imprison
поскоре́е (more) quickly, hurry it up!
посла́ть *perf.* to send
по́сле after
после́дний last; latest
послеза́втра the day after tomorrow
послу́шать *perf.* to listen
посмотре́ть *perf.* to look, to take a look
поста́вить *perf.* to put, to stand
посте́ль *f.* bed
постоя́нно constantly, always
постоя́нный steady, constant
постоя́ть *perf.* to stand; to wait
поступа́ть *imp.* to act; to enroll
поступи́ть *perf.* to act; to enroll
посту́пок *m.* action
посыла́ть *imp.* to send
посы́лка *f.* package, parcel
пот *m.* sweat, perspiration
потеря́ть *perf.* to lose
пото́м afterwards, then
потому́ что because
потороп́и́ть(ся) *perf.* to hurry
похо́жий like, resembling
поцелова́ть *perf.* to kiss

почему́ why
по́чта *f.* post office, mail
почти́ almost, nearly
почто́вый postal
почу́вствовать *perf.* to feel
по́шлина *f.* duty, customs
поэ́т *m.* poet
поэ́тому therefore, so
появи́ться *perf.* to appear, to show up
появля́ться *imp.* to appear, to show up
по́яс *m.* belt
пра́вда *f.* truth
пра́вильно correctly, right
пра́вильный right, correct, regular
прави́тельство *n.* government
пра́во *n.* right
пра́вый right (adj.)
пра́здник *m.* holiday
предлага́ть *imp.* to suggest; to propose
предложи́ть *perf.* to suggest, to propose
предме́т *m.* object; subject, topic
председа́тель *m.* chairman, president
представи́тель *m.* representative, delegate
предста́вить *perf.* to represent
предста́виться to occur, to present itself
представле́ние *n.* performance
представля́ть *imp.* to represent; to imagine
представля́ться to occur, to present itself
пре́жде before, formerly
пре́жний former
прекра́сный excellent, fine
при at, near
приба́вить *perf.* to add
прибавля́ть *imp.* to add
прибыва́ть *imp.* to arrive
прибы́ть *perf.* to arrive
прибы́тие *n.* arrival
привести́ *perf.* to bring (along, over, into)
приводи́ть *imp.* to bring (along, over, into)
привыка́ть *imp.* to get used to
привы́кнуть *perf.* to get used to

привы́чка f. habit
пригото́вить perf. to prepare
приготовля́ть imp. to prepare
придава́ть imp. to give; to add; to attach
прида́ть perf. to give; to add; to attach
приезжа́ть imp. to arrive, to come
прие́хать perf. to arrive, to come
признава́ть imp. to acknowledge, to recognize
признава́ться to admit; to confess
при́знак m. sign
призна́ть perf. to acknowledge, to recognize
призна́ться to admit; to confess
прие́м m. reception
прийти́ (придти́ ог притти́) perf. to come
прийти́сь to have to
прика́з m. order, command
приказа́ть perf. to order
прика́зывать imp. to order
приме́р m. example
принадлежа́ть to belong
принести́ perf. to bring, to fetch
принима́ть to accept, to take, to receive
приноси́ть imp. to bring, to fetch
при́нятый accepted, adopted
приня́ть perf. to accept, to take, to receive
приро́да f. nature
присла́ть perf. to send (over)
присыла́ть imp. to send (over)
прису́тствие n. presence
приходи́ть imp. to come
приходи́ться to have to
причи́на f. cause, reason
прия́тно pleasantly, pleasant
прия́тный pleasant, nice
про about
про́бка f. cork
пробле́ма f. problem
про́бовать imp. to try, to taste
про́бочник m. corkscrew
провести́ perf. to spend (time)
про́вод m. wire
проводи́ть imp. to spend (time)
провожа́ть perf. to accompany; to see off
проводни́к m. porter (on train)

провожа́ть imp. to accompany; to see off
програ́мма f. program
прогу́ливаться imp. to go for a walk
прогу́лка f. walk
прогуля́ться perf. to go for a walk
продава́ть imp. to sell
продаве́ц m. salesman
продавщи́ца f. salesgirl
прода́жа f. sale
прода́ть perf. to sell
продле́ние n. prolongation, extension
продли́ть perf. to prolong, to extend
продолжа́ть imp. to continue, to go on
продо́лжить perf. to continue, to go on
прое́зд m. passage
проезжа́ть imp. to pass (in a vehicle)
прое́хать perf. to pass (in a vehicle)
произвести́ perf. to produce
производи́ть imp. to produce
произнести́ perf. to pronounce
произноси́ть imp. to pronounce
произойти́ perf. to take place
происходи́ть imp. to take place
пройти́ perf. to pass (on foot)
пропада́ть imp. to get lost, to vanish
пропа́сть perf. to get lost, to vanish
про́пуск m. pass, permit
пропуска́ть imp. to let pass
пропусти́ть perf. to let pass
проси́ть imp. to ask, to request
просма́тривать imp. to look over, to glance through
просмотре́ть perf. to look over, to glance through
проснуться perf. to wake up
прости́ть perf. to forgive
про́сто simply
просто́й simple
простуди́ться perf. to catch cold
простужа́ться imp. to catch cold
про́сьба f. request
просыпа́ться imp. to wake up

про́тив against
проти́вник *m.* opponent
проти́вный nasty; contrary
протя́гивать *imp.* to stretch; to extend
протяну́ть *perf.* to stretch; to extend
профе́ссор *m.* professor
проходи́ть *imp.* to pass (on foot)
проце́нт *m.* per cent, percentage
проце́сс *m.* process
прочёсть *perf.* to read, to peruse
про́чий other
прочита́ть *perf.* to read, to peruse
про́шлый past, last
проща́ть *imp.* to forgive
прояви́ть *perf.* to develop (film); to display
проявля́ть *imp.* to develop; to display
пря́мо straight ahead
прямо́й straight, upright
пти́ца *f.* bird
пу́блика *f.* public, audience
пу́дра *f.* powder
пуска́ть *imp.* to let, to allow
пусти́ть *perf.* to let, to allow
пусто́й empty
пусть let (*imperative*)
пустя́к *m.* trifle
путеводи́тель *m.* guide book, itinerary
путь *m.* path, road, way
пчела́ *f.* bee
пылесо́с *m.* vacuum cleaner
пыль *f.* dust
пыта́ться *imp.* to try, to endeavor
пье́са *f.* play (drama)
пья́ный drunk
пятна́дцать fifteen
пя́тница *f.* Friday
пятно́ *n.* spot, blot, stain
пя́тый fifth
пять five
пятьдеся́т fifty
пятьсо́т five hundred
пя́тый fifth

Р

рабо́та *f.* work; job
рабо́тать *imp.* to work

рабо́тник *m.* worker
рабо́чий workers'
ра́венство *n.* equality
равно́ equally
ра́вный equal
рад glad
ра́ди for the sake of
ра́дио *indecl. n.* radio
ра́доваться *imp.* to rejoice, to be happy
ра́достно joyfully, happily
ра́достный happy, joyful
ра́дость *f.* joy, gladness
раз time, one time, once
разбива́ть *imp.* to break, to smash
разби́ть *perf.* to break, to smash
разбуди́ть *perf.* to awaken, to wake up
ра́зве ——? is that so?; really, perhaps
разгова́ривать *imp.* to converse
разгово́р *m.* conversation, talk
раздева́лка *f.* dressing room
раздева́ть(ся) *imp.* to undress
разде́ть(ся) *perf.* to undress
разли́чный different
разме́р *m.* size, dimension
ра́зница *f.* difference
ра́зный different, various
разреша́ть *imp.* to permit; to solve
разреше́ние *n.* permission; solution
разреши́ть *perf.* to permit; to solve
разуме́ется of course (*lit.,* it is understood)
разъединя́ть *imp.* to separate; to disconnect
разъедини́ть *perf.* to separate; to disconnect
рак *m.* crawfish, lobster; cancer
ра́нний early
ра́но early
ра́ньше earlier, ahead of time
расписа́ние *n.* timetable, schedule
расписа́ть(ся) *perf.* to sign, to endorse
распи́ска *f.* receipt
распи́сывать(ся) *imp.* to sign, to endorse
расска́з *m.* story, tale
рассказа́ть *perf.* to tell, to relate

расска́зывать *imp.* to tell, to relate
рассма́тривать *imp.* to look at; to
consider
рассмотре́ть *perf.* to look at; to
consider
расти́ *imp.* to grow
расхо́д *m.* expense
расчёт *m.* calculation
рвать *imp.* to tear
ребёнок *m.* child
ребя́та *pl.* fellows, guys
револю́ция *f.* revolution
регистра́ция *f.* registration
ре́дкий rare; sparse; uncommon
ре́дко seldom, rarely
ре́зать *imp.* to cut
рези́на *f.* rubber; elastic
ре́зкий harsh; sharp; biting
ре́зко sharply, harshly
результа́т *m.* result
река́ *f.* river
рекомендова́ть to recommend
рестора́н *m.* restaurant
реце́пт *m.* prescription; recipe
речь *f.* speech
реша́ть *imp.* to decide
реше́ние *n.* decision
реши́тельно definitely, absolutely
реши́ть *perf.* to decide
ро́вно equally; exactly
ро́вный even, equal
род *m.* kind, species
ро́дина *f.* native country
роди́ть *perf.* to give birth (to)
роди́ться to be born
родно́й kindred, own, native
рожа́ть *imp.* to give birth (to)
рожда́ться *imp.* to be born
ро́за *f.* rose
ро́зовый pink
роль *f.* part, role
рома́н *m.* novel; love affair
рост *m.* growth; height
ро́стбиф *m.* roastbeef
рот *m.* mouth
руба́шка *f.* shirt
рубль *m.* ruble
рука́ *f.* hand
рука́в *m.* sleeve
руководи́тель *m.* leader, guide
ру́копись *f.* manuscript

ру́сский Russian
ручно́й by hand, manual
ры́ба *f.* fish
ры́нок *m.* market
ряд *m.* row
ря́дом beside, side by side

С

с with
сад *m.* garden, orchard
сади́ть *imp.* to seat; to plant
сади́ться to sit down
сажа́ть *imp.* to seat; to plant
сала́т *m.* salad; lettuce
салфе́тка *f.* napkin
сам self; myself, yourself, himself, etc.
самолёт *m.* airplane
са́мый *pron.* same, most; *adj., adv.*
very
сапо́г *m.* boot
са́хар *m.* sugar
све́дение *n.* information
све́жий fresh
све́рху from above, on top
свет *m.* light; world
све́тлый bright; light
свёкла *f.* beet
сверх above, beyond
свида́ние *n.* meeting, rendez-vous,
date
свобо́дно freely, easily, fluently
свобо́дный free
свобо́да *f.* freedom
свой one's own
свя́занный tied (up), bound
связа́ть *perf.* to tie, to bind; to
knit
связь *f.* connection, contact; tie,
bond
свя́зывать *imp.* to tie, to bind; to
knit
свято́й holy
сдава́ть to give up, to check (baggage)
сда́ча *f.* small change (money)
сде́лать *perf.* to make, to do
сде́латься to become
себя́ oneself
сего́дня today
седо́й grey
седьмо́й seventh

сейча́с now, immediately
секрета́рь *m.* secretary
село́ *n.* village
семе́йный domestic, family-
семна́дцать seventeen
семь seven
се́мьдесят seventy
семья́ *f.* family
сентя́брь *m.* September
серди́то angrily
серди́ться *imp.* to be angry, to get angry
се́рдце *n.* heart
серебро́ *n.* silver
сере́бряный silver-
се́рый grey
серьёзно seriously
серьёзный serious, earnest
сестра́ *f.* sister
сесть *perf.* to sit down
се́ять to sow
сза́ди from behind
сиде́ть *imp.* to sit
си́ла *f.* force, power, strength
си́льно powerfully, greatly
си́льный strong, powerful
си́ний dark-blue
систе́ма *f.* system
сказа́ть *perf.* to say, to tell
сквозня́к *m.* draft, current of air
сквозь through
скла́дывать *imp.* to fold, to arrange
ско́лько how much
скоре́е quickly, sooner
ско́ро quickly, rapidly
ско́рый quick, rapid
скро́мный modest
скрыва́ть *imp.* to hide, to conceal
скрыть *perf.* to hide, to conceal
ску́льптор *m.* sculptor
скульпту́ра *f.* sculpture
скуча́ть *imp.* to be bored; to be lonely (for); to miss
сла́бость *f.* weakness
сла́бый weak, feeble
сла́ва *f.* fame, glory
сла́вный famous, renowned
сла́дкий sweet
слегка́ slightly
след *m.* trace, footprint
спеди́ть *imp.* to follow, to spy, to watch

сле́довать *imp.* to follow
сле́дующий next, following
слеза́ *f.* tear
слеза́ть *imp.* to alight, to get out
слезть *perf.* to alight, to get out
слепо́й blind
сли́шком too
слова́рь *m.* dictionary
сло́вно as if, as though
сло́во *n.* word
сло́жный complicated
сложи́ть *perf.* to fold, to arrange
слома́ть *perf.* to break
слу́жба *f.* service; job, work
служи́ть *imp.* to serve
слух *m.* hearing; rumor
слу́чай *m.* chance; case; accident
случа́йно by chance, accidentally
случа́ться *imp.* to happen
случи́ться *perf.* to happen
слу́шать *imp.* to listen
слы́шать *imp.* to hear
слы́шный audible
сме́лый daring, bold
смерть *f.* death
сметь *imp.* to dare
смешно́й funny, comical
смех *m.* laughter
смея́ться *imp.* to laugh
смотре́ть *imp.* to look (at)
смысл *m.* sense, meaning
снача́ла (at) first
снег *m.* snow
сни́зу from below
снима́ть *imp.* to take off; to snap (pictures)
сно́ва again
снять *perf.* to take off; to snap (pictures)
соба́ка *f.* dog
собира́ть(ся) *imp.* to gather; to get ready
собра́ние *n.* meeting, gathering
собра́ть(ся) *perf.* to gather; to get ready
со́бственно properly
со́бственный own (adj.)
собы́тие *n.* event.
соверше́нно entirely, completely
со́весть *f.* conscience
сове́т *m.* council; counsel, advice
сове́тский Soviet (adj.)

совреме́нный modern
совсе́м entirely, completely
согласи́ться *perf.* to agree, to consent
соглаша́ться *imp.* to agree, to consent
содержа́ние *n.* contents; maintenance
содержа́ть *imp.* to contain; to support; to maintain
Соединённые Шта́ты United States
сожале́ние *n.* regret; pity
к сожале́нию unfortunately
созда́ние *n.* creation; creature
создава́ть *imp.* to create
созда́ть *perf.* to create
созна́ние *n.* realization; consciousness
сойти́ *perf.* to get off, to alight
солда́т *m.* soldier
со́лнечный sunny; solar
со́лнце *n.* sun
соло́нка *f.* salt shaker
соль *f.* salt
сомнева́ться *imp.* to doubt
сомне́ние *n.* doubt
сон *m.* sleep; dream
сообща́ть *imp.* to inform, to notify, to communicate
сообще́ние *n.* communication, message
сообщи́ть *perf.* to communicate, to notify, to inform
со́рок forty
сорт *m.* sort, kind
сосе́д *m.* neighbor
сосе́дка *f.* neighbor
сосе́дний neighboring, adjoining
соску́читься *perf.* to be bored; to be lonely (for), to miss
сосна́ *f.* pinetree
соста́вить(ся) *perf.* to compose, to compile
составля́ть(ся) *imp.* to compose, to compile
состоя́ние *n.* condition, state; fortune
состоя́ть *imp.* to be made up, to consist of
сосчита́ть *perf.* to count
со́тня *f.* hundred

сохрани́ть(ся) *perf.* to keep, to preserve
сохраня́ть(ся) *imp.* to keep, to preserve
сою́з *m.* union, alliance
спа́льный sleeping-
спа́льня *f.* bedroom
спа́ржа, *f.* asparagus
спаса́ть *imp.* to save, to rescue
спаси́бо thank you
спасти́ *perf.* to save, to rescue
спать *imp.* to sleep
спекта́кль *m.* performance, production
спеши́ть *perf.* to hurry
спина́ *f.* back
спи́сок *m.* list
спи́чка *f.* match
споко́йно calmly
споко́йный quiet, peaceful
споко́йствие *n.* peacefulness
спор *m.* argument; debate
спо́рить *imp.* to argue, to debate
спорт *m.* sport
спо́соб *m.* way, method
спосо́бность *f.* ability; faculty
спосо́бный capable, gifted
справедли́вый just, fair
спра́вка *f.* information
спра́вочный information (adj.)
спра́шивать *imp.* to ask, to inquire
спроси́ть *perf.* to ask, to inquire
спустя́ after, later
сравне́ние *n.* comparison
сра́внивать *imp.* to compare
сравни́тельный comparative
сравни́ть *perf.* to compare
сра́зу all at once, immediately
среда́ *f.* Wednesday
среди́ in the middle of, among
сре́дний middle; average
сре́дство *n.* means
срок *m.* term, period of time
ста́вить *imp.* to put; to stand
стадио́н *m.* stadium
стака́н *m.* glass, tumbler
сталь *f.* steel
станда́рт *m.* standard
станови́ться *imp.* to stand, to become
ста́нция *f.* station
стара́ться *imp.* to try, to endeavor

стари́к *m.* old man
стари́нный ancient, antique
ста́рший senior, chief
ста́рый old
стару́ха *f.* old woman
стать *perf.* to stand, to become; to begin
статья́ *f.* article
стекло́ *n.* glass
стена́ *f.* wall
сте́пень *f.* degree; grade; extent
степь *f.* steppe, prairie
стира́ть *imp.* to wash, to launder
сти́рка *f.* laundering
стих *m.* verse
сто hundred
сто́ить *imp.* to cost
стол *m.* table
столб *m.* pole
столе́тие *n.* century
сто́лик *m.* small table
столова́ться *imp.* to board, to eat out
сто́лько so much, so many
сторона́ *f.* side
сто́янка *f.* stand
стоя́ть *imp.* to stand
страда́ние *n.* suffering
страда́ть *imp.* to suffer
страна́ *f.* country, land
страни́ца *f.* page
стра́нно strangely, oddly
стра́нный strange
стра́стный passionate
страсть *f.* passion, temper
страх *m.* fright, fear, scare
стра́шно terribly
стра́шный terrible
стреля́ть *imp.* to shoot
стреми́ться *imp.* to aim, to be anxious
стро́гий strict
стро́го strictly
стро́ить *imp.* to build, construct
строй *m.* ranks, arrangement, order
стро́йка *f.* construction
стул *m.* chair
ступа́ть *imp.* to step
ступи́ть *perf.* to step
стуча́ть *imp.* to knock
суббо́та *f.* Saturday
суд *m.* court

суди́ть *imp.* to judge, to try
судьба́ *f.* fate
суме́ть *perf.* to be able
суп *m.* soup
суро́вый strict, stern, severe
сухо́й dry; stale
суши́ть *imp.* to dry
существо́ *n.* being, creature
существова́ние *n.* existence
существова́ть *imp.* to exist
су́щность *f.* essence
схвати́ть *perf.* to catch
схва́тывать *imp.* to catch (on)
сходи́ть *imp.* to get off, to alight
сце́на *f.* stage, scene
счастли́вый happy, lucky
сча́стье *n.* happiness, luck
счесть *perf.* to count
счёт *m.* bill
счита́ть *imp.* to count; to consider
счита́ться to be considered; to take into consideration
сын *m.* son
сыр *m.* cheese
сыро́й damp; raw
сюда́ here (= to here)

Т

таба́к *m.* tobacco
та́йна *f.* mystery; secret
та́йный mysterious; secret
так so, thus
та́кже also, too
тако́й such
такси́ *indecl. n.* taxi
тала́нт *m.* talent
та́лия *f.* waist
там there
тамо́жня *f.* custom house
таре́лка *f.* plate
тата́рский Tartar-
твёрдый hard
твой thy, thine; your, yours
теа́тр *m.* theater
тебя́ *gen., acc. of* ты
телегра́мма *f.* telegram
телегра́ф *m.* telegraph
телефо́н *m.* telephone
телефо́нный telephone (adj.)
те́ло *n.* body
те́ма *f.* theme, subject, topic

темнота́ *f.* darkness
тёмный dark, obscure
те́ннис *m.* tennis
те́ннисный tennis (adj.)
тень *f.* shade, shadow
тео́рия *f.* theory
тепе́рь now
тепло́ warmly, warm
тёплый warm, cordial
терпели́вость *f.* patience
терпели́вый patient
терпе́ть *imp.* to endure, to stand, to suffer
торже́ственный solemn; gala
теря́ть *imp.* to lose
те́сный tight
тётя *f.* aunt
тече́ние *n.* current, stream
ти́хий quiet
ти́хо quietly, slowly
ти́ше more quiet, more slowly
тишина́ *f.* silence
то *pron.* that; *adv.* then
това́рищ *m.* comrade, close friend
тогда́ then, at that time
то́-есть that is; namely
то́же also, too
толка́ть *imp.* to push
толпа́ *f.* crowd
то́лстый thick; stout, fat
то́лько only
том *m.* volume
тому́ наза́д ago
тон *m.* tone
то́нкий thin, slender; delicate
торопли́во hastily, hurriedly
торопи́ть(ся) *imp.* to hurry, to hasten
торт *m.* cake
торча́ть *imp.* to stick out; protrude
тоска́ *f.* longing, distress, anguish
тот that (one)
то́тчас at once
то́чка *f.* dot, period, point
то́чно exactly
трава́ *f.* grass
трамва́й *m.* tram, street car, trolley
трамва́йный street car, trolley (adj.)
тра́тить *imp.* to spend

тре́бование *n.* claim, demand, request
тре́бовать *imp.* to demand, to request
трево́га *f.* alarm, anxiety
трево́жный anxious, alarming
тре́тий third
три three
три́дцать thirty
трина́дцать thirteen
три́ста three hundred
тро́е three
труба́ *f.* pipe; chimney; trumpet
тру́бка *f.* pipe; tube; telephone receiver
труд *m.* labor; difficulty
тру́дно difficult
тру́дный difficult, hard
тури́ст *m.* tourist
тури́стка *f.* tourist
туда́ there (to there)
тума́н *m.* fog, mist
тут here
ту́ча *f.* cloud
ту́фля *f.* slipper, shoe
тща́тельно thoroughly, with great care
тща́тельный careful, painstaking
ты thou; you
ты́сяча thousand
тюрьма́ *f.* prison
тяжело́ hard, difficult, heavy
тя́жесть *f.* weight, gravity
тяжёлый heavy, hard, difficult
тяну́ть *imp.* to pull, to drag
тяну́ться to stretch, to extend

У

у at, by
убега́ть *imp.* to run away
убеди́ть *perf.* to convince, to persuade
убеди́ться to become convinced (of)
убежа́ть *perf.* to run away
убежда́ть *imp.* to convince, to persuade
убежда́ться to become convinced (of)
убежде́ние *n.* conviction, persuasion
убива́ть *imp.* to kill

уби́йство n. murder
уби́йца m. & f. killer
убира́ть imp. to take away; to clean up
уби́ть perf. to kill
убо́рная f. toilet
убра́ть perf. to take away; to clean up
уважа́ть imp. to respect, to esteem
уваже́ние n. respect, esteem
уве́ренный sure, confident
уверя́ть imp. to assure
уве́рить perf. to assure
уви́деть perf. to see, to catch sight of
увы́! alas!
у́гол m. corner; angle
у́голь m. coal
угости́ть perf. to treat, to entertain
угоща́ть imp. to treat, to entertain
удава́ться imp. to succeed, to be successful
уда́р m. blow
уда́рить perf. to hit, to strike
ударя́ть imp. to hit, to strike
уда́ться perf. to succeed, to be successful
уда́ча f. good luck; success
уда́чный successful
удиви́тельный surprising, astonishing
удиви́ть perf. to surprise, to astonish
удиви́ть(ся) to be astonished, to be amazed
удивле́ние n. surprise, astonishment
удивля́ть imp. to surprise, to astonish
удивля́ться to be astonished, to be amazed
уди́лище n. fishing rod
удо́бный comfortable, convenient
удово́льствие n. pleasure
уезжа́ть imp. to go away, to ride away
уе́хать perf. to go away, to ride away
у́жас m. horror, terror
ужа́сно awfully, terribly
ужа́сный awful, terrible
уже́ already

у́жин m. supper
у́жинать imp. to have supper
у́зкий narrow
узлово́й main, nodal
узлова́я ста́нция junction
узнава́ть imp. to recognize
узна́ть perf. to recognize, to find out
уйти́ perf. to go away, to leave
указа́ть perf. to point out, to indicate
ука́зывать imp. to point out, to indicate
украи́нский Ukrainian
у́ксус m. vinegar
у́лица f. street
улыба́ться imp. to smile
улы́бка f. smile
улыбну́ться perf. to smile
ум m. mind
умере́ть perf. to die
уме́ть imp. to know how, to be able
умира́ть imp. to die
у́мный clever, intelligent
универма́г (= универса́льный магази́н) department store
универса́льный universal
университе́т m. university
упа́сть perf. to fall, to drop
уплати́ть perf. to pay (off)
упла́чивать imp. to pay (off)
употребле́ние n. use
употреби́ть perf. to use
употребля́ть imp. to use
управля́ющий m. manager, head
уси́лие n. effort
усло́вие n. condition
усла́вливаться imp. to agree, to reach an agreement
усло́виться perf. to agree, to reach an agreement
услу́га f. service, good turn
услы́шать perf. to hear
успева́ть imp. to have time, to manage
успе́ть perf. to have time, to manage
успе́х m. success
успе́хи progress
успока́ивать(ся) imp. to calm; to soothe

успоко́ить(ся) *perf.* to calm; to soothe
уставать *imp.* to get tired
уста́лый tired
уста́ть *perf.* to get tired
устра́ивать *imp.* to arrange
устро́ить *perf.* to arrange
усы́ *m. pl.* moustache
у́тка *f.* duck
у́тро *n.* morning
у́тром in the morning
утю́г *m.* (pressing) iron
у́хо *n.* ear
уходи́ть *imp.* to go away, to leave
уча́ствовать *imp.* to participate
уча́стие *n.* participation
уча́сток *m.* plot (of land), lot; police station
учени́к *m.* student
учени́ца *f.* student
учёный learned (person); scholar; scientist
учи́тель *m.* teacher
учи́тельница *f.* teacher
учи́ть *imp.* to teach; to learn
учи́ться *imp.* to study, to learn
учрежде́ние *n.* institution

Ф

фа́брика *f.* factory
факт *m.* fact
фами́лия *f.* family name, surname
фасо́ль *f.* beans
февра́ль *m.* February
фигу́ра *f.* figure
филиа́л branch (of an institution, store, etc.)
флаг *m.* flag
флиртова́ть *imp.* to flirt
флот *m.* fleet, navy
фо́кус *m.* trick; focus
фона́рь *m.* lantern; flashlight; headlight
фо́рма *f.* form, shape; uniform
фо́то- photographic
фра́за phrase, sentence
францу́зский French
фронт *m.* front
фунт *m.* pound
футбо́л *m.* soccer
футбо́льный soccer-

Х

хара́ктер *m.* character; disposition
хвали́ть *imp.* to praise
хва́стать(ся) *imp.* to brag
хвата́ть *imp.* to seize, to snatch; to suffice
хвати́ть *perf.* to suffice, to be enough
хвост *m.* tail; line
хи́трый cunning, sly
хлеб *m.* bread
ход *m.* movement, motion
на ходу́ in motion
ходи́ть *imp.* to go, to walk
хозя́ин *m.* landlord, host, master, owner
хозя́йка *f.* landlady, hostess, housekeeper
хозя́йство *n.* economy; housekeeping
хо́лод *m.* cold
холо́дный cold
хоро́ший good
хорошо́ very well! all right! nice, good
хоте́ть *imp.* to want
хоте́ться to want, to feel, like (impersonal)
хоть even; though; at least
хотя́ although, though
хране́ние *n.* storage
храни́ть *imp.* to keep, to store
худо́жественный artistic
худо́жество *n.* art
худо́жник *m.* artist
худо́й lean, thin; bad
ху́же worse

Ц

ца́рство *n.* kingdom, empire
царь *m.* czar
цвет *m.* color
цветно́й colored
цвето́к *m.* flower
це́лый whole, entire, intact
цель *f.* aim; target; purpose
цена́ *f.* price, value
це́нный valuable
центр *m.* center
центра́льный central
цепь *f.* chain, bonds

церко́вный ecclesiastical, church-
це́рковь f. church

Ч

чай m. tea
ча́йка f. seagull
ча́йник m. teapot
час m. hour
ча́сто often, frequently
часть f. part
часы́ m. pl. watch, clock
ча́шка f. cup
ча́ще more often
чей whose
чек m. check
челове́к m. human being, person
челове́чество n. humanity, mankind
челове́ческий human
чем than
чемода́н m. suitcase
чепуха́ f. nonsense
че́рез through, over, across
черни́ла n. pl. ink
чёрный black
черта́ f. line, trait
че́стный honest
честь f. honor
четве́рг m. Thursday
че́тверть f. quarter
четвёртый fourth
четы́ре four
четы́реста four hundred
четы́рнадцать fourteen
число́ n. number; date
чи́стить imp. to clean
чи́сто clean, neatly
чи́стый pure, clean, neat
чита́тель m. reader
чита́ть imp. to read
чиха́ть imp. to sneeze
чихну́ть perf. to sneeze
чи́ще cleaner
член m. member
чорт m. devil
чрезвыча́йно extremely, most
что what, that (rel. pron.)
чтобы in order to, so that
что за what kind of
что́-нибудь something; anything
что-то something
чу́вство n. feeling; sense

чу́вствовать imp. to feel, to sense
чуде́сный wonderful, miraculous
чу́дный wonderful, marvelous
чу́до n. miracle, wonder
чужо́й someone else's; foreign
чуть hardly
чуть ... не almost

Ш

шаг m. step; pace
шали́ть imp. to be naughty
шаль f. shawl
шампа́нское n. champagne
шампу́нь f. shampoo
шанс m. chance
ша́пка f. cap
шар m. ball; globe; sphere
ша́хматы m. pl. chess
шёл was going
шёлк m. silk
шёлковый silken
шепну́ть perf. whispeι
шепта́ть imp. to whisper
шерсть f. wool
шерстяно́й woolen
шесто́й sixth
шесть six
шестьдеся́т sixty
ше́я f. neck
ши́на f. tire
широ́кий wide, broad
шко́ла f. school
шку́ра f. skin, hide
шля́па f. hat
шокола́д m. chocolate
шофёр m. chauffeur
шпина́т m. spinach
што́пор m. corkscrew
шту́ка f. piece, item
шум m. noise
шути́ть imp. to joke
шу́тка f. joke

Щ

щека́ f. cheek
щи m. pl. cabbage soup

Э

экспози́ция f. exposition
экску́рсия f. excursion, guided tour
эне́ргия f. energy

эпóха *f.* epoch
этáж *m.* floor, story
э́тика *f.* ethics
э́то *n. nom. & acc. of* that, this
э́тот this, that
эх! eh! oh!

Ю

юбилéй *m.* anniversary, jubilee
ю́бка *f.* skirt
юг *m.* south
ю́жный southern
ю́мор *m.* humor
ю́ность *f.* youth
ю́ноша *m.* young fellow
юри́ст *m.* lawyer

Я

я I
я́блоко *n.* apple

яви́ться *perf.* to appear, to show up
явлéние *n.* appearance
явля́ться *imp.* to appear, to show up
яд *m.* poison
ядови́тый poisonous, toxic
я́зва *f.* ulcer, sore
язы́к *m.* language, tongue
яйцó *n.* egg
январь *m.* January
я́ркий bright, brilliant
я́рко brightly, colorfully
я́рус *m.* balcony, tier (theatr.)
я́сно clearly
я́сный clear, distinct
я́щик *m.* drawer, box

ENGLISH-RUSSIAN DICTIONARY

In the English-Russian Dictionary, the following points should be noted:

Nouns are always given with their gender, so that their pattern of declension can be easily located in the Outline of Grammar (**1.3-5**).

Adjectives are given only in the masculine nominative singular form. (For the declension of adjectives, see **2.3** in the Grammar section.) English words which can function both as nouns and as adjectives are marked *adj.* when used as adjectives.

Verbs: The English entry is given in the infinitive form; the corresponding Russian verb is given first in the imperfective and then in the perfective infinitive (the two forms are separated by a comma).

In phraseologic examples the entry is replaced by a mark of repetition (~).

A hyphen in Russian words indicates that a part of the preceding word is repeated, e.g.: открыва́ть, -кры́ть (i.e. откры́ть); впуска́ть, -сти́ть (i.e. впусти́ть).

When the form of the perfective is identical with that of the imperfective except that it is preceded by a prefix, the perfective is indicated by this prefix followed by a hyphen. E.g.: ду́мать, по- (i.e. поду́мать).

A

ability спосо́бность *f.*

able, to be мочь, с-; быть в состоя́нии; уме́ть, с-

about о, насчёт; о́коло; вокру́г
to be ~ собира́ться, -бра́ться

above над; (с)вы́ше
from ~ све́рху

abroad за грани́цей

absence отсу́тствие *n.*

absolutely совсе́м; соверше́нно

accept, to принима́ть, -ня́ть

accidentally случа́йно, неча́янно

accompany, to сопровожда́ть, -води́ть

according to согла́сно

account счёт *m.*

achievement достиже́ние *n.*

acid ки́слый

acknowledge, to признава́ть, -зна́ть

acquaint, to знако́мить, поto become ~ed with знако́миться, по-

acquaintance знако́мство *n.*

across че́рез, сквозь

act акт *m.*; де́йствие *n.*

act, to де́йствовать, по-

action посту́пок *m.*, де́йствие *n.*

activity де́ятельность *f.*

actor актёр *m.*

actress актри́са *f.*

actual действи́тельный

actually на са́мом де́ле

add, to прибавля́ть, -ба́вить

address áдрес *m.*
adjust, to улáживать, улáдить
admire, to восхищáться, -хитѝться
admit, to допускáть, -стѝть
advance, to продвигáть(ся), -двѝнуть(ся)
adventure приключéние *n.*
advertisement объявлéние *n.*
advice совéт *m.*
advise, to совéтовать, по-
affair дéло *n.*
affectionate лáсковый, нéжный
afraid, to be боя́ться *imp.*
after *prep.* пóсле, за; *adv.* потóм, затéм; *conj.* пóсле тогó как
afterwards потóм
again опя́ть, снóва
against прóтив
age вóзраст *m.*; век *m.*
agent áгент *m.*
aggression агрéссия *f.*
agitation волнéние *n.*
ago томý назáд
agony агóния *f.*
agree, to соглашáться, -асѝться
ahead впередѝ; вперёд
aid пóмощь *f.*
aim цель *f.*
aim, to стремѝться *imp.*
air вóздух *m.*; *adj.* воздýшный
air mail авиапóчта
airplane самолёт *m.*
airport аэропóрт *m.*
alarm тревóга *f.*
alarm clock будѝльник *m.*
alas увы́
album альбóм *m.*
alcohol алкогóль *m.*, спирт *m.*
alight, to сходѝть, сойтѝ; спускáться, -стѝться
alive живóй
all весь; всё; вся́кий
alley переýлок *m.*
alliance сою́з *m.*
allow, to позволя́ть, -вóлить; допускáть, -стѝть
all right лáдно, хорошó
almond миндáль *m.*
almost почтѝ
alone одѝн, одинóкий
along вдоль, по

aloud вслух, грóмко
already ужé
also тáкже, тóже
alteration перемéна *f.*
although хотя́
always всегдá
amaze, to поражáть, -разѝть
to be ~d удивля́ться, -вѝться
ambassador посóл *m.*
ambulance карéта скóрой пóмощи
America Амéрика *f.*
American америкáнец *m.*, -нка *f.*; *adj.* америкáнский
among мéжду
amount колѝчество *n.*, сýмма *f.*
amuse, to забавля́ть, -бáвить
amusement забáва *f.*
amusing забáвный, смешнóй
analysis анáлиз *m.*
ancient дрéвний, старѝнный
and и; а
angel áнгел *m.*
anger гнев *m.*
angle ýгол *m.*
angry сердѝтый
to be (get) ~ сердѝться, рас-
animal живóтное *n.*
anniversary юбилéй *m.*, годовщѝна *f.*
announce, to объявля́ть, -вѝть
annoy, to надоедáть, -éсть
annual годовóй, ежегóдный
another другóй
answer отвéт *m.*
answer, to отвечáть, -вéтить
ant муравéй *m.*
antique дрéвний, антѝчный
anxiety тревóга *f.*, забóта *f.*
anxious озабóченный
any какóй-нибудь, любóй
anyone ктó-нибудь; вся́кий
anything чтó-нибудь, что угóдно
apartment квартѝра *f.*
apologize, to извиня́ться, -нѝться
apparatus аппарáт *m.*, прибóр *m.*
apparently очевѝдно, повидѝмому
appeal to, to обращáться, -атѝться
appear, to появля́ться, -вѝться

appearance появле́ние *n*.; нару́жность *f*.
apple я́блоко *n*.
apple-tree я́блоня *f*.
apply to, to обраща́ться, -ати́ться
appoint, to назнача́ть, -а́чить
appointment назначе́ние *n*.; свида́ние *n*.
approach, to приближа́ться, -и́зиться; подходи́ть, подойти́
approximately приблизи́тельно
apricot абрико́с *m*.
April апре́ль *m*.
architect архите́ктор *m*.
argue, to спо́рить, по-
argument аргуме́нт *m*.
arise, to возника́ть, -ни́кнуть
arithmetic арифме́тика *f*.
arm рука́ *f*.
armchair кре́сло *n*.
arms ору́жие *n*.
army а́рмия *f*., во́йско *n*.
around круго́м, вокру́г
arrange, to устра́ивать, -ро́ить
arrest аре́ст *m*.
arrival прибы́тие *n*.
arrive, to прибыва́ть, -бы́ть
art иску́сство *n*.
article статья́ *f*.
artist худо́жник *m*.
artistic худо́жественный
as как; так; так как; когда́
~ if как бу́дто
~ to что каса́ется
ask, to спра́шивать, спроси́ть
to ~ for проси́ть, по-
asleep, to fall засыпа́ть, -сну́ть
ass осёл *m*.
assume, to предполага́ть, -ложи́ть
assure, to уверя́ть, уве́рить
astonished, to be удивля́ться, -ви́ться
astonishment удивле́ние *n*.
at в, на; при, у; о́коло, по
at all вообще́
athlete атле́т *m*.
atom а́том *m*.
attach, to придава́ть, -да́ть
attack нападе́ние *n*.
attempt попы́тка *f*.
attend, to прису́тствовать *imp*.

attention внима́ние *n*.
attentive внима́тельный
attitude отноше́ние *n*.
audience пу́блика *f*.
August а́вгуст *m*.
aunt тётя *f*.
author а́втор *m*.
authority власть *f*.
automobile автомоби́ль *m*.
autumn о́сень *f*.
avenue проспе́кт *m*.
average сре́дний
avoid, to избега́ть, -бежа́ть (*or* -бе́гнуть)
awake, to буди́ть, раз-; просыпа́ться, -сну́ться
away прочь
awful ужа́сный

B

back спина́ *f*.; спи́нка *f*.; *adj.* за́дний; *adv.* наза́д, обра́тно
bacon беко́н *m*.
bad плохо́й, дурно́й, скве́рный
bag мешо́к *m*.; су́мка *f*.
baggage бага́ж *m*.
balance бала́нс *f*.; весы́ *m. pl.*
balcony балко́н *m*.
ball шар *m*.; мяч *m*.; бал *m*.
ballet бале́т *m*.
banana бана́н *m*.
band ле́нта *f*.; ба́нда *f*.; орке́стр, *m*.
bank банк *m*.; бе́рег *m*. (*of a river*)
banknote ба́нковый биле́т *m*., банкно́та *f*.
barber парикма́хер *m*.
barber shop парикма́херская *f*.
bare го́лый
bark, to ла́ять, за-
basic основно́й
basis осно́ва *f*., основа́ние *n*.; ба́за *f*.
basket корзи́н(к)а *f*.
bath ва́нна *f*.
to bathe купа́ться, вы́-
bathing *adj.* купа́льный
bathroom ва́нная *f*.
battle би́тва *f*., бой *m*.
to be быть *imp*.

beach пляж *m.*

beam луч *m.*

beans фасо́ль *f.*

bear медве́дь *m.*

bear, to выноси́ть, вы́нести; терпе́ть, по-; нести́, по-

beard борода́ *f.*

beast зверь *m.*

beat, to бить, по-

beautiful краси́вый, прекра́сный

beauty красота́ *f.*

because потому́ что, так как
~ of из-за

become, to станови́ться, стать; де́латься, с-

bed крова́ть *f.*, посте́ль *f.*
to go to ~ ложи́ться спать

bedroom спа́льня *f.*

bee пчела́ *f.*

beef говя́дина *f.*

beer пи́во *n.*

beet свёкла *f.*

before *prep.* пе́ред, до; *adv.* впереки́; *conj.* пре́жде чем

beg, to проси́ть, по-

beggar ни́щий *m.*

begin, to начина́ть(ся), -ча́ть(ся)

beginning нача́ло *n.*

behind за, позади́, сза́ди

being существо́ *n.*

belief ве́ра *f.*

believe, to ве́рить, по-

bell ко́локол *m.*; звоно́к *m.*

belly живо́т *m.*

belong, to принадлежа́ть *imp.*

below *prep.* под, ни́же; *adv.* внизу́
from ~ сни́зу

belt по́яс *m.*

bench скаме́йка *f.*

benefit вы́года *f.*

berry я́года *f.*

beside ря́дом, во́зле, о́коло

besides кро́ме (того́)

best, the (наи)лу́чший

better *adj.* лу́чший; *adv.* лу́чше

between ме́жду

beyond сверх

big большо́й, кру́пный

bill счёт *m.*

billion миллиа́рд *m.*

bind, to свя́зывать, связа́ть

birch берёза *f.*

bird пти́ца *f.*

birthday день рожде́ния

biscuit пече́нье

bit кусо́чек *m.*
not a ~ ниско́лько

bitter го́рький

black чёрный

blank бланк *m.*

blanket одея́ло *n.*

bleach, to бели́ть, вы́-

blind слепо́й

blonde блонди́н *m.*, блонди́нка *f.*

blood кровь *f.*

blot пятно́ *n.*

blouse блу́за *f.*

blow уда́р *m.*

blow, to дуть *imp.*

blue си́ний, голубо́й

board доска́ *f.*, правле́ние *n.*; борт *m.*

board, to столова́ться *imp.*

boat ло́дка *f.*

body те́ло *n.*

boil, to кипе́ть, вс-; кипяти́ть(ся), вс-

bold сме́лый

bond связь *f.*

bone кость *f.*

book кни́га *f.*

bookcase кни́жный шкаф *m.*

book(let) кни́жка *f.*

boot сапо́г *m*, боти́нок *m.*

border грани́ца *f.*; край *m.*

born рождённый

boss нача́льник *m.*; хозя́ин *m.*

both о́ба
~ ... and и ... и

bottle буты́лка *f.*

bottom дно *n.*

bouillon бульо́н *m.*

bound свя́занный

box коро́бка *f.*, я́щик *m.*

boy ма́льчик *m.*

brag, to хва́стать(ся), по-

brain мозг *m.*

brake тормоз *m.*

branch ветвь *f.*; о́трасль *f.*; отделе́ние *n.*

brandy конья́к *m.*, во́дка *f.*

brassiere ли́фчик *m.*

brave бра́вый, хра́брый

bread хлеб *m.*
breadth ширина́ *f.*
break, to лома́ть(ся), с-; разбива́ть, -би́ть; наруша́ть, -ши́ть
breakfast за́втрак *m.*
  to have ~ за́втракать, по-
breast грудь *f.*
breathe, to дыша́ть *imp.*
breathing дыха́ние *n.*
bridge мост *m.*
brief кра́ткий
briefcase портфе́ль *m.*
briefly ко́ротко
bright я́ркий, све́тлый
brilliant блестя́щий
bring, to приноси́ть, -нести́; приводи́ть, -вести́
broad широ́кий
broadcast радиопереда́ча *f.*
brooch брошь *f.*
broom метла́ *f.*
brother брат *m.*
  ~-in-law зять *m.*
brow бровь *f.*
brown кори́чневый
brush щётка *f.*; кисть *f.*
bucket ведро́ *n.*
build, to стро́ить, по-
building зда́ние *n.*
burden бре́мя *n.*; но́ша *f.*
burn, to горе́ть, с-; сжига́ть, сжечь
bus авто́бус *m.*
bush куст *m.*
business де́ло *n.*, заня́тие *n.*
busy за́нятый
but *conj.* но, а; *prep.* кро́ме; *adv.* лишь
butcher мясни́к *m.*
butter ма́сло *n.*
butterfly ба́бочка *f.*
button пу́говица *f.*
button hole петля́ *f.*
buy, to покупа́ть, купи́ть
by *prep.* у, при, о́коло; *adv.* ря́дом; ми́мо
  ~ heart наизу́сть
  ~ and ~ вско́ре
  ~ the way кста́ти, ме́жду про́чим

C

cabbage капу́ста *f.*
cabin каю́та *f.*, каби́на *f.*
cable кана́т *m.*, ка́бель *m.*
cage кле́тка *f.*
cake торт *m.*, пиро́жное *n.*; кусо́к *m.*
calculation расчёт *m.*
calendar календа́рь *m.*
calf телёнок *m.*
call, to звать, по-; называ́ть, -зва́ть
  to ~ for тре́бовать, по-; заходи́ть, зайти́ за
  to ~ up звони́ть, по-
  to be ~ed называ́ться, -зва́ться
calm споко́йный
calm, to успока́ивать(ся), -ко́ить(ся)
camel верблю́д *m.*
camp ла́герь *m.*
can бидо́н *m.*, ба́нка *f.*
can мочь, с-
cancer рак *m.*
candle свеча́ *f.*
cane па́лка *f.*; камы́ш *m.*
cannon пу́шка *f.*
cap ша́пка *f.*, фура́жка *f.*
capable спосо́бный
capital столи́ца *f.*; капита́л *m.*
cape плащ *m.*; мыс *m.*
captain капита́н *m.*
capture, to захва́тывать, -ати́ть
car ваго́н *m.*; автомоби́ль *m.*
card ка́рта *f.*, ка́рточка *f.*
cardinal основно́й, гла́вный
care забо́та *f.*
  to take ~ of забо́титься, по-
careful осторо́жный, тща́тельный
careless беззабо́тный; небре́жный
caress ла́ска *f.*
caress, to ласка́ть *imp.*
cargo груз *m.*
carpet ковёр *m.*
carrot(s) морко́вь *f.*
carry, to носи́ть *imp.*; нести́, поto ~ on продолжа́ть, -до́лжить

to ~ out выполня́ть, вы́полнить

cart теле́га f.

cartoon карикату́ра f.

case я́щик m.; слу́чай
in any ~ во вся́ком слу́чае

cashier касси́р m.

cast iron чугу́н m.

castle за́мок m.

cat кот m., ко́шка f.

catch, to лови́ть, пойма́ть; схва́тывать, -ати́ть
to ~ cold простужа́ться, -уди́ться

cathedral собо́р m.

cattle скот m.

Caucasian кавка́зский

Caucasus Кавка́з m.

cauliflower цветна́я капу́ста f.

cause причи́на f., по́вод m.

cause, to причиня́ть, -ни́ть

caviar икра́ f.

ceiling потоло́к m.

cellar подва́л m.

cemetery кла́дбище

center центр m.

central центра́льный

century век m., столе́тие n.

certain определённый
a ~ не́который, не́кий

certainly непреме́нно, наве́рно

chain цепь f.

chair стул m.

chairman председа́тель m.

chalk мел m.

challenge, to вызыва́ть, вы́звать

chamber пала́та f.; ка́мера f.

champagne шампа́нское n.

chance возмо́жность f., слу́чай m.
by ~ случа́йно

change переме́на f.; переса́дка f.; сда́ча f.

change, to меня́ть(ся), об-, по-, переменя́ть, -ни́ть; (money) разме́нивать, -меня́ть

chap па́рень m.

chapter глава́ f.

character хара́ктер m.

charge, free of беспла́тно

charming очарова́тельный, преле́стный

chatter, to болта́ть imp.

chauffeur шофёр m.

cheap дешёвый

cheaply дёшево

check чек m.; номеро́к m.

check, to проверя́ть, -ве́рить
to ~ the luggage сдава́ть, сдать бага́ж

cheek щека́ f.

cheerful бо́дрый, весёлый

cheese сыр m.

cherry ви́шня f.

chess ша́хматы m. pl.

chest грудь f.; я́щик m.

chestnut кашта́н m.

chicken ку́рица f.; цыплёнок m.

chief нача́льник m., руководи́тель m.; adj. гла́вный

child ребёнок m.

childhood де́тство n.

childish де́тский

children де́ти pl.

chimney труба́ f.

china фарфо́р m.

chocolate шокола́д m.

choice вы́бор m.

choose, to выбира́ть, вы́брать

chop котле́та f.

Christmas рождество́ n.

church це́рковь f.

cigarette папиро́са f.

cinema кино́ n.

circle круг m.

circumstance обстоя́тельство n.

citizen граждани́н m., -а́нка f.

city (большо́й) го́род m.

claim тре́бование n.; прете́нзия f.

claim, to тре́бовать, по-

class класс m.

clean чи́стый

clean, to чи́стить, вы́-
to ~ up убира́ть, убра́ть

clear я́сный, све́тлый, поня́тный

clerk чино́вник m., слу́жащий m.

clever у́мный

climb, to ла́зить imp.; лезть, по-

cloak-room ка́мера хране́ния

clock часы́ m. pl.

close бли́зкий

close, to закрыва́ть(ся), -кры́ть(ся)

cloth ткань f.; сукно́ n.; ска́терть f.

clothed одéтый
clothes одéжда *f.*, плáтье *n.*
cloud óблако *n.*, тýча *f.*
club клуб *n.*
coal ýголь *m.*
coast морскóй бéрег *m.*, побе-
рéжье *n.*
coat пальтó *n. indecl.*
cocoa какáо *n*
coffee кóфе *n. indecl.*
coincidence совпадéние *n.*
cold хóлод *m.*; простýда *f.*;
adj. холóдный
it's ~ хóлодно
collapse обвáл *m.*, провáл *m.*
collar воротнѝк *m.*
color цвет *m.*
colored цветнóй
comb грéбень *m.*; гребёнка *f.*
come, to приходѝть, прийтѝ;
приезжáть, -éхать
comedy комéдия *f.*
comfortable удóбный
comical смешнóй
command прикáз *m.*
command, to прикáзывать,
-казáть; комáндовать *imp.*
commodity товáр *m.*
common óбщий
communicate, to сообщáть, -щѝть
communication сообщéние *n.*
company óбщество *n.*
comparative сравнѝтельный
compare, to срáвнивать, сравнѝть
comparison сравнéние *n.*
compartment отделéние *n.*;
купé *n.*
compassion сострадáние *n.*
compel, to заставлять, -áвить;
вынуждáть, вынудить
compile, to составлять -áвить
complain, to жáловаться, по
complaint жáлоба *f.*
complete пóлный
completely совершéнно
complicated слóжный
compose, to составлять, -áвить
composer композѝтор *m.*
comrade товáрищ *m.*
conceal, to скрывáть, скрыть
concerning касáтельно, относѝ-
тельно

conclude, to заключáть, -чѝть;
дéлать, с- вывод
conclusion заключéние *n.*; вывод *m.*
condition услóвие *n.*; состояние
n.; *pl.* обстоятельства *n. pl.*
conductor кондýктор *m.*; дири-
жёр *m.*
confess, to признавáться, -знáть-
ся
confidence довéрие *n.*
confirm, to подтверждáть, -рдѝть
conformity соотвéтствие *n.*
congratulate, to поздравлять,
-áвить
congress съезд *m.*, конгрéсс *m.*
connection связь *f.*
conquer, to завоёвывать, -воевáть
conscience сóвесть *f.*
consciousness сознáние *n.*
consent, to соглашáться, -асѝться
consequently слéдовательно
consider, to считáть, счесть;
рассмáтривать, -смотрéть
consideration, to take into принимáть, -нять во внимáние
consist of, to состоять *imp.* из
conspiracy зáговор *m.*
constant постоянный
construct стрóить, по-
contain, to содержáть *imp.*
content довóльный
contents содержáние *n.*
continue,   to продолжáть(ся),
-дóлжить(ся)
contract договóр *m.*
contrary протѝвный
on the ~ наоборóт
convenient удóбный
conversation разговóр *m.*, бесéда *f.*
convert, to превращáть, -атѝть;
обращáть, -атѝть
convey, to перевозѝть, -везтѝ
conviction убеждéние *n.*
convince, to убеждáть, убедѝть
cook, to варѝть, с-; готóвить
imp.
cool прохлáдный
copper медь *f.*
copy-book тетрáдь *f.*
cord верёвка *f.*

cordial *adj.* серде́чный; ликёр *m.*
cork про́бка *f.*
corkscrew што́пор *m.*
corn кукуру́за *f.*
corner у́гол *m.*
correct пра́вильный
correct, to поправля́ть, -а́вить
correspondence перепи́ска *f.*
corridor коридо́р *m.*
cost, to сто́ить *imp.*
costume костю́м *m.*
cottage да́ча *f.*
cotton хло́пок *m.; adj.* хлопчато-
    бума́жный
cough ка́шель *m.*
cough, to ка́шлять, за-
council сове́т *m.*
counsel сове́т *m.;* совеща́ние *n.*
count, to счита́ть, счесть
    to ~ on рассчи́тывать, -ита́ть
country страна́ *f.;* дере́вня *f.*
couple па́ра *f.;* чета́ *f.*
courage хра́брость *f.*
course курс *m.;* ход *m.,* тече́ние *n.*
    of ~ коне́чно
court двор *m.;* суд *m.;* корт *m.*
cousin двою́родный брат *m.;*
    двою́родная сестра́ *f.*
cover, to покрыва́ть, -кры́ть
cow коро́ва *f.*
cozy ую́тный
cradle колыбе́ль *f.*
craftsman реме́сленник *m.*
crane жура́вль *m.*
crayfish рак *m.*
cream крем *m.*
create, to создава́ть, -да́ть
creation созда́ние *n.*
creature существо́ *n.*
criminal престу́пный
cross крест *m.*
cross, to переходи́ть, перейти́
crowd толпа́ *f.*
crown коро́на *f.*
cruel жесто́кий
cry крик *m.;* плач *m.*
cry, to крича́ть, кри́кнуть; пла́-
    кать, за-
cucumber огуре́ц *m.*
culture культу́ра *f.*
cunning хи́трый
cup ча́шка *f.*

curiosity любопы́тство *n.*
curious любопы́тный; стра́нный
current тече́ние *n.;* ток *m.; adj.*
    теку́щий
curtain за́навес *m.,* занаве́ска *f.*
cushion поду́шка *f.*
custom обы́чай *m.*
customary обыкнове́нный, обы́ч-
    ный
custom-house тамо́жня *f.*
customs по́шлина *f.*
cut, to ре́зать, раз-, с-; руби́ть
    imp.; (hair) стричь *imp.*
    to ~ out выреза́ть, вы́-
cutlet котле́та *f.*
czar царь *m.*

D

daily ежедне́вный
damage вред *m.;* уще́рб *m.*
damp сыро́й, вла́жный
dance та́нец *m.*
dance, to танцева́ть, по-
danger опа́сность *f.*
dangerous опа́сный
dare, to сметь, по-
daring сме́лый, отва́жный
dark тёмный
darkness темнота́ *f.*
darling голу́бчик *m.*
date да́та *f.;* свида́ние *n.*
    up to ~ совреме́нный
daughter дочь *f.,* до́чка *f.*
day день *m.*
    ~ off выходно́й день
dead мёртвый
deaf глухо́й
dealer торго́вец *m.*
dear дорого́й
death смерть *f.*
debate спор *m.*
debt долг *m.*
December дека́брь *m.*
decent прили́чный
decide, to реша́ть, -ши́ть
decision реше́ние *n.*
deck па́луба *f.*
declare, to заявля́ть, -ви́ть
deep глубо́кий
deeply глубоко́
deer оле́нь *m.*
defeat пораже́ние *n.*

defense защита *f.*

define, to определять, -лить

definite определённый

definitely решительно

degree степень *f.*; градус *m.*

delay задержка *f.*; опоздание *n.*

delight восторг *m.*

delightful восхитительный

deliver, to доставлять, -авить

deliverance избавление *n.*

demand требование *n.*; спрос *m.*

demand, to требовать, по-

dense густой, плотный

dentist зубной врач *m.*

depart, to отбывать, -быть; уезжать, уехать

department отдел *m.*; министерство *n.*

department store универсальный магазин *m.*

departure отъезд *m.*

depend on, to зависеть *imp.* от

deposit задаток *m.*

depth глубина *f.*

describe, to описывать, описать

description описание *n.*

desert пустыня *f.*

deserve, to заслуживать, -ужить

design замысел *m.*; чертёж *m.*; узор *m.*

desire желание *n.*

desk письменный стол *m.*

despair отчаяние *n.*

dessert десерт *m.*

destiny судьба *f.*

destroy, to разрушать, -шить

detachment отряд *m.*

detail подробность *f.*, деталь *f.*

determine, to определять, -лить

develop, to развивать(ся), -вить-(ся); (*photo*) проявлять, -вить

devil чёрт *m.*

dictionary словарь *m.*

die, to умирать, умереть

differ, to отличать(ся), -читься

difference разница *f.*

different различный, разный

difficult трудный

difficulty затруднение *n.*

dignity достоинство *n.*

diligent прилежный

dimension размер *m.*

dine, to обедать, по-

dining car вагон-ресторан *m.*

dinner обед *m.*

direct прямой

direct, to направлять, -авить

direction направление *n.*

directly прямо; тотчас

director директор *m.*

dirt грязь *f.*

dirty грязный

disappear, to исчезать, -чезнуть

disappoint, to разочаровывать, -овать

disaster несчастье *n.*, бедствие *n.*

discount скидка *f.*

discovery открытие *n.*

dish блюдо *n.*

display, to выставлять, -авить, проявлять, -вить

dispose, to располагать, -ложить

disposition характер *m.*

distance расстояние *n.*

distant отдалённый

distinct ясный, отчётливый

distress горе *n.*; нужда *f.*; бедствие *n.*

distribute, to распределять, -лить

district область *f.*, район *m.*, округ *m.*

disturb, to беспокоить, о-; мешать, по-

ditch канава *f.*

divide, to делить, по-, раз-

division деление *f.*; раздел *m.*

do, to делать, с-
how do you ~ здравствуйте

doctor врач *m.*, доктор *m.*

document документ *m.*

dog собака *f.*

doll кукла *f.*

dollar доллар *m.*

domestic домашний

donkey осёл *m.*

door дверь *f.*

doorstep крыльцо *n.*

dot точка *f.*

double двойной

doubt сомнение *n.*

doubt, to сомневаться, усомниться

down *adv.* вниз, внизу; *prep.* вниз; по

downstairs вниз; внизу́
dozen дю́жина *f.*
draft сквозня́к *m.*
drag, to тащи́ть, вы́-
drama дра́ма *f.*
draw, to тяну́ть, по-
drawer я́щик *m.*
dream сон *m.*; мечта́ *f.*
dress пла́тье *n.*; оде́жда *f.*
dress, to одева́ть(ся), оде́ть(ся)
dressed оде́тый
dressmaker портни́ха *f.*
dried сушёный
drink питьё *n.*; напи́ток *m.*
drink, to пить, вы́-
drive пое́здка *f.*; езда́ *f.*
drive, to гнать, по-; е́хать, по-
driver води́тель *m.*
drop ка́пля *f.*
drop, to опуска́ть, -сти́ть
  to ~ by заходи́ть, зайти́
drugstore апте́ка *f.*
drunk пья́ный
dry сухо́й
dry, to суши́ть, вы́-
duck у́тка *f.*
due до́лжный
  ~ to благодаря́, всле́дствие
during во вре́мя, в тече́ние, в продолже́ние
dust пыль *f.*
duty долг *m.*; обя́занность *f.*; по́шлина *f.*
dwarf ка́рлик *m.*
dye, to кра́сить, о-

E

each ка́ждый
eagle орёл *m.*
ear у́хо *n.*
early ра́нний; *adv.* ра́но
earnest серьёзный
earth земля́ *f.*
earthly земно́й
east восто́к *m.*
eastern восто́чный
easily легко́
easy лёгкий
eat, to есть, съ-; ку́шать, по-
edible съедо́бный
educated образо́ванный

education образова́ние *n.*, воспита́ние *n.*
effort уси́лие *n.*
e.g. напр. (наприме́р)
egg яйцо́ *n*
  fried ~ яи́чница-глазу́нья
eight во́семь
eighteen восемна́дцать
eighth восьмо́й
eight hundred восемьсо́т
eighty во́семьдесят
either... or и́ли ... и́ли
elastic рези́нка *f.*
elbow ло́коть *m.*
elect, to выбира́ть, вы́брать; избира́ть, -бра́ть
electric электри́ческий
elephant слоа *m.*
elpehant слон *m.*
elevator лифт *m.*
eleven оди́ннадцать
else ина́че; ещё
embassy посо́льство *n.*
embroidery вы́шивка *f.*
emergency exit запасно́й вы́ход
empire импе́рия *f.*
empty пусто́й
encounter встре́ча *f.*
encourage, to ободря́ть, -ри́ть
end коне́ц *m.*
end, to конча́ть(ся), ко́нчить(ся)
endeavor, to пыта́ться, по-; стара́ться, по-
endurance выно́сливость *f.*, терпе́ние *n.*
enemy враг *m.*
energy эне́ргия *f.*
engage, to нанима́ть, -ня́ть
  to be ~d быть за́нятым
engine мото́р *m.*, дви́гатель *m.*; парово́з *m.*
England А́нглия *f.*
English англи́йский
Englishman англича́нин *m.*
Englishwoman англича́нка *f.*
enjoy, to наслажда́ться, -ади́ться
enormous грома́дный
enough дово́льно, доста́точно
enter, to входи́ть, войти́; вступа́ть, -пи́ть
enterprise предприя́тие *n.*

entertain, to развлекáть, -влéчь; угощáть, угостúть
entire цéлый, весь
entirely вполнé, совершéнно
entrance вход *m.*
envelope конвéрт *m.*
envy зáвисть *f.*
epoch эпóха *f.*
equal рáвный
equality рáвенство *n.*
equipment оборýдование *n.*
escape, to бежáть *imp. & perf.*
especially осóбенно
essay óчерк *m.*; попýтка *f.*
essence сýщность *f.*
esteem уважéние *n.*
esteem, to уважáть *imp.*
etc. и т.д., и т.п. (и так дáлее, и томý подóбное)
eternal вéчный
Europe Еврóпа *f.*
even дáже; рóвный
evening вéчер *m.*
    in the ~ вéчером, по вечерáм
event событие *n.*
ever когдá-либо
    for ~ навсегдá
every кáждый, всякий
everybody кáждый, все *pl.*
everything всё
everywhere вездé, (по)всюду
evidently по-вúдимому
evil зло *n.*; *adj.* дурнóй
exactly тóчно, рóвно; úменно
examination экзáмен *m.*; осмóтр *m.*
examine, to осмáтривать, осмотрéть
example примéр *m.*; образéц *m.*
    for ~ напримéр
excellent превосхóдный, отлúчный
except крóме
exception исключéние *n.*
excess излúшек *m.*
exchange, to обмéнивать, -нúть *or* -нять
exclaim, to восклицáть, -úкнуть
excuse, to извинять, -нúть
exhausted измýченный
exhibition выставка *f.*
exist, to существовáть *imp.*

existence существовáние *n.*
exit выход *m.*
expect, to ожидáть *imp.*
expectation ожидáние *n.*
expense расхóд *m.*
expensive дорогóй
experience óпыт *m.*
experienced óпытный
expert знатóк *m.*, экспéрт *m.*
explain, to объяснять, -нúть
explanation объяснéние *n.*
export экспорт *m.*, вывоз *m.*
express срóчный
express, to выражáть, выразить
expression выражéние *n.*
express train экспрéсс *m.*
expulsion исключéние *n.*
extend, to простирáться, -стерéться; протягивать(ся), -тянýть(ся); продлевáть, -длúть
extension продлéние *n.*
extent протяжéние *n.*
    to what ~ до какóй стéпени
external внéшний
extraordinary чрезвычáйный
extremely чрезвычáйно, крáйне
eye глаз *m.*
eyebrow бровь *f.*
eyeglasses очкú *m. pl.*

F

face лицó *n.*
fact факт *m.*
factory фáбрика *f.*, завóд *m.*
fair справедлúвый; прекрáсный
fairy tale скáзка *f.*
faith вéра *f.*
faithful вéрный
fall óсень *f.*
fall, to пáдать, (у)пáсть
    to ~ asleep засыпáть, -спáть
    to ~ in love влюблять ся, -бúться
false лóжный; фальшúвый
fame слáва *f.*
familiar знакóмый
family семья *f.*
famous знаменúтый, извéстный
far далёкий; *adv.* далекó
farmer фéрмер *m.*
fashion мóда *f.*

fast ско́рый, бы́стрый; *adv.* бы́стро
  to be ~ (*watch*) спеши́ть
fasten, to прикрепля́ть, -пи́ть
fat жир *m.*, са́ло *n.*; *adj.* жи́рный; то́лстый
fate судьба́ *f.*, до́ля *f.*
father оте́ц *m.*
  ~-in-law тесть *m.*; свёкор *m.*
fault вина́ *f.*, оши́бка *f.*
favorable благоприя́тный
fear страх *m.*
feather перо́ *n.*
feature осо́бенность *f.*
February февра́ль *m.*
feeble сла́бый
feed, to корми́ть, на-
feel, to чу́вствовать(ся), по-
feeling чу́вство *n.*
fellow па́рень *m.*
female же́нский
feminine же́нский
ferry па́ром *m.*
fetch, to достава́ть, -та́ть; приноси́ть, -нести́
fever жар *m.*, лихора́дка *f.*
few ма́ло
  a ~ не́сколько
field по́ле *n.*; о́бласть *f.*
fifteen пятна́дцать
fifth пя́тый
fifty пятьдеся́т
fight бой *m.*, дра́ка *f.*
fight, to боро́ться, по-; дра́ться, по-
figure фигу́ра *f.*; ци́фра *f.*
fill, to наполня́ть(ся), -по́лнить(ся)
  to ~ out заполня́ть -по́лнить
film плёнка *f.*; фильм *m.*
final коне́чный
finally наконе́ц
find, to находи́ть, найти́
  to ~ in заставать, -ста́ть
  to ~ out узнава́ть, узна́ть
  to be found находи́ться, найти́сь
fine прекра́сный; ме́лкий
finger па́лец *m.*
finish, to конча́ть(ся) ко́нчить(ся)
fir ель *f.*
fire ого́нь *m.*; пожа́р *m.*

firm фи́рма *f.*; *adj.* кре́пкий
first пе́рвый
  at ~ снача́ла
  in the ~ place во-пе́рвых
  the ~ time впервы́е
fish ры́ба *f.*
fishing rod уди́лище *n.*
fist кула́к *m.*
fit, to годи́ться, при-; подходи́ть, подойти́
five пять
five hundred пятьсо́т
flag флаг *m.*
flame пла́мя *n.*
flashlight фона́рь *m.*
flee, to бежа́ть *imp. & perf.*
fleet флот *m.*
flight полёт *m.*; бе́гство *n.*
floor эта́ж *m.*; пол *m.*
flour мука́ *f.*
flower цвето́к *m.*
fluently свобо́дно, бе́гло
fly му́ха *f.*
fly, to лета́ть *imp.*; лете́ть. по-
fog тума́н *m.*
fold, to скла́дывать, сложи́ть
folk(s) лю́ди *pl.*
follow, to сле́довать, по-
following сле́дующий
food пи́ща *f.*, еда́ *f.*
fool дура́к, *m.*, ду́ра *f.*
foolish глу́пый
foot нога́ *f.*
  on ~ пешко́м
football футбо́л *m.*
for *prep.* для; из-за; на; в тече́ние; за; *conj.* потому́ что, так как
forbid, to запреща́ть, -ети́ть
force си́ла *f.*
force, to заставля́ть, -а́вить
forehead лоб *m.*
foreign иностра́нный
foreigner иностра́нец, *m.*, иностра́нка *f.*
foreman ма́стер *m.*
forest лес *m.*
forget, to забыва́ть, -бы́ть
forgive, to проща́ть, прости́ть
fork ви́лка *f.*
form фо́рма *f.*; бланк *m.*; класс *m.*

form, to образо́вывать, -ова́ть
former пре́жний
formerly пре́жде, когда́-то
fortnight две неде́ли
fortunately к сча́стью
fortune состоя́ние *n.*
forty со́рок
forward вперёд; впредь
forward to отправля́ть, -а́вить
found, to осно́вывать, -ова́ть
fountain фонта́н *m.*
fountain pen авторучка *f.*
four четы́ре; че́тверо
four hundred четы́реста
fourteen четы́рнадцать
fourth четвёртый
fox лиси́ца *f.*
France Фра́нция *f.*
free свобо́дный
  ~ of charge беспла́тный
freedom свобо́да *f.*
freeze, to замерза́ть, -мёрзнуть
freight груз *m.*
French францу́зский
frequently ча́сто
fresh све́жий
Friday пя́тница *f.*
friend друг *m.,* подру́га *f.*
friendly дру́жеский
friendship дру́жба *f.*
frighten, to пуга́ть, ис-
frightful стра́шный
from от, из, с; по
front пере́дняя сторона́; фронт
  m.; adj. пере́дний
  in ~ (of) впереди́, пе́ред
frontier грани́ца *f.*
frost моро́з *m.*
fruit фру́кты *m. pl.*
fry, to жа́рить, за-
fulfil, to исполня́ть, -по́лнить
fulfilment исполне́ние *n.*
full по́лный
fully вполне́, соверше́нно
function, to де́йствовать, по-
fund запа́с *m.*
fundamental основно́й
funeral по́хороны *f. pl.*
funny смешно́й, заба́вный;
  стра́нный
fur мех *m.*

furnish, to снабжа́ть, -бди́ть;
  мебли́ровать *imp. & perf.*
furniture ме́бель *f.,* обстано́вка *f.*
further да́льше; дальне́йший
future бу́дущее *n.; adj.* бу́ду-
  щий

G

gaily ·ве́село
gain, to выи́грывать, вы́играть
gallery галере́я *f.*
game игра́ *f.*
garage гара́ж *m.*
garden сад *m.*
gasoline бензи́н *m.*
gas station запра́вочный пункт
  m.
gate(way) воро́та *pl.*
gather, to собира́ть(ся), -бра́ть-
  (ся)
gay весёлый
gear приспособле́ние *n.*
gender род *m.*
general генера́л *m.; adj.* о́бщий
generally, in general вообще́м,
  вообще́
gentleman господи́н *m.*
genuine по́длинный, настоя́щий
geography геогра́фия *f.*
geometry геоме́трия *f.*
German не́мец *m.,* не́мка *f.; adj.*
  неме́цкий
Germany Герма́ния *f.*
get, to получа́ть, -чи́ть; доста-
  ва́ть, -ста́ть; станови́ться,
  стать
  to ~ in входи́ть, войти́
  to ~ off сходи́ть, сойти́
  to ~ on пожива́ть *imp.*
  to ~ out выходи́ть, вы́йти
  to ~ up встава́ть, встать
giant велика́н *m.*
gift пода́рок *m.,* дар *m.*
girl де́вушка *f.;* де́вочка *f.*
give, to дава́ть, дать; подава́ть,
  -да́ть
  to ~ back отдава́ть, -да́ть
  to ~ in уступа́ть, -пи́ть
  to ~ up сдава́ть, сдать; бро-
  са́ть, бро́сить
glad рад
  to be ~ ра́доваться, об-

glance взгляд *m.*

glass стекло *n.*; стакан *m.*; *pl.* очки *m. pl.*

glide, to скользить, -знуть

glitter, to блестеть, -снуть

globe шар *m.*

glorious славный

glory слава *f.*

glow, to пылать, вос-

go, to ходить *imp.*; итти (идти), пойти; ехать, поto ~ away уходить, уйти; уезжать, уехать
to ~ in входить, войти
to ~ on продолжать, -должить
to ~ out выходить, выйти
to ~ up подниматься, -няться

God бог *m.*

gold золото *n.*

golden золотой

good хороший; добрый

goods товары *m. pl.*

goose гусь *m.*

government правитлеьство *n.*

grade степень *f.*; сорт *m.*; класс *m.*

gradually постепенно

grand замечательный

granddaughter внучка *f.*

grandfather дедушка *m.*

grandmother бабушка *f.*

grandson внук *m.*

grape виноград *m.*

grass трава *f.*

grateful благодарный

grave могила *f.*

gray серый, седой

grease жир *m.*; смазка *f.*

grease, to смазывать, смазать

great большой, великий

greedy жадный

green зелёный

greet, to приветствовать *imp.*; кланяться, поклониться

greeting привет *m.*, поклон *m.*

grief горе *n.*

grocer бакалейщик *m.*

ground почва *f.*; основание *n.*

ground floor нижний этаж

group группа *f.*

grow, to расти, вы-; выращивать, вырастить; становиться, стать

grown-up взрослый

growth рост *m.*

guarantee гарантия *f.*

guarantee, to гарантировать *imp.* & *perf.*

guard сторож *m.*; стража *f.*; *pl.* гвардия *f.*

guess, to угадывать, угадать; полагать *imp.*

guest гость *m.*

guide руководитель *m.*; проводник *m.*, гид *m.*; путеволитель *m.*

guilt вина *f.*

guilty виноватый

guitar гитара *f.*

gum камедь *f.*; резина *f.*

gun орудие *n.*, пушка *f.*; ружьё *n.*; револьвер *m.*

H

habit привычка *f.*, обычай *m.*

hailing, it is идёт град

hair волос *m.*; волосы *m. pl.*

hairdresser парикмахер *m.*

half половина *f.*

hall зал *m.*; передняя *f.*

ham ветчина *f.*

hammer молоток *m.*

hand рука *f.*

hand, to передавать, -дать; вручать, -чить

handbook справочник *m.*

handicraft ремесло *n.*

handkerchief носовой платок *m.*

handsome красивый

hang, to висеть *imp.*
to ~ up вешать, повесить

happen, to случаться, -читься

happiness счастье *n.*

happy счастливый, радостный

hard твёрдый, жёсткий; трудный, тяжёлый; суровый; *adv.* сильно; усердно

hardly едва (ли); с трудом

hare заяц *m.*

harm вред *m.*

harmless безобидный

harmony гармония *f.*

harsh жёсткий, грубый, резкий

hasten, to торопить(ся), по-

hastily поспешно

Why We Make This Generous Offer

There are three important reasons why the Institute for Language Study is pleased to make this special Free Record and Sample Lesson offer:

First, never before have there been so many fascinating opportunities open to those who speak foreign languages fluently. Besides the cultural and travel benefits, there are many practical dollars-and-cents advantages—and an ever-increasing number of interesting, well-paying jobs.

The Natural Method

Second, our long experience in the language field has convinced us that the "learn-by-listening" method is the fastest, most convenient and most effective one. It enables you to learn *naturally*—the way you learned English as a child. You acquire a perfect accent and perfect grammar—because that's all you hear.

Just Listen—and Learn

Finally, our professional standing in the field of languages has enabled us to make these generous arrangements with one of the foremost language schools—the inventors of the "learn-by-listening" method. And we are pleased to provide this service for those of our students who want to speak and understand a foreign language "like a native."

There is no obligation and *no salesman will call.* Just mail the card TODAY for your FREE Record.

What Others Say:

Bob Hope says... "I am studying the course in French ... I think it's a great way to study a language."

Enjoyed by Children "It is surprising how much our two children have absorbed by listening."
—Mrs. C.M.J.

"A Good Investment" "Just returned from Mexico ... Course good investment!"
—Phillips B. Iden

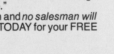

Institute for Language Study
71 Plymouth Street, Montclair, N.J. 07042

INSTITUTE FOR LANGUAGE STUDY Dept. HVP #9876
71 Plymouth Street, Montclair, N. J. 07042

Gentlemen:

Please have the originators of the famous "learn-by-listening" method send me, FREE, the Sample Record and Lesson in the one language checked below—also information which describes fully the complete course and method.

(Please check FREE Language Record and Lesson you wish)

☐ Spanish ☐ French ☐ German ☐ Italian ☐ Brazilian-Portuguese
☐ Russian ☐ Japanese ☐ Modern Greek ☐ English (for Spanish-or Portuguese-speaking people)
☐ Arabic

Name _____

Address _____

City _____ State _____

Zip Code _____ Phone _____

BK HVP/54321

BUSINESS REPLY CARD
FIRST CLASS   PERMIT NO. 1103   Montclair, N.J.

POSTAGE WILL BE PAID BY ADDRESSEE

Institute for Language Study
71 Plymouth Street
Montclair, NJ 07042

hat шля́па *f.*
hate, to ненави́деть, возненави́деть
hatred не́нависть *f.*
have, to име́ть *imp.*; получа́ть, -чи́ть;
I ~ to go я до́лжен итти́
he он
head голова́; глава́
headache головна́я боль *f.*
headlight фа́ра *f.*
health здоро́вье *n.*
healthy здоро́вый
hear, to слы́шать, у-
hearing слух *m.*
heart се́рдце *n.*
by ~ наизу́сть
hearty серде́чный
heat жара́ *f.*, тепло́ *n.*
heaven не́бо *n.*
heavy тяжёлый; *adv.* тяжело́
heel каблу́к *m.*
height высота́ *f.*; вышина́ *f.*
hell ад *m.*
hello! алло́!
help по́мощь *f.*; прислу́га *f.*
help, to помога́ть, -мо́чь
her её; свой
here здесь, тут
(to) ~ сюда́
from ~ отсю́да
~ you are вот, пожа́луйста
hereby, herewith э́тим; при сём
hero геро́й *m.*
hide шку́ра *f.*
hide, to пря́тать(ся), с-; скрыва́ть(ся), скрыть(ся)
high высо́кий; *adv.* высоко́
highly весьма́
high school сре́дняя шко́ла *f.*
highway автостра́да *f.*
hill холм *m.*
hinder, to меша́ть, по-
hire, to нанима́ть, -ня́ть
for ~ напрока́т
his его́; свой
historic(al) истори́ческий
history исто́рия *f.*
hit, to ударя́ть, уда́рить; попада́ть, -па́сть
hoarse хри́плый

to hold держа́ть(ся), поto ~ out выде́рживать, вы́держать
to ~ up заде́рживать, -держа́ть
hole дыра́, ды́рка
holiday пра́здник *m.*; *pl.* кани́кулы *f. pl.*
holy свято́й
home дом *m.*; *adj.* дома́шний; *adv.* домо́й
honest че́стный
honey мёд *m.*
honor честь *f.*
hook крючо́к *m.*
hope наде́жда *f.*
hope, to наде́яться *imp.*
horizon горизо́нт *m.*
horror у́жас *m.*
horse ло́шадь *f.*, конь *m.*
horseback, on верхо́м
hospital больни́ца *f.*, го́спиталь *m.*
host хозя́ин *m.*
hostess хозя́йка *f.*
hot горя́чий; жа́ркий
hotel гости́ница *f.*
hour час *m.*
house дом *m.*; пала́та *f.*
housekeeping (дома́шнее) хозя́йство *n.*
housewife дома́шняя хозя́йка *f.*
how как, каки́м о́бразом
~ many, ~ much ско́лько
however одна́ко, всё-таки
huge огро́мный
human челове́ческий
humanity челове́чество *n.*
humor ю́мор *m.*
hundred сто; со́тня
hundredth со́тый
hunger го́лод *m.*
hungry голо́дный
hunt охо́та *f.*
hurry, in a второпя́х
hurry, to спеши́ть, по-; торопи́ть(ся), по-
~ up! скоре́е!
hurt, to причиня́ть, -ни́ть боль; боле́ть *imp.*
husband муж *m.*
hydrogen водоро́д *m.*

I

I я
ice лёд *m.*
ice cream мороженое *n.*
idea идея *f.*, мысль *f.*, понятие *n.*
identical одинаковый
i.e. т.е. (то-есть)
if если
ill больной
illness болезнь *f.*
image образ *m,*
imagine, to представлять, -авить себе
immediately немедленно
immense огромный
import импорт *m.*, ввоз *m.*
important важный
impossible, it is невозможно
impression впечатление *n.*
imprisonment заключение *n.*
improbable, it is мало вероятно, вряд ли
improve, to улучшать(ся), улучшить(ся)
impulse порыв *m.*, побуждение *n.*
in *prep.* в, во; *adv.* внутри; внутрь
inadequate недостаточный
inasmuch as поскольку
incapable неспособный
inclination склонность *f.*
include, to включать, -чить
incomprehensible непонятный
incorrect неправильный
indeed в самом деле, действительно
increase, to увеличивать(ся), -ичить(ся)
indicate, to указывать, указать
indirect косвенный
individual личный
inflammation воспаление *n.*
influence влияние *n.*
inform, to сообщать, -щить
information справка *f.*, сведения *n. pl.*
inhabitant обитатель *m.*
ink чернила *n. pl.*
inn трактир *m.*
inner внутренний
innocent невинный
innumerable бесчисленный

inquire, to спрашивать, спросить
insane душевнобольной
inscription надпись *f.*
insect насекомое *n.*
inside внутри, внутрь
insolent дерзкий, наглый
inspect, to осматривать, осмотреть
inspection осмотр *m.*
inspiration вдохновление *n.*
install to устраивать, -роить
instalments, by в рассрочку
instance, for например
instant мгновение *n.*
instantly сейчас же
instead of вместо; вместо того, чтобы
institution учреждение *n.*
instructive поучительный
instrument прибор *m.*, инструмент *m.*
insufficiently недостаточно
insult обида *f.*; оскорбление *n.*
insurance страхование *n.*
insure, to страховать, за-
intelligent умный, толковый
intend, to намереваться *imp.*
intention намерение *n.*
interest интерес *m.*
interest, to заинтересовывать, -совать
    to be ~ed интересоваться *imp.*
interesting интересный
internal внутренний
international международный
interpreter переводчик *m.*
interrupt, to перебивать, -бить; прерывать, -рвать
interview интервью *n.*
intimate интимный; близкий
into, в, во
introduce, to вводить, ввести; представлять, -авить; знакомить, (п)о-
introduction введение *n.*
invasion вторжение *n.*, нашествие *n.*
investigate, to исследовать *imp. & perf.*
investigation исследование *n.*

investment (капитало)вложе́ние *n.*
invisible неви́димый
invitation приглаше́ние *n.*
invite, to приглаша́ть, -аси́ть
involuntarily нево́льно
iron желе́за *f.*; утю́г *m.*
iron, to гла́дить, вы-
ironic(al) ирони́ческий
irregular непра́вильный
irritate, to раздража́ть, -жи́ть
island, isle о́стров *m.*
issue вы́ход *m.*; вы́пуск *m.*
it он, она́, оно́; э́то
item пункт *m.*; статья́ *f.*; но́мер *m.*
itinerary путеводи́тель *m.*
its его́, её; свой

J

jacket жаке́т *m.*, ку́ртка *f.*
jam варе́нье *n*
January янва́рь *m.*
jar ба́нка *f.*; кувши́н *m.*
jewel драгоце́нный ка́мень *m.*
job рабо́та *f.*, слу́жба *f.*
join, to присоединя́ть(ся), -ни́ть-(ся)
joke шу́тка *f.*
joke, to шути́ть, по-
journal журна́л *m.*
journalist журнали́ст *m.*
journey путеше́ствие *n.*; пое́зд-ка *f.*
joy ра́дость *f.*
joyful ра́достный
jubilee юбиле́й *m.*
judge судья́ *m.*
judge, to суди́ть *imp.*
juice сок *m.*
July июль *m.*
jump, to пры́гать, -гнуть
    to ~ up вска́кивать, вскочи́ть
junction у́зел *m.*, узлова́я ста́нция *f.*
June июнь *m.*
just *adj.* справедли́вый; *adv.* точно, и́менно, как раз; то́лько что
    ~ now сейча́с
justify, to опра́вдывать, -вда́ть

K

keep, to держа́ть(ся), по-; со-храня́ть(ся), -ни́ть(ся)
key ключ *m.*
kill, to убива́ть, уби́ть
killer уби́йца *m.* & *f.*
kind сорт *m.*, вид *m.*, род *m.*
kind любе́зный, до́брый, ми́лый
kindly ла́сково, любе́зно
king коро́ль *m.*
kingdom короле́вство *n.*, ца́рст-во *n.*
kiss поцелу́й *m.*
kiss, to целова́ть, по-
kitchen ку́хня *f.*
knee коле́но *n.*
knife нож *m.*
knit, to вяза́ть, с-
knock, to стуча́ть, по-
    to ~ down сбива́ть, сбить с ног
know, to знать *imp.*
knowledge зна́ние *n.*
kopek копе́йка *f.*

L

label ярлы́к
labor труд *m.*, рабо́та *f.*
lace кру́жево *n.*
lack отсу́тствие *n.*, недоста́ток *m.*
ladder ле́стница *f.*
lady да́ма *f.*
lake о́зеро *n.*
lamb ягнёнок *m.*
lamp ла́мпа *f.*
land страна́ *f.*; земля́ *f.*
land, to приземля́ться, -ли́ться
landlady хозя́йка *f.*
landlord хозя́ин *m.*
lane переу́лок *m.*
language язы́к *m.*
lantern фона́рь *m.*
large большо́й, кру́пный
last после́дний; про́шлый
    at ~ наконе́ц
last, to дли́ться, про-
late по́здно
    to be ~ опа́здывать, опозда́ть
lately неда́вно, за после́днее вре́мя
later по́зже, пото́м

latest после́дний
laugh, to смея́ться, за-
laughter смех *m.*
laundry пра́чечная *f.*
lavatory убо́рная *f.*
law зако́н *m.*
lawn лужа́йка *f.*, газо́н *m.*
lawyer адвока́т *m.*, юри́ст *m.*
lay, to класть, положи́ть
lazy лени́вый
lead, to води́ть *imp.*; вести́, по-;
руководи́ть *imp.*
leader вождь *m.*, руководи́тель
m.
leaf лист *m.*
lean, to наклоня́ться, -ни́ться
  to ~ out высо́вываться, вы́сунуться
leap year висoко́сный год *m.*
learn, to учи́ть(ся), на-; узнава́ть,
узна́ть
leather ко́жа *f.*; ко́жаный *adj.*
leave, to покида́ть, -ки́нуть; уходи́ть, уйти́; уезжа́ть, уе́хать;
оставля́ть, -а́вить
  to ~ for отправля́ться, -а́виться
  to ~ out пропуска́ть, -сти́ть
lecture ле́кция *f.*
left ле́вый; *adv.* нале́во, сле́ва
leg нога́ *f.*
leisure до́суг *m.*
lemon лимо́н *m.*
lemonade лимона́д *m.*
length длина́ *f.*
lengthen, to удлиня́ть(ся), -ни́ть(ся)
less ме́нее, ме́ньше
lesson уро́к *m.*
let, to пуска́ть, пусти́ть
  to ~ in впуска́ть, -сти́ть
  to ~ out выпуска́ть, вы́пустить
  to ~ know сообща́ть, -щи́ть
  to ~ pass пропуска́ть, -сти́ть
letter бу́ква *f.*; письмо́ *n.*
  ~ of credit аккредити́в *m.*
lettuce сала́т *m.*
liberate, to освобожда́ть, -оди́ть
liberty свобо́да *f.*
library библиоте́ка *f.*
license лице́нзия *f.*

lie ложь *f.*
lie, to лга́ть, со-; врать, со-
lie, to лежа́ть, по-
  to ~ down ложи́ться, лечь
life жизнь *f.*
lift лифт
  to give a ~ подвози́ть, -везти́
lift, to поднима́ть, -ня́ть
light свет *m.*; *adj.* све́тлый;
лёгкий
light, to зажига́ть(ся). -же́чь(ся)
lighter зажига́лка *f.*
lightning мо́лния *f.*
like похо́жий, подо́бный; *adv.*
как
like, to люби́ть *imp.*
  I ~ мне нра́вится
  I would ~ я хоте́л бы
likely вероя́тно
limb член *m.*
lime ли́па *f.*
limit, to ограни́чивать, -чить
line ли́ния *f.*; строка́ *f.*; черта́ *f.*
linen полотно́ *n.*; бельё *n.*; *adj.*
полотня́ный
link звено́ *n.*
lion лев *m.*
lip губа́ *f.*
liquid жи́дкий
list спи́сок *m.*
listen, to слу́шать, по-
literature литерату́ра *f.*
little ма́ленький; ма́ло
  a ~ немно́го
live, to жить *imp.*
lively живо́й
liver пе́чень *f.*; печёнка *f.*
living room гости́ная *f.*
load, to заряжа́ть, -ряди́ть
lobster ома́р *m.*, рак *m.*
local ме́стный
lock замо́к *m.*
lock, to запира́ть(ся), -пере́ть(ся)
lonely одино́кий
long дли́нный; до́лгий; *adv.*
до́лго
  ~ ago давно́
longing тоска́ *f.*
look взгляд *m.*
look, to смотре́ть, по-; выгля́деть *imp.*
  to ~ after забо́титься, по-

to ~ around, back огля́дываться, -яну́ться
to ~ for иска́ть, по-
to ~ like каза́ться, по-
to ~ on наблюда́ть *imp.*
to ~ out остерега́ться, -ре́чься
to ~ over просма́тривать, -смотре́ть
to ~ up справля́ться, -а́виться
lorry грузови́к *m.*
lose, to теря́ть, по-; про́игрывать, -игра́ть
to ~ one's way заблужда́ться, -уди́ться
loss поте́ря *f.*; убы́ток *m.*
lost, to get пропада́ть -па́сть
lot жре́бий *m.*; до́ля *f.*
a ~ of мно́жество
loud гро́мкий; шу́мный
love любо́вь *f.*
in ~ with влюблённый в
love, to люби́ть *imp.*
low ни́зкий
lower ни́зший; ни́жний
lower, to опуска́ть, -сти́ть
lucky счастли́вый, уда́чный
luggage бага́ж *m.*
luggage room ка́мера хране́ния
lump кусо́к *m.*
lunch второ́й за́втрак *m.*
lung лёгкое *n.*
luxury ро́скошь *f.*

M

machine маши́на *f.*
mad сумасше́дший
magazine журна́л *m.*
mail по́чта *f.*
main гла́вный, основно́й
mainly гла́вным о́бразом
maintain, to подде́рживать, -держа́ть; содержа́ть *imp.*
maintenance содержа́ние *n.*
majority большинство́ *n.*
make, to де́лать, с-; заставля́ть, -а́вить
to ~up one's mind реша́ться, реши́ться
man мужчи́на *m.*; челове́к *m.*
manage, to управля́ть, -а́вить; заве́довать *imp.*; суме́ть *perf.*

manager заве́дующий *m.*, дире́ктор *m.*
manicure маникю́р *m.*
mankind челове́чество *n.*
manner спо́соб
in this ~ таки́м о́бразом
manual ручно́й
manufacture произво́дство *n.*
manuscript ру́копись *f.*
many мно́гие, мно́го
map ка́рта *f.*
March март *m.*
mark знак *m.*
market ры́нок *m.*
married жена́тый; заму́жняя
marry, to жени́ть(ся) *imp. & perf.*; выходи́ть, вы́йти за́муж; выдава́ть, вы́дать за́муж; венча́ть(ся), об-
marvelous чу́дный, чуде́сный
masculine мужско́й
mass ма́сса *f.*
massage масса́ж *m.*
master ма́стер *m.*; хозя́ин *m.*
master, to овладева́ть, -де́ть
masterpiece шеде́вр *m.*
match спи́чка *f.*; (*sports*) матч *m.*, состяза́ние *n.*
material материа́л *m.*; мате́рия *f.*
mathematics матема́тика *f.*
matter де́ло *n.*, вопро́с *m.*
what 's the ~? в чём де́ло?
as a ~ of fact на са́мом де́ле
it doesn't ~ нева́жно, ничего́
mattress матра́ц *m.*
May май *m.*
may мочь *imp.*
maybe мо́жет быть
meadow луг *m.*
meal еда́ *f.*, тра́пеза *f.*
mean, to зна́чить *imp.*
meaning значе́ние *n.*; смысл *m.*
means сре́дство *n.*
by ~ of посре́дством
by all ~ во что бы то ни ста́ло
by no ~ ни в ко́ем слу́чае
meantime, in the ме́жду тем, тем вре́менем
measure ме́ра *f.*
measure, to измеря́ть, -ме́рить

meat мя́со *n.*
mechanic меха́ник *m.*
medicine лека́рство *n.*
meet, to встреча́ть(ся), -е́тить(ся)
meeting встре́ча *f.*; собра́ние *n.*
melody мело́дия *f.*
melon ды́ня *f.*
member член *m.*
memory па́мять *f.*
mention, to упомина́ть, -мяну́ть
  don't ~ it не сто́ит благо-
  да́рности
menu меню́ *n. indecl.*
mercy ми́лость *f.*
merely то́лько, про́сто
merry весёлый
message сообще́ние *n.*, посла́-
  ние *n.*
metal мета́лл *m.*
meter метр *m.*
method ме́тод *m.*, спо́соб *m.*
midday по́лдень *m.*
middle середи́на; *adj.* сре́дний
  in the ~ of среди́
Middle Ages сре́дние века́ *m. pl.*
middleman посре́дник *m.*
midnight по́лночь *f.*
mighty могу́щественный
mild кро́ткий; мя́гкий
mile ми́ля *f.*
military вое́нный
milk молоко́ *n.*
million миллио́н *m.*
mind ум *m.*, ра́зум *m.*
  to bear in ~ име́ть в виду́
mind, to возража́ть, -ази́ть
  never ~! ничего́!
mineral минера́льный
minute мину́та *f.*
miracle чу́до *n.*
mirror зе́ркало *n.*
miserable жа́лкий
misfortune го́ре, *n.*, несча́стье *n.*
miss, to прома́хиваться, -мах-
  ну́ться; не попада́ть, не по-
  па́сть; пропуска́ть, -сти́ть;
  скуча́ть *imp.* по
missing недостаю́щий
mist тума́н *m.*
mistake оши́бка *f.*
mistress хозя́йка *f.*

misunderstanding недоразуме́ние
  n.
mixture смесь *f.*
modern совреме́нный
modest скро́мный
moment моме́нт *m.*
Monday понеде́льник *m.*
money де́ньги *f. pl.*
money order де́нежный перево́д *m.*
monkey обезья́на *m.*
month ме́сяц *m.*
monthly ежеме́сячный
monument па́мятник *m.*
mood настрое́ние *n.*
moon луна́ *f.*
moral нра́вственный
morals нра́вы *m. pl.*
more бо́лее, бо́льше
morning у́тро *n.*
most, the наибо́лее; са́мый
mostly ча́ще *or* бо́льше всего́
mother мать *f.*
  ~-in-law тёща *f.*; свекро́вь *f.*
motion ход *m.*, движе́ние *n.*
  in ~ на ходу́
motor дви́гатель *m.*, мото́р *m.*
motorboat мото́рная ло́дка *f.*
motorcar автомаши́на *f.*
motorcycle мотоци́кл *m.*
motor ship теплохо́д *m.*
mountain гора́ *f.*
mournful печа́льный
mouse мышь *f.*
moustache усы́ *m. pl.*
mouth рот *m.*
move, to дви́гать(ся), дви́нуть-
  (ся); переезжа́ть, -е́хать
movement движе́ние *n.*
movies кино́ *n.*
Mr. господи́н *m.*
Mrs. госпожа́ *f.*
much мно́го; гора́здо
  how much ско́лько
  so much сто́лько
mud грязь *f.*
muddy гря́зный
multiply, to умножа́ть, -о́жить
municipal городско́й
murder уби́йство *n.*
muscle му́скул *m.*, мы́шца *f.*
museum музе́й *m.*

mushroom гриб *m.*
music мýзыка *f.*
must дóлжен
mustard горчúца *f.*
mute немóй
mutton барáнина *f.*
mutual взаúмный
my мой, моя́, моё; мой
mysterious тайнственный
mystery тáйна *f.*

N

nail нóготь *m.*
naked гóлый
name úмя *n.;* назвáние *n.*
  family ~ фамúлия *f.*
name, to называ́ть, -звáть
  to be ~d называ́ться, -звáть-
  ся
namely тó-есть, úменно
napkin салфéтка *f.*
narrow ýзкий
nasty гáдкий, протúвный
nation нарóд *m.,* нáция *f.*
national нарóдный
native роднóй
  ~ land рóдина *f.*
natural естéственный
nature прирóда *f.*
naughty, to be шалúть *imp.*
navy (воéнный) флот *m.*
near блúзко, óколо
nearly почтú
necessary необходúмый, нýжный
necessity необходúмость *f.*
neck шéя *f.*
necklace ожерéлье *n.*
necktie гáлстук *m.*
need нуждá *f.*
need, to нуждáться *imp.*
needle игóлка *f.;* иглá *f.*
negative негатúв *m.; adj.* отри-
  цáтельный
neglect, to пренебрегáть, -брéчь
negotiations переговóры *m.pl.*
neighbor сосéд *m.,* сосéдка *f.*
neighboring сосéдний
neither... nor ни... ни
nephew племя́нник *m.*
nervous нéрвный
nest гнездó *n.*

never никогдá
nevertheless тем не мéнее
new нóвый
news нóвость *f.*
newspaper газéта *f.*
next бýдущий; слéдующий; ближáйший; *adv.* пóсле э́того
  ~ to ря́дом
nice прия́тный, хорóший
niece племя́нница *f.*
night ночь *f.; adj.* ночнóй
  at ~ нóчью
nightingale соловéй *m.*
nine дéвять
nine hundred девятьсóт
nineteen девятнáдцать
ninety девянóсто
ninth девя́тый
nitrogen азóт *m.*
no нет
noble благорóдный
nobody никтó
nod, to кивáть, кивнýть (голо-
  вóй)
noise шум *m.*
nominate, to назначáть, -áчить
none никакóй; ни одúн
nonsense вздор *m.,* чепухá *f.,*
  ерундá *f.*
noon пóлдень *m.*
norm нóрма *f.*
normal нормáльный
north сéвер *m.*
northern сéверный
nose нос *m.*
not не
not at all вóвсе не(т)
note запúска *f.*
nothing ничтó, ничегó
notice, to замечáть, -мéтить
notify, to извещáть, -вестúть
  уведомля́ть, уведомить
notion поня́тие *n.*
notwithstanding несмотря́ на
novel ромáн *m.*
November ноя́брь *m.*
now тепéрь, сейчáс
  ~ and then врéмя от врéмени
  just ~ тóлько что
nowhere нигдé; никудá
number числó *n.;* нóмер *m.*
numerous многочúсленный

nurse медсестра *f.*; няня *f.*
nut орех *m.*

O

oak дуб *m.*
oat(s) овёс *m.*
obedient послушный
obey, to слушаться, по-
object предмет *m.*
object, to возражать, -разить
objection возражение *n.*
obliged обязанный
observe, to наблюдать *imp.*
obstacle препятствие *n.*
obtain to получать, -чить
obviously очевидно
occasionally случайно
occupation занятие *n.*
occupy, to занимать, -нять
occur, to случаться, -читься;
  приходить, прийти на ум
October октябрь *m.*
odd странный
off с, со
  hands ~! руки прочь!
offend, to обижать, обидеть
offer предложение *n.*
offer, to предлагать, -ложить
office контора *f.*, бюро *n.*
officer офицер *m.*
official официальный
often часто
oil масло *n.*; нефть *f.*
oil, to смазывать, смазать
okay ладно
old старый
  how old are you? сколько вам
  лет?
omelette омлет *m.*
omit, to опускать, -стить
on на; в
once раз; однажды; когда-то
  ~ more ещё раз
  at ~ сразу
one один; некто
  ~ another друг друга
  ~ and a half полтора, -ры
oneself (самого) себя; -ся
onion лук *m.*
only *adv.* только; *adj.* единственный
open открытый
open, to открывать, -крыть

opera опера *f.*
operation операция *f.*; действие *n.*
opinion мнение *n.*
opponent противник *m.*
opportunity возможность *f.*
opposite *prep.* напротив
or или
orange апельсин *m.*
orchard фруктовый сад *m.*
orchestra оркестр *m.*
order заказ *m.*; приказ *m.*;
  строй *m.*
  to be in ~ быть в порядке
  in ~ to с тем, чтобы
order, to приказывать, -казать;
  заказывать, -казать
ordinary обыкновенный, обычный
ore руда *f.*
organ орган *m.*
organization организация *f.*
organize, to организовывать,
  -овать
origin источник *m.*; происхождение *n.*
original оригинальный
orphan сирота *m. & f.*
other другой, иной
  the ~ day на-днях
otherwise иначе
ought to должен; следует
our наш, наша, наше; наши
out из; вне; наружу
  he is ~ его нет дома
outburst вспышка *f.*
outfit оборудование *n.*
outline очерк *m.*
output производство *n.*
outside *adv.* снаружи
outstanding выдающийся
outward внешний
over над; через; на, по; за
  the work is ~ работа окончена
overcoat пальто *n. indecl.*
oversea за морем; *adj.* заморский
overshoe галоша *f.*
owing to благодаря
own собственный; родной
own, to владеть *imp.*, обладать
  imp.

owner владе́лец *m.*
ox бык *m.*; вол *m.*
oxygen кислоро́д *m.*

P

pace шаг *m.*
pack, to упако́вывать, -кова́ть
package па́чка *f.*, паке́т *m.*
page страни́ца *f.*
pain боль *f.*
paint кра́ска *f.*
paint, to кра́сить, о-
painter живопи́сец *m.*
painting жи́вопись *f.*; карти́на *f.*
pair па́ра *f.*; чета́ *f.*
palace дворе́ц *m.*
pale бле́дный
palm ладо́нь *f.*; па́льма *f.*
pants брю́ки *f. pl.*
paper бума́га *f.*
paragraph абза́ц *m.*; пара́граф *m.*
parcel посы́лка *f.*; паке́т *m.*
parents роди́тели *m. pl.*
park парк *m.*
part часть *f.*; роль *f.*
participate, to уча́ствовать *imp.*
participation уча́стие *n.*
particular осо́бенный
partly отча́сти
partner партнёр *m.*
party па́ртия *f.*; гру́ппа *f.*; вече-
ри́нка *f.*
pass про́пуск *m.*
pass, to проходи́ть, пройти́;
проезжа́ть, -е́хать; переда-
ва́ть, -да́ть
to ~ an examination сдать
perf. экза́мен
passage прое́зд *m.*, прохо́д *m.*
passenger пассажи́р *m.*
passer-by прохо́жий
passion страсть *f.*
passionate стра́стный
passport па́спорт *m.*
past про́шлый; про́шлое *n.*
paste те́сто *n.*; па́ста *f.*
paste to, кле́ить, с-
pastry пиро́жное *n.*
path тропи́нка *f.*; путь *m.*
patience терпели́вость *f.*; тер-
пе́ние *n.*

patient пацие́нт *m.*, больно́й *m.*;
adj. терпели́вый
pattern образе́ц *m.*, моде́ль *f.*
pause па́уза *f.*
pavement мостова́я *f.*
paw ла́па *f.*
pay пла́та *f.*
pay, to плати́ть, за-; опла́чивать,
-ати́ть
to ~ attention обраща́ть,
-ати́ть внима́ние
payment упла́та *f.*, платёж *m.*
pea горо́х *m.*
peace мир *m.*
peaceful споко́йный, ми́рный
peach пе́рсик *m.*
peacock павли́н *m.*
peak верши́на *f.*
pear гру́ша *f.*
pearl жёмчуг *m.*
peasant крестья́нин *m.*
peculiar осо́бенный
peculiarity осо́бенность *f.*
pedestrian пешехо́д *m.*
pen перо́ *n.*
pencil каранда́ш *m.*
penetrate, to проника́ть, -ни́кнуть
people наро́д *m.*; лю́ди *pl.*
pepper пе́рец *m.*
per че́рез, посре́дством; в, на
per cent проце́нт *m.*
perfect соверше́нный
perform, to исполня́ть, -по́лнить
performance исполне́ние *n.*;
представле́ние *n.*
perfume духи́ *m. pl.*
perhaps мо́жет быть
period пери́од *m.*
perish, to погиба́ть *imp.*; ги́бнуть,
по-
permanent постоя́нный
~ wave шестиме́сячная за-
ви́вка *f.*
permission разреше́ние *n.*
permit про́пуск *m.*
permit, to разреша́ть, -ши́ть;
позволя́ть, -о́лить
perpetual постоя́нный
perseverance насто́йчивость
person лицо́ *n.*, осо́ба *f.*, чело-
ве́к *m.*
personal ли́чный
personality ли́чность *f.*

perspiration пот *m.*
perspire, to потеть, вс-
persuade, to убеждать, убедить
petticoat нижняя юбка
pharmacy аптека *f.*
photograph фотография *f.*, снимок *m.*
phrase фраза *f.*
physician врач *m.*
piano пианино *n.*
  grand ~ рояль *m.*
pick up, to подбирать, подобрать
picture картина *f.*
pie пирог *m.*
piece кусок *m.*; штука *f.*
pig свинья *f.*
pigeon голубь *m.*
pike щука *f.*
pile куча *f.*, груда *f.*
pillow подушка *f.*
pilot лётчик *m.*
pin булавка *f.*
pincers клещи *f.pl.*; щипцы *m.pl.*
pine сосна *f.*
pineapple ананас *m.*
pink розовый
pipe труба *f.*; трубка *f.*
pitiful жалкий
pity сожаление *n.*, жалость *f.*
place место *n.*
  to take ~ иметь место
place, to помещать, -местить
plain ясный; простой
plan план *m.*
plan, to планировать *imp. & perf.*
planet планета *f.*
plank доска *f.*
plant растение *n.*; завод *m.*
plant, to сажать, посадить
plate тарелка *f.*
platform площадка *f.*, платформа *f.*
play игра *f.*; пьеса *f.*
play, to играть, сыграть
pleasant приятный
please пожалуйста
pleased довольный
pleasure удовольствие *n.*
plenty (of) очень много
plot заговор *m.*
plum слива *f.*
pocket карман *m.*
pocketbook бумажник *m.*

poem поэма *f.*; стихотворение *n.*
poet поэт *m.*
point точка *f.*; пункт *m.*
  the ~ is дело в том
point out, to указывать, указать
poison яд *m.*
poisonous, ядовитый
pole столб *m.*
police полиция *f.*
policeman полицейский *m.*
policy политика *f.*
polite вежливый, любезный
political политический
politics политика *f.*
pond пруд *m.*
pool лужа *f.*
poor бедный
popular народный, популярный
population население *n.*
porcelain фарфор *m.*
pork свинина *f.*
porridge каша *f.*
port порт *m.*
porter носильщик *m.*
portrait портрет *m.*
position положение *n.*
  to be in a ~ быть в состоянии
positive положительный
possess, to владеть *imp.*; обладать *imp.*
possibility возможность *f.*
possible возможный
post почта *f.*
postal почтовый
postcard открытка *f.*
poster афиша *f.*
postman почтильон *m.*; листоносец *m.*
post office почта *f.*, почтовое отделение *n.*
postpone, to откладывать, отложить
pot горшок *m.*
potato картофель, *m.*, картошка *f.*
poultry домашняя птица *f.*
pound фунт *m.*
pour out, to наливать, -лить
powder пудра *f.*
power власть *f.*; сила *f.* держава *f.*
powerful сильный, мощный
practical практический

practice пра́ктика *f.*
prairie степь *f.*
praise, to хвали́ть, по-
pray, to моли́ться, по-
precede, to предше́ствовать *imp.*
precise то́чный
preface предисло́вие *n.*
prefer, to предпочита́ть, -че́сть
preparation подгото́вка *f.*
prepare, to пригота́вливать(ся),
    -то́вить(ся)
prescription реце́пт *m.*
presence прису́тствие *n.*
present пода́рок *m.*; настоя́щее
    вре́мя *n.*
present тепе́решний; настоя́щий;
    прису́тствующий
    at ~ в да́нное вре́мя
    for the ~ пока́
present, to представля́ть, -а́вить
presently вско́ре
preserve, to сохраня́ть, -ани́ть
president председа́тель *m.*;
    президе́нт *m.*
press печа́ть *f.*
press, to нажима́ть, -жа́ть; гла́-
    дить, вы-
pressure давле́ние *n.*
pretty хоро́шенький; *adv.* до-
    во́льно
previous предыду́щий
price цена́ *f.*
pride го́рдость *f.*
prince принц *m.*, князь *m.*
principal гла́вный
print, to печа́тать, на-
prison тюрьма́ *f.*
private ча́стный; ли́чный
probably вероя́тно
problem пробле́ма *f.*
proceed, to продолжа́ть, -до́л-
    жить; происходи́ть, -изойти́
process проце́сс *m.*
produce, to производи́ть, -вести́
production произво́дство *n.*
professor профе́ссор *m.*
profit вы́года *f.*; при́быль *f.*
profound глубо́кий
program програ́мма *f.*
progress успе́хи *m.pl.*
prohibit, to воспреща́ть, -ети́ть
prolong, to продлева́ть, -дли́ть
prolongation продле́ние *n.*

prominent ви́дный, выдаю́щийся
promise, to обеща́ть *imp. & perf.*
prompt бы́стрый, ско́рый, неме́д-
    ленный
pronounce, to произноси́ть, -нести́
pronunciation произноше́ние *n.*
proper до́лжный; со́бственный
properly как сле́дует
propose, to предлага́ть, -ложи́ть
prose про́за *f.*
protection защи́та *f.*
protest проте́ст *m.*
proud го́рдый
    to be ~ of горди́ться *imp.*
prove, to дока́зывать, -ка́ть;
    ока́зываться, оказа́ться
proverb посло́вица *f.*
provide, to снабжа́ть, -бди́ть
provoke, to вызыва́ть, вы́звать
public пу́блика *f.*
public публи́чный; обще́ствен-
    ный
publish, to издава́ть, -да́ть
publisher изда́тель *m.*
publishing house изда́тельство *n.*
pull, to тяну́ть *imp.*; тащи́ть, вы́-
pump насо́с *m.*
punish, to нака́зывать, -каза́ть
pupil учени́к *m.*
purchase поку́пка *f.*
pure чи́стый
purpose цель *f.*, наме́рение *n.*
    on ~ наро́чно
push, to толка́ть, -кну́ть
put, to класть, положи́ть; ста́-
    вить, по-;
    to ~ down запи́сывать, -пи-
    са́ть
    to ~ in вставля́ть, -а́вить
    to ~ off откла́дывать, отло-
    жи́ть
    to ~ on надева́ть, -де́ть
    to ~ out туши́ть, по-

Q

quality ка́чество *n.*
quantity коли́чество *n.*
quarter че́тверть *f.*; кварта́л *m*
quay на́бережная *f.*
queen короле́ва *f.*
question вопро́с *m.*

questionnaire анкета *f.*
queue очередь *f.*
quick быстрый
   be ~! скорее!
quickly быстро
quiet спокойный, тихий
quite вполне, совсем, совершенно

R

rabbit кролик *m.*
race раса *f.*; гонка *f.*
radiator радиатор *m.*
radio радио *n.*
railroad железная дорога *f.*
rain дождь *m.*
raincoat дождевик *m.*
raining, it is дождь идёт
raise, to поднимать, -нять
raisins изюм *m.*
ram баран *m.*
random, at наугад
range предел *m.*
rapid скорый, быстрый
rare редкий
raspberry малина *f..*
rat крыса *f.*
rate норма *f.*; ставка *f.*
   at any ~ во всяком случае
   ~ of exchange курс *m.*
rather довольно; скорее; лучше
raw сырой
   ~ material сырьё *n.*
ray луч *m.*
razor бритва *f.*
reach, to достигать, -стичь; до-
   ходить, дойти; доезжать,
   -ехать; доставать, -стать
reaction реакция *f.*
read, to читать, про- (*or* про-
   честь)
reader читатель *m.*
ready готовый
   ~ money наличные деньги
real настоящий, действительный
reality действительность *f.*
realization осуществление *n.*
realize, to осуществлять, -вить;
   представлять, -авить себе
really действительно, на самом
   деле
reason причина *f.*, повод *m.*
reasonable разумный

recall, to отзывать, отозвать;
   вспоминать, вспомнить
receipt получение *n.*; расписка *f.*;
   квитанция *f.*
receive, to получать, -чить;
   принимать, -нять
recently недавно *f.*
reception приём *m.*
recipe рецепт *m.*
reckon on, to рассчитывать,
   -итать на
recognize, to признавать, -знать;
   узнавать, узнать
recollection воспоминание *n.*
recommend, to редомендовать
   imp. & perf.; советовать, по-
reconstruct, to восстанавливать,
   -новить
reconstruction восстановление *n.*
record пластинка *f.*; рекорд *m.*
recover поправляться, -авиться
recovery выздоровление *n.*
recreation отдых *m.*
red красный
reduction снижение *n.*; скидка *f.*
refer, to ссылаться, сослаться
   на; относиться, -нестись
reference справка *f.*; ссылка *f.*
   with ~ to относительно
reflection отражение *n.*
refreshment room буфет *m.*
refusal отказ *m.*
refuse, to отказываться, -казать-
   ся
regards привет *m.*, поклон *m.*
regiment полк *m.*
region область *f.*
registered letter заказное письмо
regret сожаление *n.*
regret, to жалеть, по-
regular правильный; регуляр-
   ный
rejoice, to радовать(ся), об-
relate, to рассказывать, -азать
relation отношение *n.*
relative родственник *m.*; *adj.*
   сравнительный
relax, to отдыхать, -дохнуть
release, to освобождать, -одить
reliable надёжный
religion религия *f.*
reluctantly неохотно
remain, to оставаться, остаться

remainder остáток *m.*

remaining остальнóй

remark, to замечáть, -мéтить

remarkable замечáтельный

remember, to пóмнить *imp.;* вспоминáть, вспóмнить

remind, to напоминáть, -пóмнить

reminiscence воспоминáние *n.*

remote отдалённый

remove, to устранять, -нить; снимáть, снять

render, to оказывать, оказáть

renew, to возобновлять, -вить

renounce откáзываться, -казáться

rent, to нанимáть, -нять

repair починка *f.,* ремóнт *m.*

repair, to исправлять, -áвить; чинить, по-

repeat, to повторять, -рить

replace, to заменять, -нить

replacement замéна *f.*

reply отвéт *m.*

reply, to отвечáть, -вéтить

report доклáд *m.;* отчёт *m.;* акт *m.*

report, to сообщáть, -щить; доклáдывать, доложить

repose óтдых *m.*

represent, to представлять, -áвить

representative представитель *m.*

reproach, to упрекáть, -кнýть

reproduction репродýкция *f.,* воспроизведéние *n.*

reptile пресмыкáющее *n.*

republic респýблика *f.*

repulsive отталкивающий

request прóсьба *f.*

request, to просить, по-

rescue, to спасáть, спасти

research исслéдование *n.*

resembling похóжий

resentment возмущéние *n.*

reserve запáс *m.*

reserve, to резервировать, за-

reside, to проживáть, -жить

residence местожительство *n.*

resist, to сопротивляться, -виться

resistance сопротивлéние *n.*

resolution решéние *n.*

respect уважéние *n.*

in ~ to в отношéнии к

respect, to уважáть *imp.*

respective соотвéтственный

responsibility отвéтственность *f.;* обязанность *f.*

responsible отвéтственный

to be ~ for отвечáть, -вéтить за

rest óтдых *m.,* покóй *m.;* остáток *m.*

rest, to отдыхáть, -дохнýть

restaurant ресторáн *m.*

restless беспокóйный

restriction ограничéние *n.*

result результáт *m.,* слéдствие *n.*

retire, to удаляться, -литься

retreat, to отступáть, -пить

return возвращéине *n.*

return, to возвращáть(ся), -вратить(ся); вернýть(ся) *perf.*

revenue годовóй дохóд *m.*

reverse обрáтный

review обзóр *m.;* журнáл *m.*

revolution революция *f.;* оборóт *m.*

revolve, to вращáться *imp.*

reward награда *f.*

rich богáтый

rid of, to get избавляться, -бáвиться

riddle загáдка *f.*

ride езда *f.*

ride, to éздить *imp.;* éхать, поéхать

right прáво *n.; adj.* прáвый; прáвильный; *adv.* вéрно; прямо

turn to the ~ поверните напрáво

all ~ хорошó, прáвильно

~ away сейчáс же

ring круг *m.;* кольцó *n.*

ring (up), to звонить, по-

rise, to вставáть, встать; поднимáться, -няться

risk, to рисковáть, -кнýть

river рекá *f.*

road дорóга *f.*

roar, to ревéть, про-

roast, to жáрить, из-

roastbeef рóстбиф *m.*

role роль *f.*

roll свёрток *m.*; рулóн *m.*; бýлочка *f.*

roll, to катúть(ся), по-

roof крýша *f.*

room кóмната *f.*

root кóрень *m.*

rope верёвка *f.*, канáт *m.*

rose рóза *f.*

rough грýбый

round крýглый; *adv.* вокрýг

row ряд *m.*

royal королéвский

rubber резúна *f.*; каучýк *m.*; *pl.* галóши *f. pl.*

ruble рубль *m.*

rug ковёр *m.*, кóврик *m.*

rule прáвило *n.*; правлéние *n.*
    as a ~ обы́чно

rumor слух *m.*

run, to бéгать *imp.*; бежáть, по-
    to ~ away убегáть, убежáть

rush, to мчáться *imp.*
    to ~ into врывáться, ворвáться

rust, to ржавéть, за-

Russia Россúя *f.*

Russian рýсский *m.*, рýсская *f.*; *adj.* рýсский

rye bread ржанóй хлеб *m.*

S

sack мешóк *m.*

sad печáльный, грýстный

safety безопáсность *f.*

sailboat пáрусная лóдка *f.*

salad салáт *m.*

salary жáлованье *n.*

sale продáжа *f.*

salesgirl продавщúца *f.*

salesman продавéц *m.*

salmon лососúна *f.*

salt соль *f.*

salt shaker солóнка *f.*

same тот же (сáмый), одинáковый
    it's all the ~ to me мне э́то безразлúчно

sample образéц *m.*

sand песóк *m.*

satisfaction удовлетворéние *n.*

satisfactory удовлетворúтельный

satisfied довóльный

satisfy удовлетворя́ть, -рúть

Saturday суббóта *f.*

saucer блюдце *n.*

sausage колбасá *f.*

savage дúкий

save, to спасáть, спастú; экономить, с-

savings-bank сберегáтельная кáсса *f.*

say, to говорúть, сказáть

scarcely едвá; вряд ли

scene сцéна *f.*

scent зáпах *m.*

schedule расписáние *n.*; грáфик *m.*

scheme схéма *f.*

scholar учёный *m.*

school шкóла *f.*

schoolboy шкóльник *m.*

science наýка *f.*

scientific наýчный

scientist учёный *m.*

scissors нóжницы *f. pl.*

scold, to ругáть, вы́-

scratch, to цáрапать(ся), -пнýть(ся)

scream, to кричáть, крúкнуть

screen экрáн *m.*

screw винт *m.*

scrupulous щепетúльный

sculptor скýльптор *m.*

sculpture скульптýра *f.*

sea мóре *n.*

seagull чáйка *f.*

seal печáть *f.*

seam шов *m.*

season сезóн *m.*

seasick, to be страдáть морскóй болéзнью

seat стул *m.*, сидéнье *n.*
    to take a ~ садúться, сесть

second вторóй

secondly во-вторы́х

secret тáйна *f.*; *adj.* тáйный

secretary секретáрь *m.*
    ~ of State минúстр инострáнных дел

section отдéл *m.*; отделéние *n.*

secure, to обеспéчивать, -пéчить; закрепля́ть, -пúть

sediment осáдок *m.*

see, to вúдеть, у-
    to ~ off провожáть, -водúть
    let me ~ дáйте подýмать
    I ~ понимáю

seed се́мя *n.*
seek, to иска́ть, по-
seem, to каза́ться, по-
seize, to схва́тывать, -ати́ть
seldom ре́дко
selection вы́бор *m.*
self сам, себя́
sell, to продава́ть, -да́ть
send, to посыла́ть, -сла́ть
   to ~ for посыла́ть за
   to ~ off отправля́ть, -а́вить
senior ста́рший
sensation ощуще́ние *n.*
sense чу́вство *n.*; смысл *m.*
sense, to чу́вствовать, по-
sensitive чувстви́тельный
sentence фра́за *f.*, предложе́ние
   n.; пригово́р *m.*
sentimental сентимента́льный
separate отде́льный
separate, to разъединя́ть, -ни́ть
September сентя́брь *m.*
sergeant сержа́нт *m.*
series се́рия *f.*
serious серьёный, ва́жный
serve, to служи́ть, по-; подава́ть,
   -да́ть
service слу́жба *f.*; услу́га *f.*
session се́ссия *f.*; заседа́ние *n.*
set набо́р *m.*; компле́кт *m.*
settle, to поселя́ть(ся), -ли́ть(ся);
   ула́живать(ся), ула́дить(ся)
settlement поселе́ние *n.*; реше́-
   ние *n.*
seven семь
seven hundred семьсо́т
seventeen семна́дцать
seventh седьмо́й
seventy се́мьдесят
several не́сколько
severe суро́вый, стро́гий
sex пол *m.*
sexual полово́й
shade тень *f.*; што́ра *f.*
shadow тень *f.*
shake, to трясти́, тряхну́ть
shallow ме́лкий
shame стыд *m.*, позо́р *m.*
shampoo шампу́нь *m.* or *f.*
shape фо́рма *f.*
share до́ля *f.*
sharp о́стрый, ре́зкий
shave, to бри́ть(ся), по-

shawl шаль *f.*, плато́к *m.*
she она́
shed, to пролива́ть, -ли́ть
sheep овца́ *f.*
sheet простыня́ *f.*; (*of paper*)
   лист *m.*
shelf по́лка *f.*
shelter прию́т *m.*; убе́жище *n.*
shepherd пасту́х *m.*
shine, to свети́ть, по-; сия́ть *imp.*;
   блесте́ть, -сну́ть
ship су́дно *n.*, кора́бль *m.*
ship, to отправля́ть, -а́вить
shipment груз *m.*; погру́зка *f.*
shirt руба́шка *f.*, соро́чка *f.*
shiver to дрожа́ть, дро́гнуть
shoe боти́нок *m.*, ту́фля *f.*, баш-
   ма́к *m.*
shoemaker сапо́жник *m.*
shoot, to стреля́ть *imp.*; застре-
   ли́ть *perf.*
shop ла́вка *f.*, магази́н *m.*
shopping, to go де́лать поку́пки
shore бе́рег *m.*
short коро́ткий
shorthand стеногра́фия *f.*
shortly вско́ре
shorts тру́сики *m. pl.*
shortsighted близору́кий
shoulder плечо́ *n.*
shout, to крича́ть, кри́кнуть
show вы́ставка *f.*; спекта́кль *m.*
show, to пока́зывать(ся), -ка-
   за́ться
   to ~ in вводи́ть, ввести́
   to ~ off хва́статься, по-
shrink, to сади́ться, сесть
shut, to закрыва́ть(ся), -кры́ть(ся)
   to ~ in запира́ть, -пере́ть
   to ~ out выключа́ть, вы́клю-
   чить
shutter ста́вень *m.*; затво́р *m.*
shy ро́бкий
sick больно́й
   I am ~ of мне надое́ло
sickness боле́знь *f.*
side сторона́ *f.*; бок *m.*
   ~ by ~ ря́дом
sidewalk тротуа́р *m.*
sieve решето́ *n.*
sigh, to вздыха́ть, вздохну́ть
sight зре́ние *n.*; вид *m.*; *pl.*
   достопримеча́тельности

sign знак *m.*; при́знак *m.*

sign, to подпи́сывать(ся), -писа́ть(ся)

signature по́дпись *f.*

significance значе́ние *n.*

silence молча́ние *n.*, тишина́ *f.*

silent безмо́лвный
to be ~ молча́ть, за-

silk шёлк *m.*

silken шёлковый

silly глу́пый

silver серебро́ *n.*; *adj.* сере́бряный

similar подо́бный

simple просто́й

simply про́сто

simultaneous одновре́менный

sin грех *m.*

since *prep.* с; *conj.* с тех пор как; так как; *adv.* с тех пор

sincere и́скренний

sing, to петь, с-

singer певе́ц *m.*, певи́ца *f.*

single еди́нственный; отде́льный

sink, to тону́ть, у-; топи́ть, у-

sister сестра́ *f.*
~-in-law неве́стка *f.*

sit, to сиде́ть, по-
to ~ down сади́ться, сесть

situation положе́ние *n.*

six шесть

six hundred шестьсо́т

sixteen шестна́дцать

sixth шесто́й

sixty шестьдеся́т

size разме́р *m.*

skate, to ката́ться *imp.* на конька́х

ski, to ходи́ть *imp.* на лы́жах

skilled квалифици́рованный; иску́сный

skin, ко́жа *f.*; шку́ра *f.*

skirt ю́бка *f.*

sky не́бо *n.*

skyscraper небоскрёб *m.*

slang жарго́н *m.*

slave раб *m.*

sled са́ни *f. pl.*

sleep сон *m.*

sleep, to спать, по-

sleeping car спа́льный ваго́н *m.*

sleepy со́нный

sleeve рука́в *m.*

slender то́нкий, стро́йный

slice ло́мтик *m.*

slide скользи́ть, -зну́ть

slightly слегка́

slip скольже́ние *n.*; оши́бка *f.*, про́мах *m.*; бума́жка *f.*

slipper ту́фля *f.*

slow ме́дленный
my watch is ~ мои́ часы́ отстаю́т

slowly ме́дленно

sly хи́трый

small ма́ленький

smart наря́дный

smash, to разбива́ть, -би́ть

smell за́пах *m.*

smell, to па́хнуть *imp.*

smile улы́бка *f.*

smile, to улыба́ться, -бну́ться

smoke дым *m.*

smoke, to кури́ть, за-

smoker куря́щий *m.*

snack заку́ска *f.*

snake змея́ *f.*

snatch, to хвата́ть(ся), (с)хвати́ть(ся)

sneeze, to чиха́ть, -хну́ть

snow снег *m.*

snowing, it is снег идёт

so так; таки́м о́бразом; ита́к
~ far до сих пор
~ long! пока́!
~ that так что; чтобы

soap мы́ло *n.*

soccer футбо́л *m.*

social обще́ственный; социа́льный

society о́бщество *n.*

sock носо́к *m.*

sofa дива́н *m.*

soft мя́гкий

soil земля́ *f.*, по́чва *f.*

soldier солда́т *m.*

sold out распро́данный

sole подо́шва *f.*; *adj.* еди́нственный

solemn торже́ственный

solid кре́пкий; соли́дный

solution реше́ние *n.*

solve, to (раз)реша́ть, -ши́ть

some како́й-нибудь; не́который; не́сколько

somebody кто́-то

somehow ка́к-нибудь
someone кто́-то
something что́-нибудь, что́-то, ко́е-что
sometimes иногда́
somewhere где́-нибудь; куда́-нибудь
son сын *m.*
song пе́сня *f.*
son-in-law зять *m.*
soon вско́ре, ско́ро
as ~ as как то́лько
sore чувстви́тельный
sorrow го́ре *n.*; скорбь *f.*
sorry, to be жале́ть, по-
I'm ~ винова́т, извини́те, прости́те
sort сорт *m.*, вид *m.*
soul душа́ *f.*
sound звук *m.*; *adj.* здоро́вый
soup суп *m.*
sour ки́слый
source исто́чник *m.*
south юг *m.*
Soviet сове́тский
~ Union Сове́тский Сою́з
southern ю́жный
sow, to се́ять, за-
space простра́нство *n.*
spare запасно́й
spare, to щади́ть, по-; эконо́мить, с-
sparrow воробе́й *m.*
speak, to говори́ть, по-
special специа́льный; осо́бый
spectacle зре́лище *n.*
spectator зри́тель *m.*
speech речь *f.*
speed ско́рость *f.*
spend, to тра́тить, по-; проводи́ть, -вести́
spider пау́к *m.*
spinach шпина́т *m.*
spirit дух *m.*
spiritual духо́вный
spit, to плева́ть, плю́нуть
spite of, in несмотря́ на
splendid блестя́щий, великоле́пный
spoil, to по́ртить(ся), ис-; балова́ть, из-
sponge гу́бка *f.*
spoon ло́жка *f.*

sport спорт *m.*
spot пятно́ *n.*; ме́сто *n.*
spring весна́ *f.*; пружи́на *f.*
spring, to пры́гать, -гнуть; вска́кивать, вскочи́ть
spy шпио́н *m.*
square пло́щадь *f.*; *adj.* квадра́тный
squeeze, to выжима́ть, вы́жать
stability усто́йчивость *f.*; про́чность *f,* сто́йкость *f.*
stadium ста́дион *m.*
stagnation засто́й *m.*
stage сце́на *f.*
stain пятно́ *n.*
staircase ле́стница *f.*
stairs ле́стница *f.*
stamp (почто́вая) ма́рка *f.*
stand стоя́нка *f.*; сто́йка *f.*; стэнд *m.*
stand, to стоя́ть, по-; выде́рживать, вы́держать
standard зна́мя *n.*; станда́рт *m.*
standpoint то́чка зре́ния
star звезда́ *f.*
starch, to крахма́лить, на-
start, to начина́ть(ся), -ча́ть(ся); отправля́ться, -а́виться; (motor) заводи́ть, -вести́
state госуда́рство *n.*; состоя́ние *n.*; *adj.* госуда́рственный
statement заявле́ние *n.*
station ста́нция *f.*; вокза́л *m.*
statue па́мятник *m.*
stay, to остава́ться, оста́ться; остана́вливаться, -нови́ться
steady постоя́нный
steak бифште́кс *m.*
steal, to красть, у-
steam пар *m.*
steamship парохо́д *m.*
steel сталь *f.*; *adj.* стально́й
step шаг *m.*; ступе́нька *f.*
step, to ступа́ть, -пи́ть; шага́ть, шагну́ть
steppe степь *f.*
stick па́лка *f.*
stick, to втыка́ть, воткну́ть; прикле́ивать(ся), -е́йть(ся)
to ~ in застрева́ть, -стря́ть
to ~ to приде́рживаться, -держа́ться
stiff жёсткий

still *adj.* ти́хий; *adv.* ещё, всё ещё; всё-таки, всё же
stimulate, to побужда́ть, -буди́ть
stir, to шевели́ть(ся), -льну́ть(ся); разме́шивать, -меша́ть
stocking чуло́к *m.*
stomach желу́док *m.*
stone ка́мень *m.*; ко́сточка *f.*; *adj.* ка́менный
stool табуре́тка *f.*
stop остано́вка *f.*
stop, to остана́вливать(ся), -нови́ть(ся); прекраща́ть(ся), -крати́ть(ся); затыка́ть, -ткну́ть
stopper про́бка *f.*
storage хране́ние *n.*
store склад *m.*; магази́н *m.*
stork а́ист *m.*
storm бу́ря *f.*
stormy бу́рный
story расска́з *m.*; исто́рия *f.*; эта́ж *m.*
stout то́лстый, по́лный; кре́пкий
stove печь *f.*, пе́чка *f.*
straight прямо́й
    ~ ahead пря́мо
strange стра́нный
stranger незнако́мец *m.*; посторо́нний челове́к *m.*
strawberries клубни́ка *f.*
stream пото́к *m.*; тече́ние *n.*
stream, to течь *imp.*
street у́лица *f.*
streetcar трамва́й *m.*
strength си́ла *f.*
stress, to подчёркивать, -черкну́ть
stretch, to протя́гивать, -тяну́ть; растя́гивать(ся), -тяну́ть(ся); тяну́ться, по-
strict стро́гий; то́чный
strike ста́чка *f.*, забасто́вка *f.*
strike, to ударя́ть(ся), уда́рить(ся); поража́ть, -рази́ть; бить, про-; бастова́ть, за-
    to ~ a match зажига́ть, -же́чь спи́чку
string верёвка *f.*; струна́ *f.*
strip, to раздева́ть(ся), -де́ть(ся)
stripe полоса́ *f.*
striped полоса́тый

strive, to стара́ться, по-
strong си́льный; кре́пкий
struggle борьба́ *f.*
struggle, to боро́ться, по-
student студе́нт *m.*
study изуче́ние *n.*; кабине́т *m.*
study, to изуча́ть, -учи́ть
stuff вещество́ *n.*, материа́л *m.*
stupid глу́пый
style стиль *m.*, слог *m.*
subject предме́т *m.*, те́ма *f.*
    to be ~ to подверга́ться, -ве́ргнуться; подлежа́ть *imp.*
subscribe, to подпи́сываться, -писа́ться
subsequently зате́м, пото́м
substance вещество́ *n.*
substitute замести́тель *m.*
substitute, to заменя́ть, -ни́ть
subtract вычита́ть, вы́честь
suburb при́город *m.*; *pl.* предме́стье *n.*
subway метро́ *n.*
succeed, to удава́ться, уда́ться
    I ~ed in мне удало́сь
success успе́х *m.*
successful уда́чный
such тако́й
suddenly вдруг, внеза́пно
suffer, to страда́ть, по-
suffering страда́ние *n.*
sufficient доста́точный
sugar са́хар *m.*
suggest, to предлага́ть, -ложи́ть
suggestion предложе́ние *n.*
suicide самоуби́йство *n.*
suit костю́м *m.*
suit, to годи́ться, при-
suitable подходя́щий
suitcase чемода́н *m.*
sum су́мма *f.*
summer ле́то *n.*; *adj.* ле́тний
summit верши́на *f.*
sun со́лнце *n.*
Sunday воскресе́нье *n.*
sunny со́лнечный
sunrise восхо́д со́лнца
sunset зака́т *m.*
superfluous (из)ли́шний
superior вы́сший, лу́чший
superiority превосхо́дство *n.*
supper у́жин *m.*
    to have ~ у́жинать, по-

supply снабжéние *n.*; запáс *m.*

support, to поддéрживать, -держáть; содержáть *imp.*

suppose, to (пред)полагáть, -ложи́ть

supreme верхóвный

sure увéренный; надёжный

surely несомнéнно

surface повéрхность *f.*

surname фами́лия *f.*

surprise удивлéние *n.*

surprise, to удивля́ть, -ви́ть
to be ∼d удивля́ться, -ви́ться

surprising удиви́тельный

surround, to окружáть, -жи́ть

surroundings окрéстности *f. pl.*

survey обзóр *m.*

suspect, to подозревáть *imp.*

suspenders подтя́жки *f. pl.*

suspicion подозрéние *n.*

suspicious подозри́тельный

swallow, to прогла́тывать, -глоти́ть

swan лéбедь *f.*

swear, to кля́сться, по-; присягáть, -гнýть

sweat пот *m.*

sweater сви́тер *m.*

sweet слáдкий

swell, to распухáть, -пýхнуть; вздувáться, вздýться

swim, to плáвать *imp.*; плыть, по-

swimmer пловéц *m.*

swing, to качáть(ся), качнýть(ся); размáхивать, -махнýть

switch, to переключáть, -чи́ть
to ∼ off выключáть, выключить
to ∼ on включáть, -чи́ть

sword меч *m.*

symbol си́мвол *m.*

sympathy сочýвствие *n.*

system систéма *f.*

T

table стол *m.*; таблица *f.*

tablecloth скáтерть *f.*

tail хвост *m.*

tailor портнóй *m.*

take, to брать, взять
to ∼ away убирáть, убрáть
to ∼ off снимáть, снять

to ∼ out вынимáть, вы́нуть
to ∼ over принимáть, -ня́ть

tale рассказ *m.*, пóвесть *f.*

talent талáнт *m.*

talk разговóр *m.*, бесéда *f.*

talk, to говори́ть, по-; разговáривать *imp.*

tall высóкий

tan, to загорáть, -рéть

tank бак *m.*, цистéрна *f.*, резервуáр *m.*; танк *m.*

tap кран *m.*

task задáча *f.*

taste вкус *m.*

taste, to прóбовать, по-; имéть (при)вкус

tax налóг *m.*

taxi такси́ *n.*

tea чай *m.*

teach, to учи́ть, на- *or* вы́-; обучáть, -учи́ть; преподавáть *imp.*

teacher учи́тель *m.*, учи́тельница *f.*; преподавáтель *m.*

team комáнда *f.*

teapot чáйник *m.*

tear слезá *f.*

tear, to рвать(ся), по-; раздирáть, разодрáть

tease, to дразни́ть, по-

teaspoon чáйная лóжка *f.*

technical техни́ческий

technique тéхника *f.*

telegram телегрáмма *f.*

telegraph, to телеграфи́ровать, *imp. & perf.*

telephone телефóн *m.*; *adj.* телефóнный

telephone directory телефóнная кни́га *f.*

telephone number нóмер телефóна

telephone receiver трýбка *f.*

telephone, to звони́ть, по- по телефóну

television телеви́дение *n.*

televison set телеви́зор *m.*

tell, to говори́ть, сказáть; расскáзывать, -азáть

temper харáктер *m.*; настроéние *n.*

temperature температýра *f.*

temple висóк *m.*

temporary вре́менный
temptation искуше́ние *n.*, собла́зн *m.*
ten де́сять; деся́ток *m.*
tenant жи́тель *m.*; жиле́ц *m.*
tendency скло́нность *f.*
tender не́жный
tennis те́ннис *m.*
tent пала́тка *f.*
tenth деся́тый
term срок *m.*; те́рмин *m.*; *pl.* усло́вия *n. pl.*
terrible стра́шный, ужа́сный
terror у́жас *m.*; терро́р *m.*
test, to испы́тывать, -пыта́ть
text текст *m.*
textbook уче́бник *m.*
textile тексти́льный
than чем
thank, to благодари́ть, по-
~ you!, ~ s! спаси́бо
thankful благода́рный
thanks to благодаря́ (чему́-либо)
that *pron.* (э)тот, (э)та, (э)то; кото́рый; *conj.* что; чтобы
~ is то-есть
the more the better чем бо́льше, тем лу́чше
theater теа́тр *m.*
their(s) их; свой
then тогда́; зате́м, пото́м
theory тео́рия *f.*
there там; туда́
from ~ отту́да
~ is есть, име́ется
therefore поэ́тому
these э́ти
they они́
thick то́лстый; пло́тный; густо́й
thief вор *m.*
thin то́нкий; худо́й
thing вещь *f.*; де́ло *n.*
think, to ду́мать, по-
third тре́тий
a ~ треть *f.*
thirsty, to be хоте́ть пить
thirteen трина́дцать
thirty три́дцать
this э́тот, э́та, э́то
thorough тща́тельный
those те
though хотя́
as ~ как бу́дто бы

thought мысль *f.*
thousand ты́сяча
thread ни́тка *f.*
threat угро́за *f.*
threaten, to грози́ть, по-; угрожа́ть *imp.*
three три; тро́е
three hundred три́ста
threshold поро́г *m.*
throat го́рло *n.*
through че́рез, сквозь; посре́дством
throw, to броса́ть, бро́сить; кида́ть, ки́нуть
thunder гром *m.*
thunderstorm гроза́ *f.*
Thursday четве́рг *m.*
thus так, таки́м о́бразом
ticket биле́т *m.*; ярлы́к *m.*
ticket window ка́сса *f.*
tie связь *f.*; га́лстук *m.*
tie, to свя́зывать, связа́ть; привя́зывать, -вяза́ть
tiger тигр *m.*
tight те́сный; туго́й
till *prep. & conj.* до тех пор пока́, пока́ не
time вре́мя *n.*; срок *m.*; раз *m.*
at that ~ тогда́
for the ~ being пока́; в настоя́щее вре́мя
on ~ во́-время
timetable расписа́ние *n.*
timid ро́бкий
tin о́лово *n.*; жесть *f.*; ба́нка *f.*
tip чаевы́е *pl.*; сове́т *m.*
tiptoe, on на цы́почках
tire ши́на *f.*
tired уста́лый
I am ~ я уста́л
to get ~ устава́ть, уста́ть
tiresome утоми́тельный
title загла́вие *n.*; ти́тул *m.*
to к, в, на
tobacco таба́к *m.*
today сего́дня
~'s сего́дняшний
toe па́лец ноги́
together вме́сте
toilet убо́рная *f.*
tomato помидо́р *m.*
tomorrow за́втра
day after ~ послеза́втра

ton тóнна *f.*

tone тон *m.*

tongue язы́к *m.*

tonight сегóдня вéчером *or* нóчью

too тáкже, тóже; сли́шком

tool орýдие *n.*, инструмéнт *m.*

tooth зуб *m.*

toothache зубнáя боль *f.*

toothbrush зубнáя щётка *f.*

tooth paste зубнáя пáста *f.*

tooth powder зубнóй порошóк *m.*

top верх *m.*; верши́на *f.*; *adj.* вéрхний
on ~ наверхý

topic предмéт *m.*, тéма *f.*

tortoise черепáха *f.*

torture пы́тка *f.*; мýка *f.*

total итóг *m.*; *adj.* весь; пóлный

touching трóгательный

tourist тури́ст *m.*, тури́стка *f.*

toward к

towel полотéнце *n.*

tower бáшня *f.*

town гóрод *m.*

toy игрýшка *f.*

trace след *m.*

tractor трáктор *m.*

trade торгóвля *f.*

traffic движéние *n.*

tragedy трагéдия *f.*

tragic траги́ческий

train пóезд *m.*

training обучéние *n.*; тренирóвка *f.*

traitor предáтель *m.*

transaction дéло *n.*, сдéлка *f.*

translate, to переводи́ть, -вести́

translation перевóд *m.*

transmission передáча *f.*

transparent прозрáчный

transport перевóзка *f.*; трáнспорт

transport, to перевози́ть, -везти́

trap ловýшка *f.*

travel путешéствие *n.*

travel to путешéствовать *imp.*

travel bureau бюрó путешéствий

traveler путешéственник *m.*

treasure сокрóвище *n.*

treat, to обращáться, обрати́ться; угощáть, угости́ть; лечи́ть, вы-

tree дéрево *n.*

tremble, to дрожáть, дрóгнуть

tremendous огрóмный

trial прóбный

trick фóкус *m.*

trifle мéлочь *f.*, пустя́к *m.*

trip поéздка *f.*, экскýрсия *f.*

triumph торжествó *n.*

trolley bus троллéйбус *m.*

tropical тропи́ческий

trouble забóта *f.*, хлóпоты *f. pl.*; гóре *n.*, белá *f.*

trousers брю́ки *f. pl*

truck грузови́к *m.*

true и́стинный; пóдлинный; вéрный

truly, yours с уважéнием

trumpet трубá *f.*

trump кóзырь *m.*

trunk сундýк *m.*

trust, to вéрить, по-; доверя́ть, -вéрить

truth прáвда *f.*

truthful правди́вый

try, to пытáться, по-; старáться, по-; попрóбовать, поto ~ on примеря́ть, -мéрить
to ~ out испы́тывать, -пытáть

tube трýбка *f.*; тю́бик *m.*

Tuesday втóрник *m.*

tumbler стакáн *m.*

tunnel туннéль *m.*

turkey индю́к *m.*

turn поворóт *m.*; óчередь *f.*

turn, to вертéть(ся) *imp.*; крути́ть(ся) *imp.*; вращáть(ся) *imp.*; повóрачивать(ся), повернýть(ся); обворáчивать(ся), обернýть(ся); обращáть(ся), обрати́ть(ся); дéлаться, с-; станови́ться, стать
to ~ off *(tap)* закрывáть, -кры́ть
to ~ on *(tap)* открывáть, -кры́ть; *(light)* включáть, -чи́ть
to ~ out *(light)* выключáть, вы́ключить
to ~ pale побледнéть *perf.*

twelve двенáдцать

twenty двáдцать

twice двáжды
~ as вдвóе

twilight су́мерки *f. pl.*
twins близнецы́ *m. pl.*
two два, две; дво́е
~ and a half два с полови́ной
two hundred две́сти
type тип *m.*
typewriter пи́шущая маши́нка *f.*
typist машини́стка *f.*

U

ugly безобра́зный, отта́лкивающий
Ukraine Украи́на *f.*
Ukrainian украи́нец *m.*, -нка *f.*; *adj.* украи́нский
umbrella зо́нтик *m.*
uncle дя́дя *m.*
uncomfortable неудо́бный
unconscious бессозна́тельный
under под; при
underclothes (ни́жнее) бельё *n.*
undergo, to подверга́ться, -ве́ргнуться
understand, to понима́ть, поня́ть
undertake, to преприпима́ть, -ня́ть
undertaking предприя́тие *n.*
underwear (ни́жнее) бельё *n.*
undress, to раздева́ть(ся), -де́ться
unemployment безрабо́тица *f.*
unexpectedly неожи́данно
unfinished незако́нченный
unfortunately к сожале́нию
unhappy несча́стный
uniform фо́рма *f.*, мунди́р *m.*
union сою́з *m.*; объедине́ние *n.*
unit едини́ца *f.*
united соединённый, объединённый
United Nations Объединённые На́ции
United States Соединённые Шта́ты
universal универса́льный
university университе́т *m.*
unknown незнако́мый, неизве́стный
unless е́сли не
unlimited неограни́ченный
unnecessary (из)ли́шний, нену́жный
unpleasant неприя́тный

until *prep.* до; *conj.* пока́ не
unusual необыкнове́нный
unwillingly неохо́тно
up наве́рх, вверх
~ and down вверх и вниз; взад и вперёд
~ to now до сих пор
upbringing воспита́ние
upon на; в
upper ве́рхний; вы́сший
upright прямо́й; *adv.* пря́мо
upset огорчённый, расстро́енный
upside down вверх нога́ми
upstairs наве́рх; наверху́
upward вверх
urgent сро́чный
use по́льза *f.*; употребле́ние *n.*
use, to употребля́ть, -би́ть; по́льзоваться, вос-; испо́льзовать *imp. & perf.*
used to, to get привыка́ть, -вы́кнуть
useful поле́зный
usual обы́чный, обыкнове́нный
usually обы́чно, обыкнове́нно
utmost кра́йний

V

vacant пусто́й; свобо́дный
vacation о́тпуск *m.*
vacuum cleaner пылесо́с *m.*
vain, in напра́сно
valid действи́тельный
valley доли́на *f.*
valuable це́нный
valuables драгоце́нности *f. pl.*
value сто́имость *f.*; це́нность *f.*
van бага́жный ваго́н *m.*
vanish, to исчеза́ть, -че́знуть; пропада́ть, -па́сть
various ра́зный, разли́чный
vast обши́рный
veal теля́тина *f.*
vegetables зе́лень *f.*
vein ве́на *f.*, жила́ *f.*
velvet ба́рхат *m.*
verb глаго́л *m.*
verse стих *m.*
very о́чень, весьма́
vessel су́дно *n.*
vest жиле́т *m.*
victim же́ртва *f.*

victory побе́да *f.*
view вид *m.*; взгляд *m.*
  point of ~ то́чка зре́ния
vigorous си́льный
village дере́вня *f.*, село́ *n.*
vinegar у́ксус *m.*
violin скри́пка *f.*
visa ви́за *f.*
visible ви́димый
vision зре́ние *n.*
visit визи́т *m.*
visit, to посеща́ть, -сети́ть; навеща́ть, -вести́ть
visitor посети́тель *m.*, гость *m.*
vodka во́дка *f.*
voice го́лос *m.*
volume объём *m.*; том *m.*
voluntary доброво́льный
vote, to голосова́ть, про-
vow обе́т *m.*, кля́тва *f.*
voyage путеше́ствие *n.*

W

wages за́работная пла́та *f.*
waist та́лия *f.*
wait, to ждать, лодо-
waiter официа́нт *m.*
waiting room зал ожида́ния
waitress официа́нтка *f.*
wake up, to буди́ть, раз-; пробужда́ть(ся), -буди́ть(ся); просыпа́ться, -сну́ться
walk прогу́лка *f.*
walk, to гуля́ть, по-; итти́, пойти́ пешко́м
wall стена́ *f.*
wallpaper обо́и *m. pl.*
waltz вальс *m.*
want нужда́ *f.*
want, to жела́ть, по-; хоте́ть, за-; нужда́ться *imp.*
war война́ *f.*; *adj.* вое́нный
wardrobe гардеро́б *m.*
warehouse склад *m.*
warm тёплый
warn, to предупрежда́ть, -еди́ть
wash, to мыть(ся), по-; стира́ть(ся), вы́-
waste, to тра́тить, по-; (*time*) теря́ть, по-
watch часы́ *m. pl.*
watch, to наблюда́ть *imp.*; следи́ть *imp.*

watchmaker часовщи́к *m.*
water вода́ *f.*
waterfall водопа́д *m.*
watermelon арбу́з *m.*
waterproof непромока́емый
wave волна́ *f.*
wave, to маха́ть, махну́ть; (*hair*) завива́ть, -ви́ть
way доро́га *f.*, путь *m.*; направле́ние *n.*; спо́соб *m.*
  ~ out вы́ход *m.*
  by the ~ ме́жду про́чим
we мы
weak сла́бый
weakness сла́бость *f.*
wealth бога́тство *n.*
weapon ору́жие *n.*
wear, to носи́ть(ся) *imp.*
  to ~ out изна́шивать(ся), -носи́ть(ся)
weather пого́да *f.*
wedding сва́дьба *f.*; *adj.* свадéбный
Wednesday среда́ *f.*
weed сорня́к *m.*
week неде́ля *f.*
weekly еженеде́льный
weep, to пла́кать, за-
weigh, to ве́сить, вз-
weight вес *m.*; тя́жесть *f.*
welcome! добро́ пожа́ловать!
well хорошо́; *interjection* ну
  as ~as и . . . и, как . . ., так и
well-known изве́стный
west за́пад *m.*
western за́падный
wet мо́крый
what что; како́й
wheat пшени́ца *f.*
wheel колесо́ *n.*
when когда́
whence отку́да
where где; куда́
  ~ from отку́да
whereas тогда́ как
whether ли; и́ли
which кото́рый; како́й
  ~ of you кто из вас
while вре́мя *n.*; *conj.* в то вре́мя как
whisper, to шепта́ть, шепну́ть
whistle, to свисте́ть, сви́стнуть
white бе́лый

who кто
whole весь; целый
whose чей
why почему, зачём
wide широкий, обширный
widow вдова *f.*
widower вдовец *m.*
wife жена *f.*
wild дикий
will воля *f.*
win, to выигрывать, выиграть
wind ветер *m.*
wind, to (*watch*) заводить, -вести
window окно *n.*; *adj.* оконный
wine вино *n.*
wing крыло *n.*
winner победитель *m.*
winter зима *f.*
wire проволока *f.*, провод *m.*; телеграмма *f.*
wisdom мудрость *f.*
wise мудрый
wish желание *n.*
   best ~es! наилучшие пожелания!
wish, to желать, по-
with с
withdraw, to отдёргивать, -рнуть; брать, взять назад
within внутри; в течение
without без
witness свидетель *m.*
wolf волк *m.*
woman женщина *f.*
wonder чудо *n.*
   no ~ не удивительно
wonder, to удивляться, -виться
wonderful чудесный, удивительный
wood лес *m.*; дерево *n.*
wooden деревянный
wool шерсть *f.*
woolen шерстяной
word слово *n.*
work работа *f.*; труд *m.*
work, to работать, по-; действовать, по-
worker работник *m.*, -ница *f.*; рабочий *m.*; трудящийся *m.*

works завод *m.*
workshop мастерская *f.*; цех *m.*
world мир *m.*; свет *m.*; *adj.* мировой
world war мировая война *f.*
worm червь *m.*, червяк *m.*
worry, to беспокоить(ся), о-
worse хуже
worth, be стоить *imp.*
worthy достойный
wound рана *f.*
wrap, to завёртывать, -вернуть; запаковывать, -ковать
wrestle, to бороться, по-
wrist watch ручные часы *m. pl.*
write, to писать, на-
   to ~ down записывать, -писать
writer писатель *m.*
writing paper писчая бумага *f.*
wrong неправильный; не тот
   something is ~ что-то не в порядке

X

X-ray рентгеновские лучи *m. pl.*

Y

year год *m.*
yearly ежегодный
yeast дрожжи *pl.*
yell, to вопить *imp.*
yellow жёлтый
yes да
yesterday вчера
   day before ~ позавчера
   ~'s вчерашний
yet ещё; всё ещё; однако, всё-таки
you вы, ты
young молодой, юный
your(s) ваш, твой
youth молодость *f.*; молодёжь *f.*

Z

zero нуль *m.*
zone зона *f.*; район *m.*
zoo зоопарк *m.*

Notes

Notes